POLITICAL INVESTIGATIONS

In this fascinating new book Robert Fine recasts three great studies of modern political life: Hegel's *Elements of the Philosophy of Right*, Marx's *Capital* and Hannah Arendt's *Origins of Totalitarianism*. The originality of this book lies in its radical reinterpretation of these individual texts which frees them from their intellectual isolation and reads them together as a living unity. In Fine's account all three emerge as formative works of critical theory which succeed in sustaining the great promises of modern politics – freedom, equality, solidarity, the new – alongside the grubbier reality of domination and violence. They are all revealed as empirical works which analyse the actual forms of political modernity, as scientific works which link external appearances to internal processes, as dynamic works concerned with the movement, trajectory and potentiality of politics and as equivocal texts which not only unmask the illusions of political life but also the illusions of unmasking itself. *Political Investigations* offers a clear and engaging read for students, academics and all who work and take pleasure in social and political thought. It also significantly reviews present-day understandings of the relation between normative political philosophy and empirically-based social theory.

Robert Fine is Convenor of the MA in Social and Political Thought and Director of the Centre for Social Theory at the University of Warwick. He is author of *Democracy and the Rule of Law: Liberal Ideals and Marxist Critiques* (Pluto) and *Beyond Apartheid: Labour and Liberation in South Africa* (Pluto). He is co-editor of *Social Theory after the Holocaust* (Liverpool University Press).

D0148723

POLITICAL INVESTIGATIONS

Hegel, Marx, Arendt

Robert Fine

London and New York

First published 2001
by Routledge
11 New Fetter Lane, London EC4P 4EE

Simultaneously published in the USA and Canada
by Routledge
29 West 35th Street, New York, NY 10001

Routledge is an imprint of the Taylor & Francis Group

© 2001 Robert Fine

Typeset in Goudy by
Keystroke, Jacaranda Lodge, Wolverhampton
Printed and bound in Great Britain by
MPG Books Ltd, Bodmin

British Library Cataloguing in Publication Data
A catalogue record for this book is available
from the British Library

Library of Congress Cataloging in Publication Data
Fine, Robert
Political investigations : Hegel, Marx, Arendt / Robert Fine.
p. cm.
Simultaneously published in the USA and Canada.
Includes bibliographical references and index.
1. Liberty. 2. Equality. 3. Solidarity
4. Authoritarianism. 5. Totalitarianism. 6. Hegel, Georg Wilhelm
Friedrich, 1770–1831. Grundlinien der Philosophie des Rechts.
7. Marx, Karl, 1818–1883. Kapital. 8. Arendt, Hannah. Origins
of totalitariansim. I. Title.
JC585 .F544 2001
320.1′01–dc21   00-069033

ISBN 0–415–23907–9 (hbk)
ISBN 0–415–23908–7 (pbk)

To my uncle, Harry Blacker,
who put a smile on our faces and knew
what is important in life
and to my daughter, Shoshi Fine,
with all my love.

CONTENTS

ACKNOWLEDGEMENTS

I should like to acknowledge the patience and support of Mari Shullaw at Routledge, and of copy-editor Tom Chandler; also, the immeasurable help I have received from many friends/colleagues/students in the Centre for Social Theory, the MA in Social and Political Thought, the Sociology Department and the University of Warwick more generally. By name I would like to offer thanks to Alan Norrie, Alison Diduck, Charlie Turner, David Hirsh, David Seymour, Gill Frith, Gillian Rose, Gillian Bendelow, Glyn Cousin, Gloesha Challice, Howard Caygill, Istvan Pogany, Kakia Goudeli, Lawrence Welch, Maria Pia Lara, Marion Doyen, Mike Neary, Peter Wagner, Simon Clarke, Simon Williams, Vic Seidler. And a special mention for family – Gillian Bendelow, Shoshi Fine, Tessa Watkinson, Sylvia Stern, Tony Fine and to the warm and wonderful Cuccuru family.

ABBREVIATIONS

Full citations, editions, etc. are given in the Bibliography.

A&J   Arendt and Jaspers, *Correspondence*
BPF   Arendt, *Between Past and Future*
Capital   Marx, *Capital*
EJ   Arendt, *Eichmann in Jerusalem*
ETW   Hegel, *Early Theological Writings*
EU   Arendt, *Essays in Understanding*
HC   Arendt, *The Human Condition*
KPW   Kant, *Kant's Political Writings*
Letters   Marx and Engels, *Letters on 'Capital'*
LM   Arendt, *Life of the Mind*
LPWH   Hegel, *Lectures in the Philosophy of World History*
MDT   Arendt, *Men in Dark Times*
MEW   Marx, *Karl Marx: Early Writings*
MJ   Kant, *The Metaphysical Elements of Justice*
OR   Arendt, *On Revolution*
OT   Arendt, *The Origins of Totalitarianism*
PH   Hegel, *Philosophy of History*
PR   Hegel, *Elements of the Philosophy of Right*
PS   Hegel, *Phenomenology of Spirit*

INTRODUCTION

This book is a study of the political thought of three writers: Hegel, Marx and Hannah Arendt. At its centre are three works: Hegel's *Philosophy of Right*, Marx's *Capital* and Arendt's *Origins of Totalitarianism*. They are all 'classics' of social and political thought and they are all texts I love to read. Beyond this subjective enthusiasm, I believe that they are also united by more substantial considerations. A central thesis of this work is that when these authors are read together, as a unity, they reveal more about themselves and about the political reality they seek to understand, than when they are read independently or in opposition to one another. These writers and their books may appear at first sight to be very different but my contention is that they resemble, complement and supplement one another in the most interesting ways. If we remain fixed at the level of contrasting Hegel's 'idealism' to Marx's 'materialism' to Arendt's 'anti-foundationalism', then not only do we freeze their thought into static philosophical categories, but political philosophy itself becomes a matter of merely choosing one philosophical presupposition over another. Far from transcending a subjective enthusiasm, we would only repeat it in a more intellectual disguise.

In his wonderful book, *Why Read the Classics?*, Italo Calvino writes that one of the things which makes a work into a 'classic' is that, when we read it, we find the most 'original and unexpected' elements that surpass all our previous conceptions of what it contained. The substance of what we find 'original and unexpected' in Hegel, Marx and Arendt might be different to different readers, and may change every time we open their books, but the crucial point is that when we read them, we cannot help questioning the images we have of them. The texts themselves never seem to exhaust what they have to say to us and the common use of terms like 'Hegelian', 'Marxist' or 'Arendtian' always seems hopelessly inadequate in relation to what we read. In order to discover what animates these authors and what might make them once again vital to our own times, we need to shake off what Calvino calls 'the pulviscular cloud of critical discourse' which has so often surrounded them (Calvino 1999: 6). *Philosophy of Right*, *Capital* and *Origins of Totalitarianism* are all texts which bear heavily the weight of previous interpretations and they trail behind themselves all manner of traces in our cultures; but one thing which makes them into classics is how much they surprise us when we read them and compare them with the images we previously had.

1

Why should we read these classics of political philosophy and social theory today? Judging by the number of recent books concerned with the political thought of Hegel and Arendt, the feeling that these two writers are still speaking to us seems to be widely shared. Marx may appear to be more exhausted at the present moment but pronouncements of his 'death' are, as it is said, premature. If anyone objects that the writings of these authors are difficult to read (which they sometimes are) and that it may not be worth the effort since it requires long stretches of time that are at odds with our current pace of life (even in academia), or that reading or rereading them may turn out to serve no useful purpose, we might refer to the pleasure of reading itself and say that 'serving a purpose' is not the only criterion for reading a book. In any case we should, as Calvino points out, leave space for reading books which might be productive of *surprising* discoveries. Social theory can never remain content with frozen images.

I try in this book to reinterpret the politics of Hegel, Marx and Arendt in a way that makes them interesting for our own times. I also try to read them in relation to the common concerns they confront – the spectres of both freedom and barbarism by which the modern world is haunted. We cannot read any 'classic' of political thought in a vacuum. We cannot cut ourselves off from contemporary experience or contemporary writing. And even if we find contemporary political culture banal and stultifying, it remains the necessary context in which we have to place ourselves. When we read any 'classic', we have to establish where we are reading it *from*, for otherwise we will tend to drift, as Calvino puts it, in a 'timeless haze'. The evocative image Calvino draws of a classic text is that it 'relegates the noise of the present to a background hum which at the same time the classics cannot exist without', and 'persists as a background noise when a present that is totally incompatible with it holds sway' (Calvino 1999: 9). This captures very well my own relation to these writers. I would only add to what Calvino says that we should not make the opposite error of turning contemporary presuppositions into an absolute standard against which to measure the validity of what these authors wrote. If there is a point in returning to the past, it is not to hear something that is merely an echo of our own voices but rather to confront afresh our own political assumptions and open up new possibilities. We have to allow the *differences* between 'them' and 'us' to become visible or audible without assuming that when a difference emerges 'they' are wrong and 'we' are right. There is not much use in setting up a contemporary standard – be it the 'open society', or the 'recognition of difference', or 'deliberative democracy' – as an Archimedian point against which to judge the worth or failings of past writers. After all, Hegel, Marx and Arendt engaged critically with most of the major and some of the minor political currents of their day, and it is in the spirit of their work if we read it as a critical engagement with our own present-day prejudices.

Let me state certain methodological guidelines which inform my own reading of these books. First, politics is *part* of our world, not the whole. It is not surprising that those who specialise in the study of politics sometimes mistake the part for the whole and confuse the forms of subjectivity, freedom and discipline which constitute *political* modernity with modernity as such. But to understand the substance of modern politics, we need to address its place within the whole, not identify it with the whole.

Second, we should not assume that the separation of politics as a separate sphere from other areas of social life is something which is naturally the case. The world has not always been divided up in this way. The separation of politics from society in general is an historical accomplishment, not a fact of nature, and we need to ask what it is about the modern age that gives rise to and maintains such divisions.

Third, we need to ask how the separation of political from other spheres of social life is achieved. I treat its emergence as a product of the actual ways in which the social world is organised. We cannot separate our ways of seeing from what is seen, nor can we treat the emergence of certain disciplinary divisions within academe independently of the subject matter which those disciplines reflect and respond to.

Fourth, in seeking to bridge the gap between a tradition of social theory which ignores or devalues the political and a tradition of political thought which ignores or devalues the social, I think we need to keep our feet firmly on the ground. What has occurred in practice is that the old neglect of politics within social theory has now been 'remedied' by all manner of over-compensatory discourses – either introducing politics into every nook and cranny of social life or turning the political into an ontology of freedom. In this respect, at least, we need to steer a middle path.

Finally, Jürgen Habermas has argued that contemporary political thought tends to be divided into two camps – on the one side, a normative political philosophy which loses contact with the world and speaks of 'the political' in a spirit of disdain for actual politics; on the other, a realist political science which contents itself with describing the world from a resolutely non-normative point of view and either accepts things the way they are or says that nothing better can be expected here. Few of us who engage in this trade would like to think of ourselves in either camp, but what Habermas says is certainly recognisable. To bridge this gap, I reach towards a form of political thought whose task is to *understand* the world as something external to itself and on this basis to make space for reflective judgement and wilful action. Understanding is itself an activity which resists indoctrination and mindless obedience, attaches us in our subjectivity to the world around us, and needs no further justification.

There is of course a subjective element in my choice of authors and their works, but my central argument is that these three writers, read together and released from the weight of prior interpretations, continue to illuminate both political life and our ways of understanding it. I start with Hegel because he put the idea of right at the centre of his political philosophy and broke radically from natural law in his conception of a science of right. I move to Marx not because he understood Hegel well, but because no one has better illuminated what Hegel was doing in his *Philosophy of Right* than Marx in his critique of *Capital*, and because reading Hegel and Marx together gives us a more complete and fruitful account of modernity than reading them apart. It allows us to see the relation between the subjective forms of right and the objective forms of the commodity as two sides of a single social order. I finish with Arendt, not because she had a profound understanding of Hegel and Marx, which she did not, but because no one has more subtly elaborated both the potentiality for barbarism and the possibilities of freedom that arise out of modern political life than she did in *Origins of Totalitarianism*. She picked up the mantle of Hegel and Marx far more than is currently recognised.

We cannot understand any of the classic texts of political philosophy in isolation. Writers write both in relation to other writers and in relation to the great political events of their times, and it is this twofold relationship, to social and political thought and reality, that gives meaning and purpose to their work. The meaning of words cannot be isolated from their use and all manner of misunderstanding arises if we abstract political concepts from the theoretical and social relations in which they are inserted. As social theorists we often lay claim to the originality both of the events we seek to comprehend and of the forms of thought we devise to make comprehension possible. We have a professional interest in stressing the innovative character of our conceptual discoveries, the disjunction of our own thought from the tradition which precedes us, and the peculiar pertinence of our ways of thinking to the problems which dominate our own times. Hegel, Marx and Arendt are no exception. They too stressed the revolutionary character both of their age and their own thought in relation to their age. Indeed, they rightly placed the idea of revolution as the most important idea of modern political life.

It is perhaps a paradox of contemporary social and political thought that the more we lose sight of the modern idea of revolution, overcome by disillusionment in the face of broken promises, the more we are infatuated with the idea of the *novum* – a sense of originality that miraculously escapes all complicity with the past. If we say today, as many do, that we must finally break with the idea of a radical break, this is not to abandon the idea of revolution, which provides after all the only possibility of escape from injustice and despair, but rather to relinquish a conceptual form of thinking which mystifies the idea of revolution, lifts it far above the mundane world, and loses sight of the fact that it is itself a product of the world it seeks to change. The proclivity of revolution to reproduce, sometimes in more irrational form, the power it overturns is not a reason for us to throw up our hands in despair, but rather to face up to the burden of events whatever message it delivers, to explore the dynamics of our own disillusionment, and see the notion of 'absolute beginning' for what it is: the merely conceptual aspect of political life divorced from its actuality. The philosophy which places its idea of the political opposite existing politics forgets that the ideal is itself a one-sided, untrue and sometimes menacing expression of the world we need both to comprehend and change.

1

READING AND
MISREADING HEGEL'S
PHILOSOPHY OF RIGHT

The state is the actuality of concrete freedom. But *concrete freedom* requires that personal individuality and its particular interests should reach their full *development* and gain *recognition of their right* for itself . . .

(Hegel PR §260A)

The old orthodoxy

If Hegel were what his critics thought he was, a philosopher who devised the most elaborate of means to justify the subjection of the individual to the state, then there would be little point in dredging up his politics today – except perhaps out of an interest in how the idea of freedom can be transformed by the modern mind into its opposite. Fortunately, however, this is not the case. Hegel was a philosopher of *right*, not of the *state*, and it is here that his contribution to contemporary political thought lies. In short, the image we are often given of the *Philosophy of Right* bears little resemblance to what we find when we actually read the text.

In his *Lectures on Hegel and his Time* (1857) Rudolf Haym set the scene for what we might call the *old orthodoxy*, when he described Hegel's *Philosophy of Right* as a 'formula for political conservatism' whose aim was to provide 'a scholarly justification of the Karlsbad police state and its political persecution'. It was Haym who branded the older Hegel 'the philosophical dictator of Germany' and discerned in his later work 'the scientific dwelling of the spirit of Prussian restoration'. He described the *Philosophy of Right* as a 'pernicious, terrifying doctrine' which 'sanctifies the existing as such', elevates the state into an object of divine worship and debases the individual into a superfluous and expendable 'moment' of the state. Worst of all, Hegel did so in the name of right and freedom. It seemed to Haym that Hegel's identity of the actual and the rational was 'absolutely scandalous', either because it rationalised the existing political order or because it was a mere tautology dressed up in the finery of speculative philosophy.[1]

Haym paved the way for the increasingly hostile judgements passed on the *Philosophy of Right* by later generations of liberal scholars, especially those who witnessed the violence of modern states manifested in the First World War and then in the rise of totalitarian regimes. After the First War, L. T. Hobhouse called Hegelianism a 'false and wicked doctrine' which uses so-called 'dialectical logic' to convert the freedom of the individual into the freedom of the state against the individual (Hobhouse 1918). The logic of the 'metaphysical theory of the state', as Hobhouse saw it, was this: first, freedom can only be attained when we think and act in conformity with our own rational will, otherwise we are determined by our passions; second, the rational will of the individual is identical to the general will, i.e. the will which expresses the good of society as a whole; third, the general will is embodied in the rational state. At the end of this dialectical dog's dinner Hobhouse argued that we find ourselves free only when our actions and thoughts conform with those demanded of us by the state. Needless to say, Hobhouse was not impressed by this 'logic', although it should be noted that his main target was not Hegel himself but the 'neo-Hegelian' theories of the state advanced by the likes of James Stirling (1865 and 1971) and Bernard Bosanquet (1918).

With the experience of totalitarianism before its eyes, 'English' liberalism became even more impassioned in its hostility to Hegel's philosophy of the state. Karl Popper wrote in 1945 that in Hegel's political philosophy 'the state is everything, and the individual is nothing'. Popper echoed the view earlier expressed by Schopenhauer, that the 'old man' debased philosophy by turning it into a tool of state interests, and he proclaimed that Hegel's 'bombastic and mystifying cant' was influential only because it had the authority of the Prussian state behind it. Popper saw in Hegel a crucial link between old Platonism and modern totalitarianism (Popper 1966: 31). His outrage was only fuelled by Hegel's insistence that 'the absolute goal of free mind is to make freedom its object, i.e. to make freedom objective' (*PR* Preface 32). It was this use of the language of freedom to deny freedom that appeared as Hegel's greatest offence. In 1946 Bertrand Russell followed suit, when he wrote that Hegel's *Philosophy of Right* 'justifies every internal tyranny and every external aggression that can possibly be imagined' (Russell 1984: 768–9). In the same year Ernst Cassirer wrote that 'no other philosophical system has done so much for the preparation of fascism and imperialism as Hegel's doctrine of the state' (Cassirer 1946: 273). Literally hundreds of other examples of such hatred toward Hegel's political philosophy could be given.

The textual support for this reading of *Philosophy of Right* was present in Hegel's characterisation of the modern state. He described it as 'the actuality of the ethical idea – the ethical spirit as substantial will, *manifest* and clear to itself, which thinks and knows itself and implements what it knows in so far as it knows it' (*PR* §257); as 'self-consciousness . . . raised to its universality' and as 'rational in and for itself' (*PR* §258); as 'an absolute and unmoved end in itself' in which 'freedom enters into its highest right' (*PR* §258), as 'the march of god in the world' and 'power of reason actualising itself' (*PR* §258A). Hegel wrote that 'one should expect nothing from the state except what is an expression of rationality' and that we should, therefore, 'venerate the state as an earthly divinity' (*PR* §272A), etc.

Hegel also wrote that as individuals we are mere 'moments' in relation to the self-sufficient power of the state, that our 'highest duty is to be members of the state' (*PR* §258) and that our existence is a matter of 'indifference' compared with that of the state (*PR* §145A). It certainly appears at face value that the old orthodoxy was right – that Hegel's *Philosophy of Right* sanctifies the state as much as it devalues the rights of individuals. There is, however, more to Hegel than meets the eye.

One major difficulty with this reading of *Philosophy of Right* has now been well rehearsed within the secondary literature: it is that it was based on a selective and one-sided reading of the text which does violence to the text as a whole. The crucial concept Hegel uses to characterise the modern state is that of 'concrete freedom', by which he means a freedom which *combines* the rights of individuals with the unity of the state. In a now famous passage Hegel writes:

> The principle of modern states has enormous strength and depth because it allows the principle of subjectivity to attain fulfilment in the *self-sufficient extreme* of personal particularity, while at the same time *bringing it back to substantial unity* and so preserving this unity in the principle of subjectivity itself. The essence of the modern state is that the universal should be linked with the complete freedom of particularity and the well-being of individuals . . . the universality of the end cannot make further progress without the personal knowledge and volition of the particular individuals who must retain their rights . . . the universal must be activated, but subjectivity on the other hand must be developed as a living whole. Only when both moments are present in full measure can the state be regarded as articulated and truly organised.

In other words, the principle of the modern state requires in Hegel's account the *complete* freedom of the individual subject. This right of subjective freedom is not only the accomplishment of the modern state, it is what defines the modern age and its ripples affect every sphere of social life:

> This right, in its infinity, is expressed in Christianity, and it has become the universal and actual principle of a new form of the world. Its more specific shapes include love, the romantic, the eternal salvation of the individual as an end, etc.; then there are morality and conscience, followed by the other forms, some of which will come into prominence . . . as the principle of civil society and as moments of the political constitution, while others appear within history at large, particularly in the history of art, the sciences and philosophy.
>
> (*PR* §124R)

Hegel argues that the right of subjective freedom is the key marker of the difference between the ancient and the modern age. In the ancient *polis*, he writes, 'universality was indeed already present but . . . particularity had not yet been released and set at liberty' (*PR* §260A). It is only in the modern age that we see for the first time in human history the desire to *reconcile the universal and the particular* in the form of the modern state.

This aspect of Hegel's philosophy of right has now been widely noted. For example, in his introduction to the Cambridge University Press edition of *Philosophy of Right* Allen Wood points out that the institutions which Hegel includes within his rational state – individual rights, the rule of law, trial by jury, a written constitution, a professional civil service, a representative legislature, a relatively autonomous civil society, the separation of church and state, etc. – were not generally present within existing Prussian political life, corresponded closely with the aims of the Prussian democratic reform movement and not with those of Prussian restorationism, and prefigured in large measure the shape of the liberal democratic polity to come (Wood 1991: ix). In Hegel's idea of the 'rational state' the monarchy was constitutional rather than absolutist (*PR* §273), the executive was in the hands of the educated middle classes rather than the nobility (*PR* §297), the legislature was based on popular representation (*PR* §300), the landed classes were corralled into a relatively powerless upper house of lords (*PR* §§302 and 304), religious authority was separated from the state (*PR* §270R), and the Reformation was celebrated for its inauguration of autonomous, reflective individuality (*PR* Preface 22). Wood concludes that the image of *Philosophy of Right* painted by the old orthodoxy was 'simply wrong' (Wood 1991: ix).

There is plenty of other material in the text to support Wood's criticisms of the old orthodoxy. First, Hegel's comment on those who in his own time sought to deny civil and political rights to Jews, on the grounds that they belonged to a 'foreign nation', may serve to illustrate his commitment to a universal conception of human rights and his opposition to any exclusionary political agenda. When we speak of Jews as *human beings*, Hegel wrote,

> this is not just a neutral and abstract quality . . . for its consequence is that the granting of civil rights gives those who receive them a *self-awareness* as recognised *legal* persons in civil society . . . If they had not been granted civil rights, the Jews would have remained in that isolation with which they have been reproached, and this would rightly have brought blame and reproach upon the state which excluded them.
>
> (*PR* §270 fn.)

For Hegel the idea of humanity was not a 'mere idea' but the solid ground on which civil and political rights were to be based.

Second, the restorationist reading of *Philosophy of Right* makes little sense of Hegel's fierce attacks on the leading figure of the Prussian Restoration, Karl Ludwig von Haller, whose *Restoration of Political Science* (1818) had appeared two years earlier and proposed a particularly thoughtless version of the doctrine that 'might is right'.[2] Hegel formulates the 'principle' of Haller's thesis thus:

just as in the inanimate world the larger displaces the smaller, the powerful the weak, etc., so also among the animals, and likewise among human beings does the same law reappear in nobler forms . . . this is accordingly the eternal and unalterable ordinance of God, that the more powerful rules, must rule and always shall rule'.

(*PR* §258)

Hegel comments with unconcealed scorn:

Herr von Haller not only consciously dispenses with the rational content of the state and with the form of thought, but fulminates with passionate zeal against them both. The *Restoration* doubtless owes part of what Herr von Haller assures us is the widespread influence of its principles to the fact that it has managed . . . to dispense with *all thoughts* and has thereby managed to make the whole work as of *one* piece in its thoughtlessness.

(*PR* §258 fn.)

Hegel describes Haller's hatred of right, law and legislation as 'the shibboleth whereby fanaticism, imbecility and hypocritical good intentions manifestly and infallibly reveal themselves for what they are, no matter what disguise they may adopt' (*PR* 258 fn.). Neither does the 'old' reading of *Philosophy of Right* make much sense of Hegel's attacks on the *historical school of jurisprudence* whose leading representative, Friedrich Karl von Savigny, sought to justify existing laws by tracing their roots back to Roman law. Hegel pointed out that the attempt to justify present-day laws by reference to their origins suffers from the genetic fallacy, that since those historical circumstances no longer exist, nothing is justified in terms of present conditions.

If it can be shown that the origin of an institution was entirely expedient and necessary under the specific circumstances of the time, the require-ments of the historical viewpoint are fulfilled. But if this is supposed to amount to a general justification of the thing itself, the result is precisely the opposite; for since the original circumstances are no longer present, the institution has thereby lost its meaning and its right.

(*PR* §3R)

One example Hegel gives is the attempt to justify the existence of monasteries in the modern world by reference to their past services 'in cultivating and populating areas of wilderness and in preserving scholarship through instruction, copying of manuscripts, etc.' Since these circumstances have now changed, he concludes, the monasteries have at least in these respects become superfluous. The key point is this: that 'a determination of right may be shown to be entirely *grounded in* and *consistent with* the prevailing *circumstances* . . . yet it may be contrary to right and irrational in and for itself' (*PR* §3R). There are numerous determinations

9

of Roman civil law which follow quite consistently from Roman institutions of patriarchalism and slavery, but are not for this reason *right*. The basic problem with the historical school of jurisprudence, as Hegel put it, is that it makes possible 'the eternally deceptive method of . . . *supplying a good reason for a bad thing* and believing that the latter has thereby been justified . . . the truly essential issue, the concept of the thing, has not even been mentioned' (*PR* §3).[3]

Hegel was equally dismissive of the hatred of right, law and the state that was expressed by radicals in the name of the people. Taking as his example the German nationalist, Jacob Fries, he characterises his doctrine thus:

> In a people among whom a genuine communal spirit prevails, all business relating to public affair would gain its *life from below, from the people itself*; *living* societies, steadfastly united *by the sacred bond of friendship*, would dedicate themselves to every single project of popular education and popular service.
>
> (*PR* Preface 15)

As Hegel saw it the superficiality of Fries's self-styled philosophy lay in the fact that it was not based on 'the development of thought and the concept but on immediate perception and contingent imagination'. It reduced 'the complex inner articulation of the ethical, i.e. the state, the architectonics of its rationality . . . to a mush of "heart, friendship and enthusiasm"' (*PR* Preface 16). It substituted for the *work* of understanding *feeling* which reserves the right to do as it pleases and *conscience* which identifies right with subjective conviction. It declared its contempt for reason and science on the grounds that truth cannot be known, while at the same time it declared this truth to be incontrovertible. It reduced truth and ethics to subjective convictions, with the result that the most criminal of principles, since they too are convictions, were accorded the same status as the most democratic and ethical (*PR* Preface 19). Hegel described this radical hatred of right and law (no less than the conservative hatred expressed by von Haller) as the 'chief shibboleth whereby these false friends of "the people" give themselves away' (*PR* Preface 17).[4]

The new orthodoxy

The natural conclusion to be drawn from these arguments is that Hegel's philosophy of right was far more embedded in the liberal tradition than it seems at first sight. Certainly the image of Hegel as the philosopher of Prussian restoration or as the precursor of totalitarianism is shattered once we read these parts of the text. It is not surprising, therefore, that the image that has replaced the old orthodoxy is that Hegel was after all a liberal and that his philosophy was aimed at displaying the fundamental rationality of modern liberal institutions. From within the perspective of this 'new orthodoxy' Hegel is now celebrated both as an heir to classical liberal theories of the state and as their arguably most advanced interpreter. Many commentators now praise him for three major achievements: first, overcoming the *ahistorical* and *asocial* conceptions of natural right present within *natural law* theories of liberalism and instead locating the idea of right in the infrastructure of modern political life; second, overcoming the one-sided viewpoint of a 'vulgar' liberalism which treats rights of private property as *everything* and political intervention on behalf of the public good as *nothing*; and third, reminding liberalism of its own forgotten origins when the aim was not to affirm private right over the public good but rather to achieve *harmony, reconciliation, synthesis* between these poles. From this perspective Hegel's *Philosophy of Right* was a critique of a vulgarised liberalism but not of liberalism as such.

The new orthodoxy has taken many different forms. For example, one of the landmarks of its development within contemporary social theory was the publication in 1972 of Shlomo Avineri's study, *Hegel's Theory of the Modern State*. Avineri argued that Hegel rescued liberalism from its own limitations by radicalising its conception of the state and thereby prefiguring the actual path liberalism was to take. He read Hegel's idea of the 'rational state' as a modern, social democratic welfare state 'free . . . from the shackles of the old absolutism, based on representation, served by a rationally ordered bureaucracy, allowing ample space for voluntary associations and trying to strike a balance . . . between *homo economicus* and *zoon politikon*' (Avineri 1972: 240). For Avineri, the social democratic state really was the 'actuality of the ethical idea'; its citizens really were linked to it by a relation more like 'identity' than 'faith or trust'; the feeling of patriotism was based on the awareness of citizens that their interests are preserved in the state's interests. Avineri echoed Hegel's comment that when we walk the streets at night in safety, we do not often enough reflect on how this is due solely to the working of state institutions (*PR* §268A). He echoed Hegel's opposition to social contract theories which confuse the state and civil society, arguing that the state should not be equated exclusively with the protection of civil society and that the private interests of individuals should not be the ultimate end for which they are united. Avineri endorsed Hegel's theory of the 'rational state' because it was invested with the task not merely of guaranteeing private property but of offering a successful reconciliation of the class conflicts endemic within civil society and of embodying the political self-consciousness of its members (Avineri 1972: 181).

In some versions of the new orthodoxy Hegel's philosophy of right is associated with a radical republicanism. For example, in their introduction to *Hegel's Political Writings* Lawrence Dickey and H. B. Nisbet read the *Philosophy of Right* as a philosophy of 'ethical life' (*Sittlichkeit*) based on a metaphysical belief in the spiritual essence of humanity which, with God's help and our own determination, can be cultivated and actualised in our social and political lives. They read it as a critique of a subjectivism which in its material aspect focuses exclusively on the pursuit of private interests and in its moral aspect focuses exclusively on inner-directed feelings of piety. They see it as a critique of a civil society in which people are fixated on their immediate concerns at the expense of public life and of

11

a self-centred morality which has lost contact with communal concerns. The rehabilitation of Hegel as a political thinker is here linked to his support for a comprehensive public life beyond both the official political institutions of government and the narrow world of private right.

This republican reading of the text is echoed in the work of Andrew Arato. He acknowledges that there are 'two Hegels' fighting an internal battle within the text: an *étatist* Hegel who treats the state as a secular deity whose claims upon its citizens are always unquestionable and irresistible, and a *social* Hegel who identifies universality with the free body of citizens. For the *étatist* Hegel the state must impose order on civil society by means of the police, executive, crown and other administrative organs. The *social* Hegel posits 'the autonomous generation of solidarity and identity' by means of the associations of civil society (estates and corporations), their representatives in the state parliament (the assembly) and public opinion. Arato calls on us to *decide* in favour of the social Hegel: the Hegel who sees civil society as a site for the effective participation of individuals in public life, the Hegel who recognises that citizens have only a restricted part to play in the business of the existing state but who regards it as essential to 'provide people with activity of a general character over and above their private business' (Arato 1991: 316). Hegel's contribution to political thought, as Arato presents it, was to derive the category of civil society from the republican tradition in such a way as to expand public life from the single level of the political state to a series of levels, including 'the public rights of private persons, the publicity of legal processes, the public life of the corporation, and finally the interaction between public opinion and the public deliberation of the legislature' (Arato 1991: 318). In short, he presents the *Philosophy of Right* as at least *containing* within the text a theory of civil society which extols its associational life, representative institutions and rule of law against the external power of the state.

Some recent American commentators read Hegel's philosophy of right as offering a 'middle road' or 'third way' between the conflicting demands of libertarianism and communitarianism, individualism and collectivism, liberalism and Marxism, property and community. For example, in their introduction to *Hegel and Legal Theory*, Drucilla Cornell and her co-editors read him as a critic both of a narrow liberalism which fetishises the right of private property and of an equally narrow socialism which fetishises the authority of the state. They argue that the strength of the *Philosophy of Right* lies in its recognition that property rights are *necessary*, because they make possible 'relationships of mutual recognition and respect among autonomous social actors', but *insufficient* because they 'cannot alone bring about the common good' and individuals must also be educated in the ethical life of the community. The third way, neither liberal nor socialist, is given the name of Hegel (Cornell *et al.* 1991: x).

In a book entitled *Hegel's Critique of Liberalism* Steven Smith writes in a similar vein that Hegel's rational state combines 'the ancient emphasis on the dignity and even architectonic character of political life with the modern concern for freedom, rights and mutual recognition' in such a way as to avoid both the

Arato, as we have seen, admits that there are two Hegels, statist and social, fighting it out in the text and ask us simply to choose. K.-H. Ilting draws on Hegel's earlier lectures on *Natural Law and the Science of the State* to argue that his *basic* political commitment was to a republicanism in which individuals no longer focus *exclusively* on their private rights but also recognise that they must co-operate in the preservation of the political community which guarantees them their private rights in the first place. He argues that in these earlier lectures it is clear that what was important for Hegel was that citizens consciously acknowledge the 'universal', for only by this means can the political order be prevented from splitting into two mutually hostile armies – the public and the private (Ilting 1984: 95). What is entailed is a kind of contract: if the state is to support the personal rights of individuals, the citizens must in return support the state which grants them such rights and without which their so-called natural liberty would be worthless. Ilting admits that the *Philosophy of Right* itself has a more *étatist* character compared with the republicanism of his earlier work, but he explains this mainly as the result of Hegel's personal and political compromises designed to placate the state censors established under the Karlsbad Decrees. T. M. Knox refers simply to the difficulties Hegel had in steering a course between the Scylla of individual right and the Charybdis of state despotism, and surmises that it was only human if he should from time to time founder on one or other of these rocks (Stewart 1996: 79). Although the new orthodoxy has done great service in rehabilitating the liberal, rights-based aspect of Hegel's philosophy of right, it too loses sight of the integrity of the text as a whole. How, for example, are we to reconcile this republican reading with Hegel's declaration that Kant's republicanism would 'destroy the absolutely divine principle of the state, together with its majesty and absolute authority' (*PR* §258R), or his belittling of the doctrine of popular sovereignty as a 'confused idea' (*PR* §§257–68)?

The additional cost of breaking up the unity of the text is also to break up the unity of the system of right itself. Thus while the new orthodoxy has focused on forms of free association and social solidarity within civil society, Hegel presented civil society as an integrated sphere of social life linking the corporations and other forms of association with the system of needs and the police. Or while the new orthodoxy has separated what it sees as the democratic aspects of the state, its representative institutions and constitutional framework, from the 'external' elements of the state which it finds less acceptable, Hegel presents the state as an 'organism' which includes the constitution, the crown, the legislature and the executive as elements of a larger totality. Or while the new orthodoxy has drawn a line between Hegel's critique of the social antagonisms present within civil society and the resolution of these antagonisms provided by the state, Hegel presents the state as *preserving* as well as overcoming the contradictions of civil society and expresses this idea in the concept of 'sublation'. At issue here is not just the difficulty of distinguishing those aspects of Hegel's political philosophy we approve from those we disapprove, nor just the difficulty of preserving the integrity of the text as a whole, but the difficulty of facing up to the equivocations of modern political life. The dimension of Hegel's *Philosophy of Right* that I find missing within the new orthodoxy is that illustrated in Walter Benjamin's comment in *Theses on the Philosophy of History* that 'there is no document of civilisation which is not at the same time a document of barbarism' (Benjamin 1968: 256), or in Thomas Mann's comment that there are not two sides at war, the evil and the good, but only one which 'through the devil's cunning transforms its best into evil'. It is the dimension of Hegel's work that German 'critical theory' was more alert to.

In any event, if it were true that the instruction Hegel gives in the *Philosophy of Right* is to accept the basic rationality of the modern political order, to outlaw all forms of revolutionary criticism, to make the idea of the rational state the only standard of judgement against which to measure existing states, to treat social theory as a necessary aid in revealing the rationality of a world experienced as oppressive – if all this were true, then the outrage expressed by the 'old orthodoxy' might well be more appropriate than the current urge to rehabilitate Hegel's philosophy of right. The strength of the old orthodoxy lay in the outrage it expressed over the violence of the modern state: it was wrong in its assessment of Hegel but its defence of individual right does not thereby lose its validity. The new orthodoxy exposed the limitations of the old reading of Hegel, but it has somehow lost the nerve of outrage against the violence of the state. From the misplaced outrage of the old orthodoxy to the increasingly uncritical pronouncements of the new, liberalism itself remains strangely unquestioned. One declares that Hegel was an enemy of liberal values, the other that he was their champion. Both treat liberalism itself as the standard against which the text must be judged. Neither puts at risk the liberal view of the world. We may conclude that there has been no single path of progression in our reading of this elusive text.

Critical theory

> Today, the doctrines exalting the state, notably Hegelianism, have been thrown overboard . . . Hegel's idea of the state is basically incompatible with the German racial myth. Hegel asserted the state to be 'the realisation of reason' . . . Hegel's theory is rational; it stands also for the free individual. His state is predicated upon a bureaucracy that guarantees the freedom of the citizens because it acts on the basis of rational and calculable norms.
>
> (Neumann 1986: 171–2)

Against the charge of fostering totalitarianism levelled against Hegel by the old liberal orthodoxy in the inter-war period, critical theory defended Hegel on the grounds that Hegel's rational concept of the state was incompatible with the ideas of *Volk* and *Führer* which infused National Socialism. It was argued that Hegel and fascism were impossible bedfellows: why? because Hegel offered a doctrine of the state supremacy and this doctrine was abandoned in Germany when the claims of the Nazi movement conflicted with the claims of the state. For the Nazis, the state represented not an end in itself but a means for their movement, and the idea of the state was subsumed to the authority of the 'true community' bound together by blood and soil and subject to no rational norms. According to the critical theorists, Hegel was attacked because rationality and the right of subjective freedom remained the basis of his view of the state. For Hegel, as Herbert Marcuse put it, the state rules civil society; under Nazism civil society (or at least its most powerful economic and political components) rules the state.

Critical theory situated Hegel firmly within the liberal tradition, but its twist was to indict the liberal tradition itself. It recognised that the *aim* of Hegel's philosophy of right was not to subsume the individual to the power of the state but rather, as Karl Löwith put it in *From Nietzsche to Hegel*, to 'harmonise principles of political community derived from the ancient *polis* with principles of individual freedom derived from modern Christianity' (Löwith 1967: 240). Löwith read the *Philosophy of Right* as a momentous effort to achieve 'moderation' in the face of extremes. In *Reason and Revolution* Herbert Marcuse read it as an attempt to construct a form of state which would preserve the rights of property-owners, resolve the social problems besetting civil society, and embody the universal will. Marcuse wrote:

> The anarchy of self-seeking property owners could not produce from its mechanism an integrated, rational and universal social scheme. At the same time, a proper social order . . . could not be imposed with private property rights denied, for the free individual would be annulled . . . The task of making the necessary integration devolved therefore upon an institution that would stand above the individual interests . . . and yet would preserve their holdings.
>
> (Marcuse 1979: 201)

Reconciliation, moderation, harmony, synthesis . . . these were the keywords that critical theory associated with Hegel. It was convinced, however, that Hegel's attempted reconciliation was spurious. According to Löwith, this was because he failed to address the social questions that were determining the future of bourgeois society: 'how to control the poverty brought about by wealth . . . the progressive division of labour . . . the necessity of organising for the masses forcing their way upward . . . the collision with liberalism . . . the increasing claims of the will of the many . . . who now seek to rule by force of numbers' (Löwith 1967: 241). Löwith thought that Hegel displayed the characteristic political naivety of a philosopher when he stated his belief that modern social antagonisms could be successfully reconciled by the modern state or even by the Prussian state! Franz Neumann and Herbert Marcuse were harsher in their judgements. Neumann wrote that Hegel's Preface to the *Philosophy of Right* was an 'inexcusable paean' to the Prussian state, 'the state of broken promises, of disappointed hopes, a state which cared nothing for free institutions' (Neumann 1986). Marcuse also saw extremely authoritarian tendencies within the *Philosophy of Right* but he maintained that they were a mirror of the trajectory of liberalism itself. His argument was this: as the class inequalities and conflicts endemic in capitalist society were exacerbated, so too the only solution *within the existing conditions* was to turn the state into an increasingly independent power. Marcuse held that it was this practical imperative that impelled Hegel to betray his philosophy of freedom, and that this betrayal could not be undone as long as totality was conceived, as he thought Hegel conceived it, as a 'closed ontological system, finally identical with the rational system of history' (Marcuse 1979: 314). Hegel's fault, so it seemed, did not lie in his naivety but in his hard-headed realism: he knew what had to be done if the state was to achieve the necessary integration in a modern capitalist society.

The only way out, as Marcuse saw it, was to move beyond Hegel's 'abstract, logical, speculative expression of the movement of history' and detach the dialectic from its ontological base (Marcuse 1979: 315). Marcuse considered the positive moment in Hegel's political thinking to be the discovery that the 'possibility and truth' immanent within the modern state is that of humankind becoming 'the conscious subject of its own development'. To realise this end, however, he concluded that it was necessary to foster new forms of individualism (beyond abstract right), new forms of association (beyond civil society) and new forms of human self-consciousness (beyond the state). Against the existing system of 'universal negativity', Marcuse advanced an 'affirmative materialism' which would privilege the idea of happiness and material satisfaction over that of right (Marcuse 1979: 294).

Marcuse's 'solution' was premised on destroying and overcoming the actual system of right which constitutes the modern political order. He turned the key *concepts* associated with the system of right (individuality, association, and self-determination) into abstract ideals whose achievement required the destruction of the system itself. Marcuse's colleague, Theodor Adorno, recognised the impossibility of this kind of utopian critique when he argued that Hegel's speculative identity of the rational and the actual in the *Philosophy of Right* proceeded out of the *collapse* of all attempts at radical separation between a totally irrational 'is' and an abstractly rational 'ought'. Adorno acknowledged that utopian thinking may be a 'necessary moment' in the evolution of critical consciousness, but he argued that it leaves the 'ought' without substance and the 'is' without intelligibility (Jarvis 1998: 169). What appeared to Marcuse as a genuine reconciliation was premised on an opposition between 'what is' and 'what ought to be' which leaves both sides equally empty.

Adorno radicalised Marcuse. In *Negative Dialectics* he vented the full force of critical theory's outrage against Hegel's 'betrayal' and the text reverberates with phrases which might have put a smile on Popper's face. He wrote that in the *Philosophy of Right* Hegel turned the state into an object of worship, degraded individuals into its mere executors, dissolved the everyday experience of alien and oppressive power from an allegedly higher philosophical vantage point, associated political 'fault-finding' with an inferior consciousness, disguised decisions of state as democratic procedures emanating from the will of the people, identified the rational individual with obedience to the state, and held that the individual was always in the wrong whenever he was 'too benighted to recognise his own interest in the objective legal norm' (Adorno 1990: 309). Adorno asserted that Hegel's nationalistic doctrine of the 'popular spirit' was reactionary in relation both to Kant's idea of a cosmopolitan order and his own earlier idea of the 'world spirit'; that his degradation of the individual corresponded to the actual indifference of modern states to the lives of individuals; that his ideology of 'great men' corresponded to the actual cult of the leader in modern polities. In an extremely evocative passage Adorno maintained that the world which the *Philosophy of Right* sanctified, consists of 'an endless procession of bent figures chained to each other, no longer able to raise their heads under the burden of what is'. It is a world which compresses the particular 'like a torture instrument' (Adorno 1990: 345). And Hegel was the philosopher who 'with serene indifference . . . opts once again for the liquidation of the particular', who nowhere in his work doubts 'the primacy of the whole', and who puts the reflective capacity of philosophy into the service of the state.

The strength of the *Philosophy of Right*, according to Adorno, lay in its recognition of the increasing dominance of the universal over the particular in bourgeois society and in its repudiation of the individualistic illusions of liberal thought. Its vice was to mystify the political primacy of the state over the individual by translating it into the logical primacy of the universal over the particular in speculative thought. Adorno's reading of the text was, however, no less one-sided than that of the liberal orthodoxies. This may be illustrated by his impatient dismissal of passages in the *Philosophy of Right* where Hegel apparently argued in defence of subjective freedom. For example, Hegel says that 'a conscience which makes right a matter of subjective conviction will *with good reason* consider the positive forms of duty and law as hostile to itself . . . a dead, cold letter and shackle'; Adorno replies that the phrase 'with good reason' was a mere 'slip of the pen', something that Hegel just 'blurted out', and that Hegel was in fact always on the side of the objective legal norm against individual conscience. Hegel says that 'from the moral standpoint the urge to be something particular can never be content with a notion of the universal which demands that individuals must do only what is prescribed to them'; Adorno replies that Hegel merely 'blackens' the rights of individuals 'as a form of narcissism – like a father chiding his son, "Maybe you think you're something special"' (Adorno 1990: 329). Adorno announces that 'social analysis can learn incomparably more from individual experience than Hegel conceded' *as if* Hegel conceded nothing, but it was Adorno who displayed the real equivocation over the rights of individuals when he grudgingly conceded that 'in the face of the totalitarian unison with which the eradication of difference is proclaimed as a purpose in itself . . . part of the social force of liberation may have *temporarily* withdrawn to the individual sphere' (Adorno 1996: 17). For Hegel the state could *never* be an idea before which all individuality must kneel and there could be nothing temporary about the relationship between social liberation and the individual freedom (*PR* §182A).

It may not be surprising that Adorno, writing under the shadow of Auschwitz, saw only the 'consummate negativity' of the existing system of right. He could offer no solution except to face up to it from the 'standpoint of redemption' – perhaps more in hope than expectation that this standpoint would delineate the 'mirror-image of its opposite'. In a characteristic trope, however, he declared the impossibility of even this 'solution':

> It presupposes a standpoint removed . . . from the scope of existence, whereas we well know that any possible knowledge must not only be first wrested from what is, if it shall hold good, but is also marked for this very reason by the same distortion and indigence which it seeks to escape. The more passionately thought denies its conditionality for the sake of the unconditional, the more unconsciously and so calamitously it is delivered up to the world.
>
> (Adorno 1996: 247)

There appeared to be no exit. The system of right was fated to produce a world of chained and defeated figures, walking through social life as in a prison-yard exercise, and to represent its barbarism in the language of freedom. The overcoming of the system of right was both an absolute necessity and impossible to achieve inasmuch as the overcoming would be marked by the same distortions as that which is overcome. The affiliation of freedom to the idea of 'right' no longer had any substance but the divorce of freedom from right offered no way out. Adorno read the *Philosophy of Right* as a reflection of a totally administered society in which the individual had become superfluous and the universal had become absolute, and as a recognition that this was a fatality which the modern system of right could not escape as long as it remained intact. What is revealed in this account is the sociological aspect of Hegel's depiction of the system of right as a social reality and the potentiality Hegel saw for the growth of fanaticism and barbarism within it. What is lost is any sense of tension, contradiction or other possible outcomes.

Critical theory accepted that in his youth Hegel was revolutionary in both political and philosophical terms, and that he was profoundly inspired by the French revolution. In *The Young Hegel* Georg Lukacs was only the first to point out how far the young Hegel pre-empted the ways of thinking that the young Marx was later to echo (Lukacs 1975). The consensus within critical theory, however, was that the older Hegel came to reject his own earlier radicalism and subsumed his philosophy of freedom to the authority of the state. This is now a widely held view. There is disagreement over the precise *timing* of this rupture. Some locate it around 1800, when Hegel was about thirty years old, in his shift from an emphasis on human individuals and political action to a cosmic *Geist* in which human beings have no active part to play (e.g. Taylor 1993: 74). Others locate it later than 1800, seeing in the *Phenomenology of Spirit* an echo of Hegel's earlier radical themes (e.g. Marcuse 1979: 173). There is disagreement over the *causes* of this change: whether it was the result of merely personal compromises (with age and academic success doubtless playing their part), or of the conflict between Hegel's 'revolutionary method' and 'conservative system' (Marcuse 1979), or of the conservative nature of the dialectical method itself (Colletti 1973), or of the aftershocks of revolutionary terror (Habermas 1974). There is disagreement over the direction of the change: whether it led Hegel to Prussian restorationism or to a prefigurative totalitarianism or less dramatically to what Jürgen Habermas calls an 'emphatic institutionalism'. Wherever the dividing line is placed, whatever reason is adduced to explain it, and however abruptly it is conceived, the consensus is that Hegel's later political writings – and especially his *Philosophy of Right* – express a movement away from youthful radicalism to at best a naive liberalism and at worst a deeply authoritarian state-mind. I think (following Rose 1981) we need to suspend these stereotypical views of a movement from the radicalism of youth to the conservatism of old age and see instead the unity of Hegel's *oeuvre* if we are to uncover what is valuable in the *Philosophy of Right*.

New critical theory

Perhaps more than any other critical theorist, Jürgen Habermas has taken up the challenge of putting the idea of 'right' at the centre of contemporary political thought, and his own magisterial work, *Between Facts and Norms*, may be read as an extended commentary on Hegel's *Philosophy of Right*. Habermas follows in Hegel's footsteps when he expresses his concern that contemporary political theory is disintegrating into what he calls 'normative' and 'realist' camps that have no more to say to one another. The normative approaches of political philosophy are in danger of losing all contact with social reality and are open to the criticism that they take insufficient notice of the hard facts that have long contradicted the self-understanding of the modern constitutional state. The realist approaches of the social sciences are intent on screening out all normative considerations and recommend a disillusioning if not downright cynical view of the political process. They focus only on places where illegitimate forms of power force their way into the constitutionally regulated forms of right and stress only those tendencies in the administrative complex to become autonomous of democratic decision making and to join forces with the social power of organised corporate interests. If the characteristic mode of political philosophy is normative abstraction, the characteristic mode of political sociology is that of normative defeatism. The question Habermas raises is how to bridge the gap between normative and realist theorising, political philosophy and political science, idealism and empiricism, in order to make space for the reconstruction of critical thought.

Hegel's effort to reconcile the rights of individuals with a universal political community provides Habermas with the starting point from which to reintegrate private right, public life and political democracy as elements of a coherent whole.

Habermas argues that this project entails recovering the missing link between the revolutionary tradition of radical, participatory democracy and the liberal tradition of natural law theory which was shattered when on the one hand Marxism discredited the idea of legality and on the other liberalism imposed all manner of institutional and constitutional constraints on the idea and practices of democracy.[5] Habermas seeks to attain what he sees as a new recognition: that today the individual right and the rule of law cannot be thought without radical democracy and that radical democracy cannot be thought without the rule of law. Or to put the same point in another way, private legal subjects cannot enjoy individual liberties if they do not themselves participate in the process of deciding what rights individuals should have, and citizens cannot participate publicly in collective decision making unless they themselves are endowed with legally defensible private and public rights.

In seeking to work through this project, however, Habermas situates Hegel's *Philosophy of Right* firmly within the natural law tradition. He comments that 'natural law up to [and including] Hegel wanted to single out normatively the only reasonable social and political order'. According to Habermas, Hegel only added an historical dimension to the eighteenth-century conceptual repertoire of natural law theory and otherwise remained firmly within its ways of thinking. Hegel, he says, was still in the business of providing 'a direct blueprint for a normative theory of law and morality', and 'remained convinced, just like Aristotle, that society finds its unity in the political life and organisation of the state' (Habermas 1997: 1–5). I want to suggest that there is another Hegel whose signature can be read on the text of the *Philosophy of Right* – a Hegel whom Habermas cannot or will not see.

I do not think that Hegel could have *added* the historical dimension to the repertoire of natural law since, as he himself recognised, the historical dimension had already been added to natural law by Adam Smith and the school of Scottish political economy. After all, Smith's 'state of natural liberty' is achieved self-consciously at the *end of history*, not at its beginning. Second, I do not think Hegel intended to 'single out normatively the only reasonable political order' since the central argument of the Preface in the *Philosophy of Right* was to reorient philosophy away from this natural law perspective and toward a 'scientific and objective treatment' of the actual political order. Third, I do not think that Hegel presents the modern political state as the ultimate principle of political unity, since the nub of his argument in the introduction to the *Philosophy of Right* is that the violence already present in the simplest forms of abstract right is reproduced, not overcome, both in the *internal* constitution of the state and in its *external* relations with other states.

This is not the place to criticise Habermas's immense achievement in reconstructing Hegel's philosophy of right for our own period, but only to suggest that Habermas reads Hegel in the way he does because he, Habermas, remains within the eighteenth-century repertoire of natural law theory. To be sure, he declares his interest in not offering a direct 'blueprint' for a normative theory of law, but a 'guide for reconstructing the network of discourses that . . . provides the matrix from which democratic authority emerges' (Habermas 1997: 5). However, the difference between a 'blueprint' and a 'guide' is one of degree and may not be fundamental inasmuch as the latter still aims at providing what natural law theory has always sought to provide: 'a critical standard against which actual practices – the opaque and perplexing reality of the constitutional state – could be evaluated' (Habermas 1997: 5). When Habermas reconstructs the *Philosophy of Right* for our own time, he approaches it on the basis of his own inheritance from natural law and it is this inheritance that makes it difficult for him to recognise Hegel's far more critical relation to the natural law tradition.[6]

Notes

1 In the *Encyclopaedia* Hegel distinguished between what is 'actual' and what is 'existent' by saying that philosophy must know 'not only that God is actual, the most actual, indeed alone truly actual, but also that existence in general is partly appearance and partly actual'. If this is so, then the identity of the actual and the rational could be read as another way of proclaiming the identity of the rational and the rational – seemingly a mere tautology.

2 Haller was the political philosopher most closely associated with the *Junker* aspiration to re-establish a feudal state and their own overriding authority. Hegel concludes this discussion with the following comment: 'On top of all this incredible crudity, perhaps the most amusing touch is the emotion with which Herr von Haller describes his inexpressible pleasure at his discoveries: "a joy such as only the friend of truth can feel when, after honest enquiry, he attains the certainty that . . . he has, so to speak, found the utterance of nature, the word of God himself"' (*PR* §258 and fn.).

3 Hegel mentions another 'abominable law' which used to give creditors the right to cut off the flesh of debtors. According to this law, if anyone had cut off too much or too little, he would incur no consequent legal disadvantage: a clause which Hegel notes would have benefited Shylock in *The Merchant of Venice*. The appeal to so-called 'old rights' may be used to justify any old barbarity.

4 Hegel's target was well chosen. Fries was 'radical', but he represented the anti-Semitic, xenophobic wing of student fraternity politics. He published a pamphlet called *On the danger posed to the welfare and character of the German people by the Jews*, in which he suggested that Jews should be prohibited from establishing their own educational institutions, marrying Gentiles, employing Christians as servants or immigrating into Germany. He also wrote that Jews should be forced to wear a distinctive mark on their clothing and be encouraged to emigrate from Germany (Avineri 1974: 119–20). Shlomo Avineri had good reason to characterise the political current which Fries represented as 'proto-fascist' (Avineri 1972: 121).

5 According to Habermas, the problem with the traditional view of the socialist project is that in its design and implementation of a concrete form of life, it forgets that the participants themselves must first reach an understanding of what socialism is and that the democratic self-organisation of a legal community constitutes its normative core. Everything then hangs on substance – on *what* understanding they reach.

6 Habermas argues that there is an intrinsic relationship between the rule of law and radical democracy: 'only those laws may claim legitimacy that meet with the agreement of all citizens in a discursive law-making process that is itself legally constituted' (Habermas 1997: 141). He argues that in the 'post-metaphysical' context of the present day, when comprehensive world views and collectively binding ethics

have disintegrated, democratic procedures for the production of rights and laws form the only possible source of political legitimacy. Based on the premise that the integration of differing life-worlds can only be achieved today by 'the actors themselves reaching an understanding about the normative regulation of strategic interaction', including the question of what rights citizens must mutually grant each other if they decide to constitute themselves as a voluntary association of legal subjects, the task he sets social theory is to offer a guide for reconstructing the matrix from which the democratic processes of forming opinions and preparing decisions can emerge. He draws the conclusion that the requirements of self-legislation and self-determination can only be fulfilled with a code that implies the guarantee of individual rights, and by the same token that the equal distribution of these rights can only be satisfied by democratic procedures. This 'reconstructive' way of thinking expresses very well a widely felt desire to reconcile right and democracy, but it is satisfied at the cost of dissolving the actual conflicts which exist between the different forms and shapes of right and of obscuring the distinction between morality and ethical life. It leaves unspoken what happens to those rights which fail to meet this democratic legitimacy test but whose actual legitimacy lies in the substance of the freedom they embody; and equally unspoken what happens to those democratic procedures which fail to produce this rights-effect. Habermas maintains that it is the freedom that allows us to deliberate and reflect on decisions we ourselves have made that is ultimately constitutive of democracy, but everything then depends on the *substance* of such deliberations. Deliberation is certainly a value, but like any other form of right it is *relative* to other forms. The consensus it engenders should not be made into an absolute standard of right.

2

THE IDEA OF HEGEL'S
PHILOSOPHY OF RIGHT

Now I am ready to tell how bodies are changed into different
bodies.

(Ted Hughes, *Tales from Ovid*)

Understanding, politics and the task of philosophy

Hegel's *Philosophy of Right* is a study of the idea of right as it is conceived and
actualised in the modern age. It explores the various forms and shapes which the
idea of right assumes, how one form and shape of right is transmuted into another,
how these different forms and shapes are connected with one another as elements
of a system of right, and how in the course of such metamorphoses the possibilities
of freedom are enhanced and denied. It is an investigation into the dynamics of
subjectivity – not in abstract but as it is made concrete and real in our own social
and political lives.

The task Hegel sets for a philosophy of right is not to express the author's own
moral and political opinions concerning what is right and wrong, not to prescribe
'what ought to be' but rather to understand 'what is'. If something is to be discussed
philosophically, Hegel declares, then it will bear 'only *scientific* and *objective*
treatment' and philosophy will treat with indifference 'any criticism expressed
in a form other than that of scientific discussion of the matter itself' (*PR* Preface
23). Philosophy is not a statement of the philosopher's own 'opinions, feelings
or convictions'; it is not 'what *wells up from each individual's heart, emotion
and enthusiasm*' (*PR* Preface 15); its task is that of understanding rather than
prescription. Hegel writes of the *Philosophy of Right* that:

As a philosophical composition, it must distance itself as far as possible
from the obligation to construct a *state as it ought to be*; such instruction
as it may contain cannot be aimed at instructing the state on how it ought
to be, but rather at showing how the state, as the ethical universe, should
be recognised.

(*PR* Preface 21)

Hegel presents the shift of emphasis contained in the *Philosophy of Right* as a theoretical leap from one kind of political philosophy to another – from a philosophy which prescribes what a reasonable political order should be to a philosophy whose task is to *understand* what the actual political order is. '*Hic Rhodus, hic saltus*' (here is Rhodes, here make the leap).

In case we miss the point, Hegel repeats it in many ways. If a philosopher 'builds a world *as it ought to be*', he writes, 'then it certainly has an existence, but only within his opinions – a pliant medium in which the imagination can construct anything it pleases' (*PR* Preface 22). Philosophy is not about 'inventing and propounding *yet another theory*' of political community, as if the philosopher had to imagine that 'no state or constitution had ever previously existed or were in existence today, but that we had *now* . . . to start right from the beginning and that the ethical world had been waiting only for such intellectual constructions, discoveries and proofs as are now available' (*PR* Preface 12). The task of political philosophy is 'the comprehension of the present and the actual, not the setting up of a world beyond, which exists God knows where – or rather . . . in the errors of a one-sided and empty ratiocination' (*PR* Preface 20). Hegel's repeated instruction is to read the *Philosophy of Right* as a scientific and objective treatment of the actual political order rather than as a normative prescription for an ideal political order. It is in my opinion the inability of commentators to take seriously Hegel's instruction on how to read his text that has been at the root of all the wild and conflicting interpretations which have been made of it.

There is nothing *uncritical* in Hegel's stress on understanding rather than prescription. It is not a recipe for quietism, cynicism or indifference in the face of injustice. I quote:

> Reason is not content with . . . that cold despair which confesses that, in this temporal world, things are bad or at best indifferent, but that nothing better can be expected here, so that for this reason alone we should live at peace with actuality. The peace which cognition establishes with the actual world has more warmth in it than this.
>
> (*PR* Preface 22)

The peace Hegel seeks with the modern world has fire in its belly. He describes it as 'a great obstinacy, the kind of obstinacy that does honour to human beings, that they are unwilling to acknowledge in their attitudes anything which has not been justified in thought' and he presents this 'obstinacy' as one of the great achievements of the modern age (*PR* Preface 22). He sees his own 'science of right' as a creature of this age in its refusal to accept any dogma or doctrine or given authority: 'For such thinking does not stop at what is *given*, whether the latter is supported by the external positive authority of the state or of mutual agreement among human beings, or by the authority of inner feeling and the heart . . .' (*PR* Preface 11). It does not 'adhere with trusting conviction to the publicly recognised truth' nor does it fix any 'position in life' on this so-called 'firm foundation'. Equally it does not turn '*divergence* from what is universally acknowledged as right' into an alternative principle of thought (*PR* Preface 12). When it encounters difficulties in distinguishing what is valid among a variety of opinions, it bases its judgement on 'genuine concern for the matter itself . . . the substance of the right and the ethical', not on the 'vanity and particularity of opinions' (*PR* Preface 12). It locates 'genuine thought' not in an opinion about something but in 'the concept of the thing itself' (*PR* Preface 14). Hegel's idea of a 'science of right' accepts no predetermined authority, whatever its source or however appealing its message. It has nothing in common either with a *positivism* that dogmatically identifies 'what is' with 'what ought to be', or with an *empiricism* which identifies the appearance of things with their whole being.

When things are bad in the world, philosophy as Hegel sees it is not a substitute for *changing* the world, nor is its task that of *interpreting* the world, as if the experience of alienation and domination could be dissolved by some dialectical slight of hand. The task of philosophy is to '*comprehend* what is, because *what is, is reason*' (*PR* Preface 21). Using the allegory of the 'rose in the cross', Hegel writes:

> To recognise reason as the rose in the cross of the present and thereby to delight in the present – this rational insight is the reconciliation with actuality which philosophy grants to those who have received the inner call to *comprehend*, to preserve their subjective freedom in the realm of the substantial and at the same time to stand with their subjective freedom . . . in what has being in and for itself.
>
> (*PR* Preface 22)

In this imagery I find a number of interwoven threads. First, reason is to be found *in the present* and not in pure thought. The point, therefore, is to *recognise* reason in the real world, not to construct abstract ideals that exist only in the philosopher's head. Second, the present is conceived as a *cross*, a world of suffering, and not as the actualisation of reason. Whatever reason it contains, therefore, requires the work of recognition. Third, the specific value of *understanding* is that it preserves the subjective freedom of individuals while at the same time attaching it to the external world, to the realm of the substantial, to what has being in and for itself. In other words, the activity of understanding the world, which is the call of philosophy, is at once a resistance to what Hannah Arendt called 'unworldliness' or the isolation of human subjectivity from the world around it.

Hegel expresses his idea of a philosophy of right in the form of a famous 'doubledictum' or *doppelsatz*: 'What is rational is actual; and what is actual is rational' (*PR* Preface 20). In this speculative identity of the rational and the actual, the first proposition indicates that the so-called abstract ideals we place opposite the real are only the real world reconstructed 'in the shape of an intellectual realm' (*PR* Preface 23). The proverbial example Hegel gives is that of Plato's *Republic*, which he describes as 'essentially the embodiment of nothing other than the nature of Greek ethics'. According to Hegel, the *Republic* expresses Plato's recognition that 'the ethics of his time were being penetrated by a deeper principle . . . [which] within this context could appear . . . only as a destructive force' (*PR* Preface 20). This deeper principle was that of 'free infinite personality' and from the point of view of Greek ethics it appeared destructive because the individual's right to private property 'now filled his entire world' and the ends which individuals set before themselves became those of 'gain, self-maintenance and perhaps vanity' (*PH* 157). Compared with ancient virtue, the materialism of the new world seemed vulgar and the *Republic* was Plato's heroic attempt to counteract this force from above, by invoking the 'external form of Greek ethics' and suppressing individual personality and private property (*PR* Preface 20). Hegel does not wish to 'trash' Plato's opposition to private property or his struggle to defend Greek ethics; on the contrary, he argues that it proves Plato's greatness since 'the principle on which the distinctive character of his Idea turns is the pivot on which the impending world revolution turned' (*PR* Preface 20). However, he argues that Plato's failure to come to terms with the 'principle of self-sufficient particularity' helped to establish a philosophical tradition which regards 'the *present* as vain', looks beyond it 'in a spirit of superior knowledge', and displays the vanity of its own 'superior wisdom' (*PR* Preface 21).

Hegel's second proposition, 'what is actual is rational', states that the modern political world has a rational structure, that its forms and shapes are organised into a system and that it is intelligible in terms of scientific analysis. To say that the modern political world is intelligible is not, of course, to say that it is just or immune to criticism. It is not to say that there is anything wrong in passing negative judgements upon it. There is something wrong only when philosophy 'looks down on the matter in hand with a superior and supercilious air, without having gone into it thoroughly enough to understand its true nature' (*LPWH* 76). Hegel attempts to reconstruct the relation between philosophy and politics in such a way that philosophy abandon both its disdain for the actual political world and its hubris of thinking that it can transform the world in accordance with its own abstract ideals. Political life is not a void waiting for philosophy to give it meaning and content. Hegel's conception of political philosophy does not try to outlaw our rightful need and desire to oppose 'what ought to be' to 'what is', but he is against the presumption that philosophy can deduce 'what ought to be' from *a priori* conceptions of right or from transcendental principles of history, morality and language, and then impose this *sollen* on the rest of us. Hegel's philosophy of right preserves the space which separates our understanding of political life from the practicalities of political action and leaves us *free* to make our own political choices. He does not abandon the struggle to bridge the gap between what is and what ought to be, but he addresses this gap in a way that is designed to forestall the use of violence, terror and annihilation to bring the 'is' in line with the 'ought'.

The *Philosophy of Right* is a contribution to the critique of modern political life. Hegel makes no claim to bird's-eye wisdom, let alone to absolute knowledge. 'The owl of Minerva begins its flight only with the onset of dusk' (*PR* Preface 23), he wrote, but he was writing at the *dawn* of the modern state – at a time when

The subject matter of a philosophy of right, as Hegel presents it, is the *idea* of right. In the term 'idea' Hegel includes both the *concept* of right and what he calls its *actualisation* or *existence*. The idea of right is the *unity* of the concept and its actualisation. Hegel puts the matter thus:

> The subject matter of the *philosophical science of right* is the *Idea of right* – the concept of right and its actualisation. Philosophy has to do with Ideas and therefore not with what are commonly described as *mere concepts*. On the contrary, it shows that the latter are one-sided and lacking in truth. The *shape which the concept assumes in its actualisation*, and which is essential for cognition of the *concept* itself, is different from its *form* of being purely as concept, and is the other essential moment of the Idea. The concept and its existence are two aspects (of the same thing), separate and united, like soul and body . . . A soul without a body would not be a living thing, and vice versa. Thus the existence of the concept is its body . . . the unity of existence and the concept, of body and soul, is the Idea. The Idea of right is freedom, and in order to be truly apprehended, it must be recognisable in its concept and in the concept's existence.
>
> (PR §1)

The *concept* of right and its *existence* are equally 'real' and each viewed in isolation from the other is 'one-sided' and 'lacking in truth'. Conceptual thinking considers only the conceptual aspect and ignores the shapes in which the concept is actualised; realist thinking considers only the existence of right and knows nothing of its concept. Like the body and soul of an individual, Hegel writes, the idea of right contains both concept and existence.

Hegel analyses the forms and shapes of right as a logical progression, starting from the simplest and the most abstract and moving step by step to the more complex and concrete. He begins with abstract right and its internal division into personality, property, contract and wrong. He moves from abstract right to morality (*Moralität*) and its internal division into responsibility, welfare and conscience. From morality he moves to the forms of ethical life (*Sittlichkeit*) which include the family, civil society, the state and relations between states. The family is in turn differentiated into marriage, property and children. Civil society is differentiated into the system of needs, the system of rights, the police and the corporations. The state is differentiated into the constitution, the sovereign, the executive, the legislature and external sovereignty. International law is differentiated into treaties between states, war between states and what Hegel calls the transition from the state to 'world history' (Table 2.1). The spheres of ethical life are further differentiated as shown in Table 2.2. It is a complicated schema, appropriate to the complications of modern political life. The science of right, as Hegel sees it, must observe 'the proper *immanent* development of the thing itself' (PR §2). In this process of 'self-division' and 'self-determination', the concept of right is not only the beginning but also 'the soul which holds everything together

Table 2.1 Transition from abstract right to the modern state

Abstract right	Morality	Ethical life
Personality	Responsibility	Family
Property	Intention	Civil society
Contract	Conscience	State
Wrong		Relations between states

Table 2.2 Spheres of ethical life

Family	Civil society	State	Relations between states
Marriage	System of needs	Constitution	External sovereignty
Property	System of rights	Monarch	International law
Children	Police and welfare	Legislature	World history
	Corporations	Executive	

and which arrives at its own differentiation only through an immanent process' (PR §32). Every form and shape of right develops through an internal process into the next form and shape of right, thus displaying them all as a connected series or *system*. The 'higher dialectic', as Hegel puts it, is the movement of right through its various 'concepts and shapes'. As the movement of right from one form and shape to another, the dialectic is not an 'external activity of subjective thought . . . but the very soul of the content which puts forth its branches and fruit organically' and which thought merely observes (PR §31). The 'science of right' is not content with describing the outward appearances of this movement; its aim is rather to detect the 'inner pulse' that beats within the wealth of forms, appearances and shapes that constitute the field of right as a whole (PR Preface 21). Nor does it presuppose some *resultat* at the end of this journey, some final moment of reconciliation, be it a teleology of progress culminating in the modern state or a cosmopolitan global order or a teleology of regress culminating in barbarism and destruction. In Hegel's philosophy of right we are presented with a radically incomplete drama of human struggle. In this dialectic the pulse of freedom does not stop beating.

Hegel's 'higher dialectic' contrasts with the 'vulgar dialectic' (the famous triad of thesis, antithesis and synthesis) he discerned in natural law theory. Put at its simplest, the *thesis* or *positive moment* of natural law is the idea of abstract right and its embodiment in personality and private property. The right of property is associated with liberation from relations of personal dependency, the freedom to use and abuse one's own property as one wishes, the legal equality of property owners, the wealth of nations, etc. The *antithesis* or *negative moment* consists in the clash of interests which occurs when individuals, as owners of private property, overcome their mutual isolation and associate with one another on the basis of generalised relations of exchange and contract. The society thus formed, 'civil society', is beset by new forms of social antagonism and systemic contradiction, including social inequalities, moral corruption, political tyranny and economic instability. The *synthesis* or *moment of reconciliation*, as conceived within natural law, is achieved through the formation of a rational state designed to unify the political order as a whole. The rational state guarantees the rights of persons and their property, reconciles the antagonisms of civil society and provides the space for popular participation in the general administration of society that is otherwise missing in an age of private concerns (Fine 1985: ch. 1). Many commentators treat the *Philosophy of Right* as if the schema of natural law theory were also Hegel's schema (e.g. Habermas 1997: 1–5), but Hegel objected to the *naturalistic* foundations of this schema, to the *external* ways in which relations between the different forms of right were conceived, and to the premature sense of *completion* it proffered in the idea of the rational state as a unifying force.

Hegel argues that each stage of the movement of right represents the existence of right in one of its determinations: as personality, property, morality, family, civil society, the state, representation, etc. Each form represents a distinctive variety of right and gives determinate shape to freedom. None, however, can be understood except in relation to the system of right as a whole:

> its particular determinations should not be considered in isolation and in the abstract, but rather as a dependent moment within *one* totality, in the context of all the other determinations which constitute the character of a nation and age; within this context they gain their genuine significance and hence also their justification.
>
> (PR §3R)

It is one of the errors of *abstract thought* to consider a particular determination – be it private property or the state or civil society or the system of representation or the constitution – in isolation from the rest, as if right were embodied in this particular determination alone and all the rest were external to it. The fact that property, morality, ethics and the interests of the state can come into collision, indicates that they are all forms of right and relative in relation to one another. As Hegel puts the matter, 'only the right of the world spirit is absolute in an unlimited sense' (PR §30R). The error of *abstract thought* is to isolate one particular form and shape of right from the rest and treat it as privileged. This tendency is present in political doctrines which privilege either private property (neo-liberalism), or the state (official socialism), or the system of representation (radical democracy), or the bureaucracy (bureaucratic collectivism), or civil society (civil society theory), or public participation (republicanism). In every case, the 'other' forms of right are not recognised as such and are viewed instead as instances of illegitimate power. When battles rage between these different doctrines, no one can be indifferent to their outcome; but they share a common inability to recognise the system of right as a whole and the *articulation* of these different forms within the system as a whole.

Hegel's philosophy of right forgoes the purely *historical* task of viewing 'the emergence and development of determinations of right as they appear in time' (*PR* §3R). It explores the *logical* progression of the forms and shapes of right which may or may not coincide with their order of historical emergence. The development from the most abstract to the most concrete forms of right is a conceptual sequence which may or may not coincide with the temporal sequence of their actual appearance. For instance, the family certainly comes into existence before private property, but private property is nonetheless dealt with first on the ground that the family, as it is in the modern world, is only 'the subsequent and further stage (of the concept of abstract right), even if it should itself come first in actuality'. Hegel describes his own methodology thus:

> We merely wish to observe how the concept determines itself, and we force ourselves not to add anything of our own thought and opinions. What we obtain in this way, however, is a series of thoughts and another series of existent shapes, in which it may happen that the temporal sequence of their actual appearance is to some extent different from the conceptual sequence. Thus we cannot say, for example, that property existed before the family, although property is nevertheless dealt with first. One might accordingly ask at this point why we do not begin with the highest instance, that is, with the concretely true. The answer will be that we wish to see the truth precisely in the form of a result, and it is essential for this purpose that we should first comprehend the abstract concept itself. What is actual, the shape which the concept assumes, is therefore from our point of view only the subsequent and further stage, even if it should come first itself in actuality. The course we follow is that whereby the abstract forms reveal themselves not as existing for themselves, but as untrue.
>
> (*PR* §32A)

The word 'untrue' at the end of this passage indicates that the point of departure may not be what comes first in time but that it is determined by what constitutes the most abstract and simple forms of the modern age. When Hegel says that the notion of a person possessed of free will is the *first* form of modern subjectivity, or that property is the *first* form in which 'the free will must first give itself an existence' (*PR* §33A), his use of the word 'first' is not temporal but conceptual.

In the course of the self-determination of the idea of right, as both concepts and shapes change, the concrete institutions of modern political life may appear to be independent of their origins. But this appearance of independence is illusory in that the determination of each concept and shape presupposes those determinations from which it results. The starting point should *not*, therefore, be the 'highest instance' or the 'concretely true', such as the state itself, because it is itself the result of many determinations and can only be understood if we break it down into its simpler and more abstract elements. 'Sublation' (*Aufhebung*) is the name Hegel gives to the movement from the simple and abstract to the complex and concrete. It indicates that the characteristics belonging to the simpler forms (say, private property) enter into the higher forms (say civil society) and that the relation between them is *intrinsic*, not *external*. The relation between the simpler forms and the more complex is not merely one of *progression*, as if the state is a 'higher form of right' than individual personality; still less is it one of *transcendence*, as if the emergence of the state somehow makes individual personality redundant; nor is it one of *reconciliation*, as if the state resolves the conflicts and contradictions that previously tore civil society apart. The use of the term 'sublation' indicates a relation between *preservation* and *transcendence* in which both sides are kept in mind: it indicates that the contradictions present within the simpler forms of right are preserved as well as transcended in the more complex. The contradictions present in abstract right enter into civil society, those present in civil society enter into the state, those present in the state enter into the cosmopolitan order.

The movement of right is complicated by the inversions suffered by the presuppositions of the state once they become in the course of their development objective moments of the state itself. When the simple and abstract changes into the complex and concrete, the former becomes in turn determined as that which the latter has posited. What originally appears as the presupposition, now appears as that which is itself posited. Thus originally the state presupposes civil society, but after the formation of the state it is the state which posits civil society as a moment of its own existence. It is now civil society that presupposes the state and it is only when this is the case that civil society can attain its own full development (PR §182A). Rights which originally appear to belong to us by virtue of our personality become the property of a legal system whose prerogative is to enact, adjudicate and enforce our rights and punish those who violate them. The subject who starts life as the autonomous, self-directing atom of natural law theory, becomes in the course of this movement a bearer of rights whose actualisation depends on the legal system. All the differences between natural right and legal positivism have their origin in this dialectic. As Hegel puts it, 'Natural law or philosophical right is different from positive right, but it would be a grave misunderstanding to distort this difference into an opposition or antagonism' (PR §3R). The mutation of positive law into the state can create all manner of confusion when properties belonging to *state* law are attributed to law as such, or when properties belonging to state *law* are attributed to the state as such. The form is identical in each case, so that from the juridical point of view either the law appears as something posited by the state or alternatively the state appears to be no more than a sum of laws. The effect is particularly disorienting when the ills of the modern state are loaded on to the legal form or when the virtues of the legal form are projected on to the modern state.[1]

The task of the philosophy of right, as Hegel presents it, is not to dissolve the experience of domination, nor to declare that at some deeper level we have consented to whatever the state commands, nor to say that the experience of oppression is merely superficial on the grounds that the concept of the state is invisible to natural consciousness, nor to embrace a 'dialectic' which, as Hegel puts it, 'takes an object, proposition, etc., given to feeling or to the immediate consciousness in general, and dissolves it, confuses it, develops it this way and that, and is solely concerned with deducing its opposite' (*PR* §31). The dialectic is the movement of right. To understand it is to explain the experience of subjection, not to annul it from a higher philosophical standpoint. The state is not the endpoint of freedom or the culmination of the idea of right, it is not the telos at the end of any line of progression, and nothing would be more ridiculous than to invert this logic and see the movement from abstract right to the state as a fall from grace or as a step which can and should be retraced. The movement from an initial stage of freedom, as the right to do as you please with what is yours congruent with the freedom of others to do as they please with what is theirs, to the actualisation of freedom in a concrete political form, cannot be reversed or undone.

The fetishism of the subject and the total state

Hegel's philosophy of right at once embraces the *right of subjective freedom* as the supreme achievement of the modern age, and it stands in opposition to a *subjectivism* which fetishises the subject, converts it into the absolute and fixes on this moment in its 'difference from and opposition to the universal' (*PR* §124R). Hegel's insistence that the goal of a free mind is to 'make freedom *objective*' has a twofold meaning: on the one hand, it indicates that the right of subjective freedom is not merely an idea but has to be actualised in the world as something substantial and politically real; on the other hand, it indicates that pure subjectivity – i.e. the metamorphosis of the subject into an independent power, supreme in status, unrestricted by any spiritual or material constraint – is not the goal of a free mind. For Hegel, the distinction between subjectivity and *subjectivism* (or the fetishism of the subject) is crucial. If the former is the greatest achievement of the modern age, the latter constitutes its characteristic pathology. The subject becomes 'like a God'. It presents its will as absolute. It demands worship. What starts life as a principle of critical thought becomes in the course of its own development a new source of superstition and subjection.

Nowhere is the importance of this distinction between subjectivity and subjectivism drawn out more sharply than in Hegel's analysis of the subjectivism of the modern state. In the system of right, the state represents freedom in its most *concrete* form, inasmuch as 'the momentous unification of self-sufficient individuality with universal substantiality takes place' within it, and for this reason is 'superior to the other stages' of right (*PR* §33A). However, Hegel does not present the modern state as the completion or culmination of ethical life. He demonstrates rather that the *concept* of the modern state is itself *irrational, one-sided, untrue*. It presents itself as an earthly God, as having God-like characteristics. It assumes its own divinity and demands to be worshipped. It equates itself to the power of reason itself. This is the language of megalomania. The state does not appear as what it is, a form of right relative to other forms, but as the Absolute.

The essential contradiction of the modern state, as Hegel presents it, does not lie in the difference between the *concept* and its *actualisation* but in the concept itself. The difference between the concept of the state and its actual 'disfigurements' is not a difference to be overcome in the name of the concept. We cannot take the *concept* of the state to be rational and ideally given, and then criticise or transform the existing state from that standpoint, for it makes no sense to try to bring empirical reality up to the level of the concept if the concept itself is irrational, untrue and one-sided. When Hegel declares that the *idea* of the state is the unity of its *concept* and *existence*, he does not mean that the existing state is only *realised* to the extent that it realises its concept, as if the latter alone comprises its essential being or rational structure. On the contrary, if the distance between the concept and existence of the state is treated as a deficiency to be overcome in the name of their rational identity; this will not dispel the political illusions of our age but replicate them in their most irrational form. The pretension of the modern state to be 'absolute' is already dangerous enough without political philosophy demanding that all obstacles to the realisation of this pretension be overcome.

The Italian idealist philosopher, Giovanni Gentile, may serve to illustrate what Hegel opposed. He thought that he was drawing on Hegel's *Philosophy of Right* when he coined the term 'totalitarianism' in the 1920s to express the actuality of 'total freedom' in which the self-realisation of the individual is identified with the universality of the state and the state itself is seen as 'comprehensive, all embracing, pervasive . . . total' (Bellamy 1988). Gentile criticised Hegel for having an *a priori* view of individual right and sought to overcome what he saw as a rationalistic conception of atomised individuals still surviving within Hegel's philosophy. For Gentile, Hegel may himself have been a liberal but his conceptualisation of the state provided the resource for a far more radical, i.e. totalitarian, conclusion. He argued that it was above all Hegel who had the insight that the state is the *one true subject* and that the our self-realisation as individuals consists in our identity to the state. My will is subordinate to the state only to the extent that it is identical to it, he wrote, I want what the law wants me to want (Gentile 1961). Gentile turned Hegel's depiction of the 'God-like' *concept* of the state, as the 'divine idea as it exists on earth', into an ideal to be actualised and named the philosophy which undertakes this task 'actualism'. In so doing, he turned Hegel's argument on its head.

In the *Philosophy of Right* Hegel demonstrated the 'immense contradiction' present in the idea of the modern state, the madness that lies within the heart of reason. Mere conceptual thinking forgets that the *concept* of the state, taken in isolation from its content, is 'untrue' and 'one-sided', and in its active, political form the attempt to actualise the concept of the state is necessarily consumed in an endless destruction. Gentile's 'actualism' was *precisely* what Hegel warned against: a way of thinking which sought to actualise the divinity of the state and *thus* make man master of his own fate. From this standpoint, the manifold guarantees provided by the system of right appear only as a limitation on the 'divine idea' and therefore as something to be overcome. Gentile himself may have still retained an idea of the 'rational architectonic' of the state, though not of individual right, but the more radical totalitarian mind was ready to take this line of reasoning further – beyond and against the very idea of the state. Hegel discerned the destructive potencies of the modern state, of which 'totalitarianism' was one exemplar, and even if he could not imagine the full extent of its capacity for destruction, he had a profound sense of the struggle between the modern Leviathan and the equally modern Behemoth.

The moral point of view: the 'fanaticism of destruction'

> Abstract reflection may turn the idea of 'doing as you please' into the main aim of life, or it may view morality as a perennial and hostile struggle against one's own satisfaction, as in the injunction 'Do with repugnance what duty commands' (Schiller), or it has a view of biography which fixes on the subjective side of great individuals, i.e. those passions which are declared in advance to be inherently inferior, and overlooks the substantial element.
>
> (Adapted from *PR* §124R)[2]

Nowhere in his *Philosophy of Right* was Hegel's foreboding of future catastrophe more evident than in his discussion of morality. In the system of right Hegel places *Morality* before the emergence of *Ethical Life* and after *Abstract Right*. He does this because morality presupposes a consciousness on the part of individual subjects that their decisions depend not on any outside power but only on themselves, and is not yet attached to the institutions of ethical life. Hegel argues that the moral point of view came into being with Christianity but was developed only in modern times.

It was Kant's great achievement to articulate this viewpoint and show that the determinations of the will are a matter for itself alone and not for any external power. Kant sought to demonstrate that the moral point of view comes into being when 'the will contains the element of pure indeterminacy . . . in which every limitation, every content, whether present immediately through nature, through needs, desires and drives, or given and determined in some other way, is dissolved' (*PR* §5). Hegel called this the 'limitless infinity of *absolute abstraction*, the pure thinking of oneself', and he formulated the principle of 'pure indeterminacy' as follows:

> This subjectivity, as abstract self-determination and pure certainty of itself alone, *evaporates* into itself all *determinate* aspects of right, duty and existence, inasmuch as it is the power of *judgement* which determines solely from within itself what is good in relation to a given content, and

36

at the same time it is the power to which the good, which is at first only
an idea and an *obligation*, owes its *actuality*.

(*PR* §138)

There is of course nothing wrong, and Hegel saw nothing wrong, in looking
inwards in order to determine what is right from within oneself. Such self-
determination is the life-enhancing consequence of those epochs in which 'what
is recognised as right and good in actuality and custom is unable to satisfy the
better will' and appears to have no value. Socrates provides an early exemplar
of this moral subjectivity at a time when ancient democracy was falling into ruin
and becoming increasingly 'hollow, spiritless and unsettled'. Socrates 'evaporated',
to use Hegel's term, all determinate aspects of rights, duties and existence, and
retreated into himself to search for the right and the good. Hegel saw it as the
strength and depth of our own times that 'reverence for the existing order is in
varying degrees absent' and that people seek to 'equate accepted values with their
own will' (*PR* §§138R and 138A).

Hegel maintained that this negative freedom contains within itself 'an essential
determination and should therefore not be dismissed'; but he also held that it is a
defect of the understanding to treat this 'one-sided determination as unique and
elevate it to supreme status' (*PR* §5). Contradiction arises when subjectivity
becomes the *sole and exclusive* principle of self-determination and when the will
turns to *pure inwardness*. Once self-consciousness acquires the formal right of self-
determination, it can show that everything we normally recognise as right or good
is 'null and void, limited and in no way absolute'. Everything then depends
on what content self-consciousness gives to itself (*PR* §138A). As long as I am
inactive and do nothing, I rest content with this awareness of freedom within me.
As soon as I proceed to act and look for principles, I reach out for determinations
deduced purely from the concept of free will itself. This is the principle that Kant
expressed when he wrote that the individual consciousness *must* make self-
determination into its principle. Everything else must be 'vaporised' and re-formed
into a new determination – even if the new determination turns out to be a replica
of the old.

According to Kant, the individual self-consciousness must turn 'the universal
in and for itself' into its principle. Kant's definition of right declares that the
essential element of right is 'the *limitation* of my freedom or *arbitrary will* in such a
way that it may coexist with the arbitrary will of everyone else in accordance with
a universal law' (*PR* §29). Hegel observed that the individual self-consciousness
could equally well give precedence to the 'arbitrariness of its own particularity'
and thereby become capable of being 'evil' (*PR* §139). The capacity for evil is
present within the moral point of view because morality and evil have a common
root in the 'self-certainty' with which the question of right is resolved (*PR* §139R).
The moral point of view and evil are not opposites; the triumph of the one does
not presuppose the suppression of the other. I may refuse to commit myself to any
determination at all, in which case I remain suspended in indeterminacy, but

equally well I may try to destroy whatever determination I make in the belief that all determination is a limitation on my freedom and that indeterminacy is the only true freedom. The Kantian definition of right contains only a *negative* determination, that of limitation by the arbitrary will of others, and it can naturally give rise to the demand that all such limitations be abolished. In this case, what is advanced as 'rational' appears as a limitation on my freedom, as an 'external and formal universal' which must be overcome.

Where the essential element of freedom appears as the possibility of abstracting from every determination in which I find myself, freedom becomes the 'freedom of the void' and it is this *freedom of the void* which is raised to the status of an 'actual shape and passion'. In its theoretical aspect, it becomes the 'fanaticism of pure contemplation' (as in the meditative dimension of Hindu religion). In the more active realm of politics and religion it becomes the 'fanaticism of destruction', destroying the existing social order, destroying individuals regarded as suspect, destroying any determinate organisation which attempts to rise up anew. It is only in destroying something that this negative will has a feeling of its own existence. It may believe that it wills some positive condition, such as universal equality or a properly religious life or a new world order, but it does not in fact will the positive actuality of this condition because this would gives rise to some kind of institutional order and the negative self-consciousness demands the annihilation of every objective determination. Every positive determination of freedom appears as an alien form of representation, so that the actualisation of freedom can only be done through the fury of destruction. The example Hegel gives is that of the Reign of Terror in the French Revolution:

> This was a time of trembling and quaking and of intolerance towards everything particular. For fanaticism wills only what is abstract, not what is articulated, so that whenever differences emerge, it finds them incompatible with its own indeterminacy and cancels them. This is why the people, during the French revolution, destroyed once more the institutions they had themselves created, because all institutions are incompatible with the abstract self-consciousness of equality.
>
> (*PR* §§5R and 5A)

Fanaticism does not arise from my capacity to cut myself off from everything, even from my own life, for it is in this reflective power of thinking that I distinguish myself from my animal-existence. The danger lies rather in elevating negative freedom to 'supreme status'. Self-determination becomes 'sheer restless activity which cannot yet arrive at something *that is*' (*PR* §108A). 'What is' is, therefore, devalued against 'what ought to be' and appears worthless, fit only for destruction.

If I do reach some kind of conclusion, as Kant did in the maxim that the principle of my action must be the universal law, this may be a pure formalism without content, a preaching of duty for duty's sake which offers no criteria for deciding whether a specific action is or is not a duty, in which case any criminal line of conduct may be justified. Or it may be given a more determinate content which relates to my 'natural, subjective existence – my needs, inclinations, passions, fancies, in short, my *happiness*'. Happiness is a *relationship* in which I count as 'something *particular*' and the content of my natural existence makes its appearance (*PR* §123R). To make happiness my end, therefore, is to recognise that I am a living being and that I have the right to satisfy my needs as a living being. There is nothing wrong in this – 'nothing degrading about being alive', and in any case the alternative of 'existing in a higher spirituality' is not available to us (*PR* §123A). From the moral point of view, however, the determinations of happiness are not true determinations of freedom. They are either despised, as if there were something degrading about being alive and wanting happiness, or they are treated as if they were true determinations of freedom. In the latter case, I pass off my own inclinations, needs, passions and fancies as if they were the good and the universal. This turns into hypocrisy when imposed upon others and a form of 'absolute subjectivity' when imposed upon myself. I may become convinced that the goodness of my will consists only in willing the good and that to will anything else, including the satisfaction of my inclinations, is bad; or I may adopt the view that my *conviction* that something is good and right determines its ethical character; or I may mystify everything by presenting the authority to which my duty is owed as the product of a free mind and by declaring that in doing my duty, I am free (*PR* §133A).

From reading Hegel's discussion of morality in the *Philosophy of Right*, the conclusion we are invited to draw is that there is a definite connection between the 'moral point of view' and the fanaticism of destruction. If 'what is' is devalued against 'what ought to be', if duty for duty's sake is emptied of all content, if subjective conviction becomes its own justification, if subjectivity only knows *itself* as the absolute, and if freedom lies in the destruction of all that is determinate, then there arises the capacity for 'evil'.[3] Hegel's argument is provocative and radical. It is that evil is rooted not so much in the suppression of morality or in its subordination to instrumental rationality (Bauman 1990), but in the moral point of view itself or more precisely in the elevation of the moral point of view to a supreme status within the system of right as a whole. The moral point of view is a creature of our age. Born of abstract right, it surpasses the limitations of private property and individual personality in the sphere of self-reflection and self-determination and so reaches the 'higher ground' of freedom. What Hegel argues, however, is that on this higher ground where morality prevails, there are also sown the seeds of something far more troubling: the dark clouds of a thoroughly modern barbarism to come.

Notes

1 A useful analogy could here be made between Hegel's analysis of the difficulties in distinguishing between law as law and law as state law and Marx's analysis of the

3

HEGEL AND KANT
Natural law and the science of right

Hegel's science of right

Kant and Hegel had this in common: that they both put the recognition of right at the centre of their political thought. We may, however, pursue how Hegel undertook the task of 'recognising precisely what right is', by considering what Hegel did *not* mean, that is, by re-examining his relation to the natural law thinking of Kant. In contemporary commentaries, the relation between Hegel's *Philosophy of Right* and Kant's *Metaphysics of Morals* remains very much in question. One version, which corresponds roughly to what I have called the 'old orthodoxy', is to read Hegel's critique of Kant as symptomatic of Hegel's own anti-rights, anti-liberal, anti-cosmopolitan and anti-humanist convictions. Another, which corresponds roughly to what I call the 'new orthodoxy', emphasises Hegel's debt to Kant and on this basis seeks to reconstitute him as a liberal thinker in the natural law tradition.[1] My own argument embraces a third possibility: that Hegel did construct a critique of Kantian natural law – one that was neither illiberal nor anti-rights but on the contrary pushed Kant's 'critical philosophy' beyond the rather narrow confines of criticism which Kant himself permitted.

In an earlier essay *On the Scientific Ways of Treating Natural Law* (1802) Hegel distinguished two camps in modern natural law theory, 'empirical' and 'formal', and expressed his dissatisfaction with both. He argued that the governing principle of the formalists was the *a priori* of reason and of the empiricists the *a posteriori* of experience, but both turned isolated individuals as they appear in modern civil society into a starting point and hence into a condition of all political cohesion. Eighteenth-century natural law theory asked philosophy to choose between 'empiricism' and 'theory', but in the first case philosophy was swallowed up in experience and in the second it was abstracted from experience. The result was the same: each wing of natural law posited a 'true absolute' in what was only a one-sided 'negative absolute' (Hegel 1975a: 75). In order to bring life back into philosophy, Hegel maintained that we must no longer regard the system of right as 'absolute and eternal' but see it for what it is, as 'wholly finite' (Hegel 1975a: 102).

Hegel's project was to construct for the first time a 'science of right'. But what is a science of right and how is it to be constructed? According to Hegel, we must take our cue from the natural sciences and their ways of understanding the natural world. Observing that in the natural sciences it is uncontentious that 'the philosopher's stone lies hidden . . . *within nature itself*', but that in political science the philosopher's stone still seems to lie within our own heads, Hegel challenged this account of the opposition between natural and social science (*PR* Preface 12). He argued that a science of right ought to study laws of right in roughly the same way as the natural sciences study laws of nature. It should recognise that both the laws of right and the laws of nature are 'external to us' and that our cognition 'adds nothing to them' (*PR* Preface 13). Hegel acknowledged that there are major differences between these different kinds of law. Laws of right, unlike laws of nature, are derived from human beings. Their diversity shows that they are not absolute. Unlike laws of nature, they are never *valid* simply because they exist and there is always the possibility of conflict between what they are and what they ought to be. Our own inner voice of conscience may or may not come into collision with them and consequently, when we are subjected to the power of rightful authority, it is never in the same way as we are subjected to the power of natural necessity. However, while recognising the importance of these distinctions, Hegel still insisted that the task of political philosophy is to 'recognise precisely what right is' – as something knowable beyond our own feelings, opinions, convictions and judgement.

Kant's metaphysics of right

Hegel's *Philosophy of Right* was a sustained commentary on and critique of Kant's *Metaphysics of Justice* and the two texts parallel one another in interesting ways. According to Kant, the idea of right guarantees to individuals freedom from constraint compatible with the freedom of others. The only obligation it imposes on individuals is to respect the rights of others. It is the ground on which justice, universal freedom and the legitimacy of the state are based. Kant presented his *Metaphysics of Justice* as a *critical* philosophy whose starting point is the courage to think for oneself about what is right. It accepts no substitute for reason, no doctrine or dogma, no custom or positive law. From this idea of a critical philosophy Kant drew the conclusion that the determination of right must not be confused with 'what can be learned from experience' (*MJ* Introduction to *The Metaphysics of Morals* 15), because the latter would confound what is right with what is merely the case. Right must be seen, therefore, as having an *a priori* basis, as a pure concept of reason, and the discovery of what right is must be based on logical deductions from the postulates of practical reason alone. Beware, Kant warned, of spurious *a priori* reasoning that is 'basically nothing but experience raised to generality through induction':

> Instruction in the laws of morality is not drawn from observation of oneself and the animality within him, nor from the perception of the course of the world as to how things happen and how men in fact do act

42

... reason commands how one ought to act, even though no instance of such action may be found.

(MJ Introduction to *The Metaphysics of Morals* 15–16)

Kant argued that for the *Metaphysics of Justice* to be a *critical* philosophy, it has to be a system of *a priori* knowledge which can be applied to the world of experience but whose application must not detract from the purity of its laws or cast doubt on its *a priori* origin (MJ Introduction to *The Metaphysics of Morals* 16–17). It is only *a priori* reasoning that can recognise precisely what right is and any empirical determination would detract from its validity.

Kant's method of analysis was that of logical deduction from the juridical postulates of practical reason. First, he purported to deduce the idea of the 'person' (*persona*). The person is a possessor of rights whose 'actions are susceptible to imputation' and whose 'moral personality is nothing but the freedom of a rational being under moral laws' (MJ Introduction 24). Then he deduced the idea of a 'thing' (*res*). A thing is 'an object of free will that itself lacks freedom' and is 'not susceptible to imputation'. Then he deduced the separation of property from mere possession: 'an external thing is mine ... only if I can assume that it is still possible for me to be injured by someone else's use of the thing even when it is not in my possession' (MJ §1). Then he deduced the idea that there is nothing in the world which cannot be made into property:

> It is possible to have any and every external object of my will as my property ... a maxim according to which, if it were made into a law, an object of will would have to be in itself (objectively) ownerless (*res nullius* – property of no one), conflicts with Law and justice.
>
> (MJ §2)

Kant placed rights of property within the realm of 'natural laws' which he defined as those laws to which 'an obligation can be recognised *a priori* by reason without external legislation' (MJ Introduction to *The Metaphysics of Morals* 26). He argued, in line with the natural law tradition, that natural laws provide the immutable principles on which all positive legislation must be based (KPW 132, MJ §A). The close resemblance between his own deductions and the designation of personality and property within Roman law served to demonstrate to Kant's satisfaction the rationality of a legal system in which rights of personality and private property constitute its nucleus.

Kant postulated the unity of freedom and coercion. His basic proposition was that 'everything that is contrary to right is a hindrance to freedom based on universal laws' and that right therefore entails 'the authority to apply coercion to anyone who infringes it' (KPW 134, MJ §D). He presented right as the basis on which the 'freedom of everyone' can be identified with 'the law of reciprocal coercion' and argued that right depends on and has no existence apart from the possibility of external coercion. The right of freedom under law is at once a right of lawful coercion (*KPW* 134–5, *MJ* §E). In his analysis of public law Kant argues that the movement from the 'state of nature' to 'civil society' (again Kant uses the traditional language of natural law theory) is a *rational necessity* that people *must* recognise and accept and which has nothing to do with experience. He conceives the state of nature as a society in which property rights are already *valid* because they are deduced *a priori* from the postulates of practical reason, but he argues that citizens *must* abandon this 'wild and lawless' state of freedom in order to find their 'whole freedom' in civil society. He maintains that civil society draws its laws from the natural laws of society, but it provides in addition the juridical conditions under which each person's property is secured through the formation of *public law*. He insists that it is not experience that teaches us that we act in a violent and malevolent manner to one another in the state of nature and so must construct a means of public legal coercion; it is rather the '*a priori* rational idea of a non-lawful state' that tells us that in the state of nature we can never be secure and that a 'public and legal state' *must* therefore be established (*KPW* 137, *MJ* §44). In other words, for Kant it is a rational necessity that the unilateral will of the property owners *must* give way to a 'collective, universal and powerful Will that can provide the guarantee required' (*MJ* §8). He writes:

> the first decision the individual is *obliged* to make, if he does not wish to renounce all concepts of right, will be to adopt the principle that one must abandon the state of nature in which everyone follows his own desires, and unite with everyone else (with whom he cannot avoid having intercourse) in order to submit to external, public and lawful coercion. He must accordingly enter into a state wherein that which is to be recognised as belonging to each person is allotted to him *by law* and guaranteed to him by an adequate power . . . In other words, he should at all costs enter into a state of civil society.
>
> (*KPW* 137, *MJ* §44)

From the concept of the person as 'nothing but the freedom of a rational being under moral laws', Kant deduces the principle that 'a person is subject to no laws other than those that he (either alone or at least jointly with others) gives to himself'. The public and legal state, then, is one in which those who are *subject* to the law are also its *authors*. From this 'Idea of the state as it ought to be', Kant then deduces the particular institutional forms of a republican constitution: a representative legislature to establish universal norms, an executive to subsume particular cases under these universal norms, a judiciary to determine what is right in cases of conflict, and the constitutional principle of the separation of their powers to maintain the distinct spheres of state activity in accordance with 'the moments of its concept' (*KPW* 138, *MJ* §45). Kant's ideal state corresponds closely enough to a liberal republic in which the law is autonomous, the civil service is professional and government is based on popular representation.

With the formation of this ideal state, Kant identifies reason, that is, obedience to our own laws, with obedience to the laws of the state and conversely identifies transgression of the laws of the state with disobedience to our own laws.[2] Originally, sovereignty may have resided directly in the hands of the people, but Kant maintains that once a republic is instituted, it must no longer 'let the reins of government out of its hands and return them to those who had them previously'. If it did, the people would 'by their absolute and arbitrary will destroy the new institutions again' (*KPW* 163, *MJ* §52). Since the legislature is deduced from the idea of the 'general united will', Kant concludes that it can do 'absolutely no injustice to anyone'. Whatever it decides, the citizens have already consented to. Citizens can lodge complaints about unjust laws but Kant stipulates that they must not resist or disobey them. There can be no such thing as legitimate resistance, because this would mean that the people want to act as judge of their own cause – and that, Kant tells us, is 'absurd' (*KPW* 145, *MJ* §49A). Kant declares that it is 'the people's duty to endure even the most intolerable abuse of supreme authority' (*KPW* 145, *MJ* §49A), that any alteration required for a defective constitution may be undertaken only by the legislature, and that no attempt to coerce the government to act in a certain way is permitted on the part of 'an arbitrary association of the people'. If they tried to 'coerce' the government, they would be no better, according to Kant, than a 'riotous mob' (*KPW* 162, *MJ* §52).

Kant maintains that the 'well-being of the state' refers only to that condition in which 'the constitution conforms most closely to the principles of justice' and must not be confused with 'the welfare or happiness of the citizens of the state'. We have the right and duty to think for ourselves, but for Kant this right is restricted to 'the use which anyone may make of it as a man of learning addressing the entire reading public' (*KPW* 55, 'What is enlightenment?'). Otherwise, as in the case of an officer receiving a command from his superiors or a clergyman receiving an order from his church, we must obey. Kant's critical philosophy commands everyone to obey the law 'without regard to his inclinations' (*MJ* Introduction to *The Metaphysics of Morals* 15) and it dictates that the duty to obey the law can take no account of the pleasure or displeasure with which it is combined. Our freedom, as Kant defines it, does not lie in our capacity to choose for or against the law, but only in our 'internal legislation of reason' (*MJ* Introduction to *The Metaphysics of Morals* 28), and the use of *coercion* is justified if this internal legislation leads us astray (*KPW* 134, *MJ* §D). Kant argues that we have the right to *force* other people into a civil condition if they fail to do so of their own accord, and once they have entered into a civil condition (whether voluntarily or under coercion) their binding imperative is to obey the law. Criminals who violate the rights of others must be punished and since the authorisation for their punishment comes from reason itself, the humanitarian and utilitarian arguments put by penal reformers against certain forms of punishment like capital punishment, should be seen as mere 'sophistry and a juristic trick'. Since the definition of civic personality presupposes a certain capacity for practical reason, Kant infers that those who lack this capacity (or are deemed to lack it) must be excluded from the definition of civic personality and therefore from rights of political participation. Kant's own list of exclusions includes apprentices, personal servants, minors, women and anyone who depends for support 'not on his own industry but on arrangements by others' (*KPW* 139, *MJ* §46).

Hegel's argument against Kant's metaphysics of right

The nub of Hegel's argument is that Kant's critical philosophy turns out not to be critical enough. State-consciousness haunts the antechambers of Kant's discussion of public law as much as property-consciousness haunts his discussion of private law. The language of right and freedom is transmogrified into a language of coercion and necessity. The word 'must' pervades the discourse, so much so that the first decision the free individual *must* make is to submit to external coercion. The force of this *must* is all the stronger since the decision is not based on experience, which could be modified in the light of new experience, but rather on an *a priori* rational law which is binding regardless of our inclinations. The closer Kant comes to conceptions of personality, property, civil society and the state as they exist in a modern bourgeois republic, the more he insists that 'all propositions about rights are *a priori*, for they are laws of reason' (*MJ* §6). Hegel argues that this insistence hides the spuriousness of Kant's deductions. What is in fact a predicate of the state, the idea of the 'general united will', is turned into a mystical subject, while the real subject, the modern state, is turned into a deduction from this mystical substance. Kant's concern, according to Hegel, is simply to rediscover the idea of right in every sphere of private and public law that he depicts. He gives an empirical account of property and power in modern constitutional states and uses critical philosophy to convert these empirical facts into deductions from the postulates of practical reason. These deductions are spurious because they cannot derive the *specifica differentia* of particular institutions from the Idea of the 'united will' and because they dress the determinate historical forms of personality, property, civil society and the state in the cloth of rational necessity. By presupposing the rationality of bourgeois right, Kant's *Metaphysics of Justice* leaves the world much as he finds it. His critical philosophy ends up as an uncritical positivism.[3]

Hegel acknowledged that Kant's *Metaphysics of Justice* represented a big step forward. It advanced the idea of moral laws as laws of autonomy which individuals impose on themselves and follow for their own sake; the idea of laws of freedom which the will determines from itself and which express the independence of reason; the idea of will as the activity of thought which 'throws off the deficiency of mere subjectivity' and 'translates the subjective end into objectivity through the mediation of activity' (*PR* §§8 and 8A); the speculative identity of 'good and reality' as a demand on practical reason which says that 'the good attains the "highest good" only when it is realised in external reality'; the analysis of the *movement* of right from its simplest form as abstract right to the increasingly more complex forms of civil society, the state and the cosmopolitan order. For Hegel, however, the key to understanding Kant's *Metaphysics of Justice* is that freedom is present only as an abstraction. The postulated harmony 'is determined as something merely *subjective* – as only what *ought* to be; i.e. what does *not* at the same time have *reality*. It is something *believed* that can only claim subjective certainty, not truth; i.e. *not* that objectivity which corresponds to the Idea' (Hegel 1991b: §60). It is as if there are two realms: 'a realm of *subjectivity* in the pure regions of transparent thought' and 'a realm of *objectivity* in the element of an externally manifold actuality that is an undisclosed realm of darkness' (Hegel 1993: 11. 231–2). In this duality external reality is a void, without truth or reason, given meaning by a subjectivity which subsumes it to thought. It is in opposition to this dualism that Hegel commits himself to the unity of the actual and the rational and to the transformation of practical philosophy, based on the conviction that to neglect concrete analysis of the actual political order is to be condemned to an abstract normativity.

Persons and things

It may appear at first sight that personality and property were for Hegel what they were for Kant: *a priori* deductions from the idea of practical reason. This reading *seems* to be justified by the fact that Hegel starts his *Philosophy of Right* with a single person in a pre-social condition, describes the right of private property as a rational necessity for humanity, and criticises *empirical* natural law theories on the ground that they postulate private property as a merely *accidental* feature of human history with a merely *external* and *contingent* relation to human freedom. Hegel begins the section on property with the claim that:

> The rational aspect of property is to be found not in the satisfaction of needs but in the superseding of mere subjectivity of personality. Not until he has property does the person exist as reason.
>
> (*PR* §§41 and 41A)

It *seems* that the ethical significance of private property for Hegel lay in its intrinsic and essential relation to our humanity. If what makes us human is our non-restriction to natural instincts or to fixed ways of satisfying them, then private property appears as the mark of a humanity finally recognised at the end of history and released from its long ordeal.[4] This appearance, however, is deceptive. For Hegel, abstract right is a social form and comes first in his exposition because it is the simplest and most abstract social form of the subject. Historically the notion of a 'person' was first developed in ancient Rome when personality was instantiated as an estate in contrast with slavery, and when rights of property (including property over slaves) became 'the first embodiment' of the relative freedom of members of this estate (*PR* §40). In the modern age every human being is now in principle a *person* endowed with rights over *things*, and is obliged to relate to all other human beings *as persons*.

Personality is understood by Hegel as a social form taken by individuals under given historical conditions and generalised in the modern age. The difference between Kant and Hegel may be encapsulated thus: if Kant turns individuals as they appear in our own society into an *a priori* condition of political cohesion, Hegel begins with individuals as they are found within our society in order to denature their form of existence and unpack what is distinctive about the modern subject.

Hegel maintained that the concept of 'personality' marks the distinction between 'persons' and 'things', and he criticised the confusion he saw in Kant's division of rights into the *right of things* and the *right of persons*. He argued that this division was fundamental to Roman law only because personality was instantiated as an 'estate' or 'condition' which contrasted with that of slavery and expressed its relative freedom (PR §40). In this context rights of property included both rights over 'things' and rights over slaves (and to a large extent children) conceived as things. The so-called *rights of persons* in Roman law had to do with slavery and with dependent family relationships, and Kant only confused the matter further by categorising these relations under yet another heading, that of *personal rights of a real kind*. Kant enhanced this confusion by arguing that *rights of persons* are those rights which arise out of a contract in which I agree to give something or perform a service (in Roman law the *ius ad rem* which arises out of an *obligatio*). But a right based on contract is not a right over a person but only over a thing which a person disposes of. In his attachment to Roman law, Kant confounds the nature of right in the modern age – an age in which slavery is abolished, children are no longer chattels, and everyone is in principle endowed with personality and obliged to relate to others as *persons*.[5]

The *concept* of personality, as Hegel depicts it, expresses the fact that an individual is conceived as a free spirit who has rights over things and an obligation to respect others as persons. Freedom constitutes its substance and destiny, but the freedom in question is abstract. Personality begins where 'the subject has not merely a consciousness of itself in general as concrete and in some way determined, but a consciousness of itself as a completely abstract 'I' in which all concrete limitation and validity are negated and invalidated' (PR §35R).

> When I say 'I', I leave out of account every particularity such as my character , temperament, knowledge and age. 'I' is totally empty; it is merely a point – simple, yet active in this simplicity.
>
> (PR §4A)

The emergence of personality entails the self-division of the subject: I both know myself to be free and I have knowledge of myself as an object. I am at the same time something free and determinate. I am an 'I' who is wholly indeterminate, and I am someone of a particular age, height, religion and class, located in a particular place, endowed with particular desires. Personality is at once 'sublime and ordinary' – the unity of the infinite and the finite. The *person* has a twofold character, a double existence, and Hegel describes it as the supreme achievement of the modern subject to support this contradiction:

> It is inherent in *personality* that, as *this* person, I am completely determined in all respects (in my inner arbitrary will, drive and desire as well as in relation to my immediate external existence) . . . and know myself in my finitude as *infinite, universal* and *free*.
>
> (PR §35)

Personality is a form of subjectivity which from the start contains within itself 'division and opposition'. Since the person is not the living body but the 'I' who owns her own body, then even the death of an individual as a physical being does not signify the death of the individual as a person. Thus after the death of an individual, the independence of his or her spirit may be expressed legally through laws of inheritance which seek out new physical forms of expression: 'The death of merely immediate and individual vitality is the emergence of spirit' (Hegel 1991b: §222).

As a person, I stand in opposition to the world of *things* – an opposition which is expressed in Roman law in terms of *persona* and *res*. This separation and opposition fills the world. A thing is anything that is external to my freedom and into which I can place my will. This includes things in the tangible sense of the term, e.g. land, corn, bread, machines, money, etc., but equally

> intellectual accomplishments, sciences, arts, even religious observances (such as sermons, masses, prayers and blessings at consecrations), inventions and the like become objects of contract . . . bought and sold . . . treated as equivalent to acknowledged things.
>
> (PR §43R)

We may be reluctant to treat knowledge, talent, piety and honour as things, since they are internal attributes of a human being or processes of personal development, but in the system of right they are relevant as things. As a person I have the right to place my will in anything. To the extent that I am an object of the senses and have a natural existence, I am myself a thing as well as a person. As a person, I possess my life and body like other things.

> All things can become the property of human beings, because the human being is free will and as such exists in and for himself, whereas that which confronts him does not have this quality. The will alone is infinite, absolute in relation to everything else, whereas the other, for its part, is merely *relative*. Thus to appropriate something means basically only to manifest the supremacy of my will in relation to the thing and to demonstrate that the latter does not have being in and for itself and is not an end in itself. This manifestation occurs through my conferring

upon the thing an end other than that which it immediately possessed; I give the living creature, as my property, a soul other than that which it previously had; I give it my soul.

(PR §44A)

This split between *persons* and *things* puts all freedom and spirit on the side of the subject and none on the side of the object. As a person, I am or I have free will, but the only way I can actualise my freedom is through the ownership of things. Property becomes the 'first *existence* of freedom' and an 'essential end in itself' (PR §45R). The force of the word 'essential' is that the actualisation of freedom in property is not a choice but a determination, and the rational aspect of this determination is not to be found in the satisfaction of needs but in the superseding of 'mere subjectivity of personality'. In the system of right, it is not until I have property that I exist as a rational human being and give my free will actuality (PR §49).

In the modern world, as opposed to the ancient, all human beings are in principle persons. If nothing else, we are at least owners of our own lives, bodies and labour power.

The human being, in his immediate existence in himself, is a natural entity . . . it is only through the development of his own body and spirit . . . that he takes possession of himself and becomes his own property as distinct from that of others . . . this taking possession of oneself consists also in translating into *actuality* what one is in terms of one's concept (as possibility . . .) . . . what one is in concept is posited for the first time as one's own . . . and it thereby becomes capable of taking on the *form of the thing* . . .

(PR §57)

In the ancient world subjection was expressed in the conflict between a person as a free human being and the institution of slavery, that is, of people who were not persons. In the modern world, the point of view of the free will goes beyond that 'false' point of view in which the human being exists only as a natural being and is therefore capable of enslavement. Persons cannot be property and cannot be enslaved. Thus by asserting the *concept* of freedom, the modern age refutes the basis of all historical justifications of slavery which depend on regarding the human being simply as a natural resource. As Hegel puts it, the claim that slavery is contrary to right is firmly tied to 'the *concept* of the human being as spirit, as something free *in itself*'.

This is familiar ground, but Hegel adds that this viewpoint too is *one-sided* and *false* inasmuch as it regards the human being as *by nature* free and 'takes the concept as such in its immediacy . . . as the truth'. He writes:

This antinomy, like all antinomies, is based on formal thinking which fixes upon and asserts the two moments of an Idea in separation from each other, so that both are lacking in truth and do not conform to the Idea. The free spirit consists precisely in not having its being as mere concept . . . but in overcoming this formal phase of its being.

(PR §57R)

The strength of conceptual thinking is that it goes beyond the false appearances of 'conceptlesss existence' in which there is neither rationality nor right; but it makes no space for 'objective spirit', that is, the *content* of right, and it annihilates all evidence of conflict between the concept of personality and its social existence.

In the system of right every human being becomes a person and the personality is given existence at least through ownership of one's own life and body. The generalisation of abstract right turns my capacity to labour, my labour power, into a form of property which can itself be bought and sold on the market place. In this context, subjection is displaced but it is by no means eliminated. The rational aspect of private property is only that I own property: '*what* and *how* much I possess . . . is purely contingent as far as right is concerned . . . equality can only be equality of abstract persons as such, which thus *excludes* everything to do with possessions' (PR §49). The system of private property remains 'indifferent to particularity'. It does not require that everyone's property be equal, only that everyone ought to have some property. In this system one cannot speak of an 'injustice of nature' in the unequal possession of goods, and the moral wish that all human beings should have a livelihood and that no one should starve has 'no objective being'. Thus recognition of one person by another takes the form of a contract in which owners of property freely exchange the things they own for other things. In contractual relations anything can be alienated so long as it is a thing: i.e. that it is not free, not personal, without rights (PR §42). Individuals cannot alienate themselves if they are to remain persons, but they can alienate their bodies, their minds and their capacity to labour – in pieces or by the hour: 'I can alienate individual products of my particular physical and mental skills and active capabilities to someone else and for him to use them for a limited period . . . The distinction here is that between a slave and a modern servant or hired labourer' (PR §67). The alienation of *things* (be it labour power or material things or intellectual property) is not something external to private property, it is an *essential* element of what private property is, and the idea of a contract entails that it is 'by common will and with due respect for the rights of both' that we exchange our goods. The crucial point is that this 'indeterminacy is itself determinate': neither the form nor the terms of the contract are the product of will.

Hegel argues that within the system of right abstract right is the starting point for the long and arduous process of education (*Bildung*) required before individuality can be realised. Yet the relation of abstract right to the institutions of ethical life (family, civil society and the state) is not settled once and for all. If individuality were *fixated* at a stage of life in which the right of private property appears as everything, it would in Hegel's words be 'trivial' (PR §35A), 'false'

(PR §§41A and 57R), 'merely formal' (PR §30R), even 'contemptible' (PR §35A). The determinations of abstract right do not have to be treated as the *exclusive* aspect of social relations. Hegel comments that if someone were interested *only* in his or her formal rights, this would be a sign of 'pure stubbornness, such as is often encountered in emotionally limited people; for uncultured people insist most strongly on their rights, whereas those of nobler mind seek to discover what other aspects there are to the matter in question' (PR §37A). The determination of right is *one* aspect of a relationship but it is merely formal in character compared with the relationship as a whole. It is a permission or warrant. I do not have to pursue my rights. The only necessity of right is negative, to respect others as persons and not to violate their rights, and the development of ethical life presupposes that there is more to a human relationship than right alone. If I relate to others and they to me *exclusively* in terms of rights, then everything which depends on particularity would become a matter of indifference. As far as other needs are concerned, indifference would be the only rule.

Hegel argues that although the spheres of ethical life (family, civil society and the state) are developed forms of abstract right, it would be totally confusing simply to introduce the idea of a contractual relationship in an unmediated way into the family or civil society or the state. The right of private property necessarily grows into a 'higher sphere of right' (PR §46R), but once morality, the family, civil society and the state are brought into the picture, all kinds of restrictions may be imposed on the rights of property. Thus in his discussion of *Morality* Hegel writes of how the right of private property may in extreme situations, where the requirements of personal survival come into collision with the rights of property, be subsumed to the 'right of necessity'. Where the alternatives are on one side a finite injury to property and on the other 'an infinite injury to existence with total loss of rights', Hegel wrote that the latter must prevail:

> Life as the totality of ends, has a right in opposition to abstract right. If, for example, it can be preserved by stealing a loaf, this certainly constitutes an infringement of someone's property, but it would be wrong to regard such an action as common theft. If someone whose life is in danger were not allowed to take measures to save himself, he would be destined to forfeit all his rights; and since he would be deprived of life, his entire freedom would be negated. There are certainly many prerequisites for the preservation of life, and if we look to the future, we must concern ourselves with such details. But the only thing that is necessary is to live *now*; the future is not absolute, and it remains exposed to contingency. Consequently, only the necessity of the immediate present can justify a wrong action, because its omission would in turn involve committing a wrong – indeed the ultimate wrong, namely the total negation of the existence of freedom . . . no one should be sacrificed completely for the sake of right.
>
> (PR §127A)

The proposition that no one should be sacrificed completely for the sake of rights of property does not deny the validity of the latter but it reveals its one-sided and relative character. In his discussion of civil society Hegel writes of how free contract may be profoundly affected by the norms and goals of the corporations, notably in relation to welfare for the poor. In his discussion of the state Hegel writes that the state may in times of war demand a widespread abrogation of property rights or even the sacrifice of life itself (PR §324), and in peaceful times it makes all manner of exceptions to private property in order to curb the excesses of civil society (PR §46R). In the system of right there is nothing absolute about the right of private property when it comes into conflict with the demands of morality and ethical life, and it would be the mark of an 'uncultured mind' to think that there is something absolute about private property (PR §30R). This does not mean that private property has no right at all, or that it can be violated at will, or that it is external to the institutions of ethical life; but it does mean that the state and other spheres of ethical life not only maintain or restore the right of private property when it is threatened or usurped, but can and do make exceptions too. If the state were determined to expropriate all forms of private property, however, such as we see prefigured in Plato's *Republic* and actualised in certain Communist societies, the effect of this expropriation would be to annul one form of property, that of individual private property, and replace it with another, that of state property. The abolition of private property by the state would transfer ownership of all things (including my body, my mind and my capacity to labour) to the state and the state would emerge as the sole 'person' whose personality is given *existence* in the ownership of things.

Morality and ethical life

As an empirical description of the system of right, Hegel maintained that Kant's *Metaphysics of Justice* lacked crucial categories and distinctions necessary to understand the modern political order. Most important, Hegel argued that Kant had an inadequate understanding of the category of *Sittlichkeit* (ethical life) or of the distinction between morality and ethics. Hegel writes:

> Morality and ethics, which are usually regarded as roughly synonymous, are taken here in essentially distinct senses . . . Kantian usage prefers the expression morality, as indeed the practical principles of Kant's philosophy are confined throughout to this concept, even rendering the point of view of *ethics* impossible and in fact expressly infringing and destroying it. But even if morality and ethics were etymologically synonymous, this would not prevent them, since they are now different words, from being used for different concepts.

(PR §33)

Hegel's criticism of Kant's lack of distinction between morality and ethics is often taken to mean that Kant concentrates only on inner-directed feelings of morality at the expense of any orientation toward the social and political institutions of the community, while Hegel reorients philosophy to the importance of the political order in conditioning and setting the bounds of moral choices and judgements. This is true as far as it goes, but when Hegel identifies the family, civil society and the state as spheres of *ethical life*, this does not in and of itself distinguish him from Kant who considers these spheres under the heading of *public law*. The difference cannot lie only in the claim that Kant stresses private morality whereas Hegel also stresses political engagement, for Kant too is committed to an active public life. The difference lies rather in how the institutions of ethical life (family, civil society and state) are understood: whether as deductions of practical reason or, as Hegel puts it, as 'an objective sphere which . . . posits distinctions within itself which are . . . determined by the concept' (PR §144). Hegel writes:

> These distinctions give the ethical a fixed content which is necessary for itself and whose existence is exalted above subjective opinions and preferences; they are law and institutions which have being in and for themselves.
>
> (PR §144)

In other words, Hegel is saying here that if we view these institutions from the point of view of morality rather than that of ethics and treat them as actual or potential emanations of our will, we will fail to recognise their 'objective existence' as ethical powers. Ethical life is a system of determinations which *govern* the lives of individuals and in relation to which 'the vain pursuits of individuals are merely a play of the waves' (PR §145A).

> In relation to the subject, the ethical substance and its laws and powers are . . . an object, inasmuch as *they are*, in the supreme sense of self-sufficiency. They are thus an absolute authority and power, infinitely more firmly based than the being of nature . . . All these substantial determinations are *duties* which are binding on the will of an individual . . .
>
> (PR §§146 and 148)

The illusion of *Morality* is that the social and political institutions of *Sittlichkeit* are, actually or potentially, the products of the will and it is this point of view that Kant professes. Hegel responds that 'moral subjectivity in fact determines nothing' for ethical relations are *necessary* relations and impose on subjects *binding duties* that can never be understood as emanations of their will – even in their most rational manifestation (PR §148R). Hegel affirms the existence of subjectivity in modern ethical life, but he argues that subjectivity is a 'mere moment' within it. Individuals may bear 'spiritual witness' to ethical powers as to their own essence and may find their '*liberation* in duty', not least their liberation from natural drives and inclinations. In an ethical community duty does not appear as a limitation on freedom but only as a limitation on 'freedom in the abstract' or on the 'arbitrary will of subjectivity'. In ethical life the individual must do what is prescribed and it is this which is given the name of virtue: 'the *habit* of the ethical appears as a *second nature . . .*' (PR §§149–50).

For Hegel the paradigmatic case of ethical life was that of ancient Greece where the relation of the individual to the *polis* really was more like one of identity than faith and trust, both of which presuppose some degree of self-reflection. To its citizens the ethical life of the *polis* was always already present as the presupposition of their activity. Modern ethical life, in contrast to the ancient, grants 'the right of individuals to their subjective determination to freedom, in so far as they belong to ethical actuality' (PR §153) and this subjectivity becomes in turn the 'outward appearance in which the ethical exists'; but subjectivity is always already contained within the ethical as one of its subordinate moments. Hegel writes that there are only two possible viewpoints on the ethical realm: 'one proceeds atomistically and moves upward from the basis of individuality' (the viewpoint of *Morality*); the other starts from 'substantiality', the unity of the individual and society. This is the perspective of *Sittlichkeit* and it is the 'road of science' of which Kant had no understanding.

Hegel criticised the lack of distinction between 'morality' and 'ethical life' not only in Kant himself, who drew rather cautious liberal conclusions, but also in those who reproduced the viewpoint of *Morality* for more radical ends. Since the institutions of ethical life (family, civil society, the state) are *supposed to be* emanations of our will but *in fact* have an independent existence apart from our will, it would be natural to conclude that they ought to be destroyed and replaced with institutions which are in fact emanations of our will. Hegel argued that this perspective, which is elaborated within the modern revolutionary tradition, replaces illusion with illusion. It holds that the moral point of view is right in theory but not yet realised in practice. In a passive mode it lives unhappily with this knowledge; in an active mode it seeks to destroy those institutions which now appear as obstacles to the realisation of our freedom and replace them with institutions which accord precisely with the idea of right. In both its conventional Kantian form and in its more radical expression, the inability to distinguish morality from ethical life dresses the latter in the cloth of the former. It gives ethical life the 'outward appearance' of being the self-determination of the will and thereby conceals the 'self-sufficiency' of its authority and power. It is the source, as we might say, of many democratic illusions.

The beginning of ethical life, for Hegel, is marked by the emergence of the family and its most distinctive innovation, love. Love introduces a level of recognition between individuals that goes far beyond mere respect for one another's rights. It cannot be reduced to any form of contract. It renounces a purely independent existence; it seeks unity with another; and it looks for self-fulfilment in this unity. But love also contains the contradictions of abstract right.

Hegel describes love as 'the consciousness of my unity with another, so that I am not isolated on my own but gain my self consciousness only through the *renunciation of my independent existence* and through knowing myself as the *unity of myself with another* and of the other with me' (*PR* §158). It contains an 'immense contradiction'. Its first moment is the feeling that 'I do not wish to be an independent person in my own right, and that, if I were, I would feel deficient and incomplete'. Its second moment is that 'I find myself in another person' and that 'I gain recognition in this person who in turn gains recognition in me'. My willing renunciation of an independent life in favour of unity with another presupposes my independence in the first place but also the possibility of regaining it in a relation to another. Love is thus predicated on the 'simultaneous renunciation and affirmation of individual personality' (*PR* §§158 and 158A). It both negates and affirms self-consciousness and it is the capacity of the modern subject to sustain this contradiction that Hegel calls our 'genius'.

The love of which Hegel speaks is not an abstract ideal; it is love as it is shaped in our own world within the setting of the family. Its 'first moment' is marriage. Hegel argues that in seeking to understand marriage we face an array of erroneous interpretations: that it is a purely sexual relationship conceived only in its physical aspect; that it is a civil contract based on arbitrary relations between individuals which can be taken up and dismissed at will (a notion Hegel sees in Kant); that it is simply based on the *feeling of love* and open to all its contingencies. Hegel calls marriage 'rightfully ethical love' to capture the fact that the transient, capricious and purely subjective aspects of love are excluded, for marriage externalises the contradiction present within love. Hegel argues that the *origin* of marriage is subjective in that it depends on the particular inclinations of the two persons who enter this relationship (or in a 'traditional marriage' on the initiative of the parents who arrange it); but he also points out that the 'free consent' of the individuals concerned, to give up their individual personalities and to constitute between themselves a single person, is itself an 'objective determination'. It even becomes the duty of the individuals concerned not to focus on the 'self-limitation' which marriage brings, but on the feeling of 'liberation' they derive from it (*PR* §§162 and 162A).

Hegel observes that in modern times the subjective factor, that of being in love, is increasingly regarded as the only important factor in the origin of marriage: 'it is imagined that each must wait until his hour has struck, and that one can give one's love only to a specific individual' (*PR* §162A). The sharing of love becomes the most vital end of our personal lives. But what starts off as an effect of feeling soon asserts itself as a substantial factor. Marriage becomes an institution 'exalted above the contingency of passions'. If it begins life in the form of a feeling, this aspect is soon superseded as the family becomes a person and its members its mere accidents. Marriage is exalted so that everything else appears powerless against it and subject to its authority (*PR* §§163 and 163A). In some circumstances it even becomes an object of religious worship, as it did in ancient Rome in the shape of the *Penates*, and in modern times it still appears as the exemplary institution in which 'piety finds its place'. The marriage ceremony confirms a bond that is set above all contingency of feeling. At the same time it sets the genders apart. The man is supposedly endowed with qualities of personal self-sufficiency; he is powerful and active; he finds his 'actual substantial life in the state, in learning, etc.' (*PR* §166). The woman occupies the role of 'concrete individuality and feeling', she is passive and subjective, she finds her vocation in the family itself, her ethical disposition is to piety and she relates more to the 'law of the emotive' rather than to the higher sciences or philosophy or artistic productions, all of which require a 'universal element'. In this 'pure type' of marriage, Hegel writes,

> The difference between man and woman is the difference between animal and plant; the animal is closer in character to man, the plant to woman, for the latter is a more peaceful process of unfolding whose principle is the more indeterminate unity of feeling. When women are in charge of government, the state is in danger, for their actions are based not on the demands of universality but on contingent inclination and opinion. The education of women takes place imperceptibly . . . more through living than through the acquisition of knowledge, whereas man attains his position only through the attainment of thought and numerous technical exertions.
>
> (*PR* §166A)

These passages engender outrage in every thinking being committed to equality. They are not an expression of Hegel's view of what love *should* be but his account of what love all too often *is*. As he points out, when the family is treated as a single person in terms of property, this 'difference' between men and women is further consolidated through the representation of the family by the 'husband as its head' (*PR* §171). This pure type of family life may thankfully be 'disfigured' in all manner of ways (and today the institution of marriage is meant to accommodate an equality between husband and wife that denies such gender differences), but the movement which Hegel explores – from the *idea of love* as the 'consciousness of my unity with another' to the *actuality* of family life – remains no less troubling. In the face of such contradictions Hegel argues we may be tempted by a romanticism which declares that the marriage ceremony is superfluous, that it is a formality that can be dispensed with, and that love alone is the essential element. Hegel cites the case of Friedrich von Schlegel's *Lucinde* where Schlegel represents 'physical surrender' as the sign that is necessary to prove the freedom and intensity of one's love. A beautiful idea, Hegel comments, but also 'an argument with which seducers are not unfamiliar'. Do not forget, he says, that under existing conditions 'a girl loses her honour in the act of physical surrender, which is not so much the case with a man who has another field of ethical activity apart from the family' (*PR* §164A). For Hegel, 'Lucinde's shame' reveals that the 'immense contradiction' present within love is not so easily resolved.

Kant's inability to distinguish between morality and ethical life is replicated in a parallel inability to distinguish between civil society and the state. Kant wrote interchangeably of *civil society* (*status civilis*) and the *state* (*civitas*) and referred indifferently to a *civil state* or a *state of civil society*. The difference between them appeared to him only as one of viewpoint. In a seminal chapter on Hegel's use of the concepts 'state' and 'civil society', Manfred Riedel has shown that Kant's identification of civil society and the state inherited an old European tradition whose origins go back to the concept of κοινωνία πολιτική (political community) in Aristotle's *Politics* (Riedel 1984). The fusion of state and civil society was the classical formula of European political philosophy before the modern era, and as long as Kant remained confined within this framework, he could find no way of understanding civil society in its modern form: as a de-politicised and de-traditionalised society, forming a system of complete interdependence among otherwise isolated, self-interested and private individuals, separated on one side from the state and on the other from the family. As Riedel notes, Hegel was the first political philosopher to conceptualise civil society in its modern sense as 'the stage of difference which intervenes between the family and the state' (*PR* §182A). Hegel's philosophy of right is punctuated by criticisms of the propensity of the natural law tradition, up to and including Kant, to equate the state simply with the protection of civil society and treat the private interests of the members of civil society as the 'ultimate end' for which they are politically united.

Hegel wrote that the development of civil society was the achievement of the modern age which provided institutional support for the *liberation of the subject*, but that it also provides the ground on which *subjectivism* thrives. Members of civil society are private persons who 'have their own interest as their end', regard the universal 'as a hostile element prejudicial to their own ends', try to 'keep it at a distance' and *imagine* that they can 'do without it' (*PR* §184A). But in fact civil society is a 'system of all-round interdependence' in which the needs and rights of individuals are interwoven with the needs and rights of everyone else. Civil society is a system of social interdependence since, as Hegel put it, individuals cannot satisfy any of their particular needs except through the 'exclusive *mediation* of the form of *universality*' (*PR* §182). It is a sphere of *ethical life* inasmuch as its members recognise one another as 'rightful individuals' who satisfy their needs through the free exchange of the products of their labour with other free individuals, as 'human beings' who educate themselves through their work, and as members of social groups who develop a sense of collective responsibility and solidarity with fellow-members. It is also, however, a system of ethical life that is 'lost in extremes'. It consists not only in the multiplication of needs and the means of their satisfaction, but also in an 'equally infinite increase in dependence and want' (*PR* §195).

> Civil society affords a spectacle of extravagance and misery as well as of the physical and ethical corruption common to both . . . Particularity in itself is boundless extravagance and the forms of this extravagance are themselves boundless . . . But on the other hand, deprivation and want are likewise boundless, and this confused situation can be restored to harmony only through the forcible intervention of the state.
>
> (*PR* §§185 and 185A)

Hegel speaks of the deprivation and poverty which mar civil society and the sense of injustice felt by the poor when the feelings of right which normally come from supporting ourselves by our own activity are contradicted by their social existence. Hegel writes that it is not enough to speak of right and freedom in the abstract when these ideas appear as a mere sham to those who are deprived of all the advantages of civil society, or when they are used to justify the indifference of those who say that support for the poor is contrary to the principles of civil society. Despite an excess of wealth, Hegel writes, civil society is 'not wealthy enough . . . to prevent an excess of poverty', and the principal means it has of dealing with poverty is merely to 'leave the poor to their fate and direct them to beg from the public' (PR §245). If civil society can find no better answer to the question of poverty, then Hegel adds, 'the boundlessness of deprivation and want can only be restored to harmony through the forcible intervention of the state' (PR §185A). In this sense, we would have to say that, as Hegel put it, a well functioning 'civil society . . . pre-supposes the state . . . as something self-subsistent' (PR §256). We have come a long way from Kant's idealised account of civil society as the 'law-governed decisions of a united will'. We have come to Hegel's theory of the modern state, the character of which I shall now address through a re-examination of the young Marx's rightly renowned, spirited, but ultimately misjudged critique.

Notes

1 In terms of Hegel's own intellectual biography, Habermas goes along with mainstream of critical theory when he contrasts the radical and intersubjective character of Hegel's early writings to what he calls the 'emphatic institutionalism' of his later *Philosophy of Right* (Habermas 1990: 23–43). Thus in *The Philosophical Discourse of Modernity* (first published in 1985) he presents the younger Hegel as committed to a community based on second-order, constitutional norms which recognise the heterogeneity and plurality of modern society and which regulate social differences without imposing any absolute conception of social morality. By contrast, he presents the older Hegel as having moved towards a position in which 'the individual will is totally bound to the institutional order and only justified to the extent that the institutions are one with it'. Habermas applauds the younger Hegel for recognising the importance of intersubjectivity in a heterogeneous and pluralistic society, but admonishes the older Hegel as repeating the inability of liberalism to face up to the demands of democratic self-determination which it could only hear as a 'note of discord offending against reason'. What ensued, according to Habermas, was the 'blunting of critique' (Habermas 1990: 43). Not only does this account repeat the conventional view of a movement from the radicalism of youth to the conservatism of old age (which is not true of Habermas either) but more importantly to my mind, it calls a '*blunting* of critique' what was in fact an *extension* of critique to critique itself.

2 Compare with Hobbes who writes: the law of the sovereign can 'never be against reason' and every member of society 'must acknowledge himself to be the author . . . of whatever he that is already their sovereign shall do and judge fit to be done' (Hobbes, *Leviathan*, quoted in Fine 1985: 25).

3 There is a certain irony in how closely the young Marx's later critique of Hegel followed the more original lines of Hegel's own critique of Kant. To Marx it seemed

that Hegel was merely a more realistic, hard-headed apologist for the modern state than Kant, and that his special offence was to see through the conceptual illusions of this system of rule and still give it a philosophical certificate of health. What Marx did not see is that Hegel's philosophy of right was a *critique* of Kant's inversion of subject and predicate and of the spurious 'deductions' he made from the postulates of practical reason.

4 Chris Arthur comments that 'instead of making the historical judgement that in this society freedom means freedom of property, he [Hegel] makes the philosophical judgement that the concept of freedom actualises itself in the private property system' (Arthur 1986: 96). Jeremy Waldron reads *Philosophy of Right* more favourably as a sophisticated natural law theory, criticising Hegel for his failure to see that private property can be justified only if it can be made available in significant quantities to every person (Waldron 1988). Laurence Dickey writes that Hegel was acutely aware of the close ties that many eighteenth-century natural law theorists had been drawing between economic and civil developments in history, and of how they had moved beyond a 'fixation' on property toward the more 'ethical' dimensions of civil society. He argues that Hegel continued in this tradition when he sought to reactivate the virtues of 'magnanimity, courage and the love of mankind' without trying to reverse the development of commercial society (Dickey 1989: 192–220). These otherwise diverse readings have in common the fact that they all situate Hegel's analysis of property firmly within the natural law paradigm.

5 The concept of personality also marks the distinction between *human beings* and *animals*: the former appear as thinking beings who translate their thoughts into action and thereby determine themselves as free beings; the latter appear as instinctual beings impelled by nature to certain behaviours but without will because they do not represent to themselves what they desire. The *person* in this sense is the nucleus of a system of rights in a way that the *animal* cannot be. The system of right distinguishes between personality and subjectivity in general. Any living thing whatever may be a subject, but *as a person* I am a subject who is aware of my subjectivity. This distinction between *persons* and *animals*, like that between *persons* and *things*, is a social distinction established within the system of right; it is *not* an 'ontology' nor does it determine how the distinction between persons and animals is applied.

4

STATE AND REVOLUTION
Hegel, Rousseau, Marx

The young Marx's critique of Hegel's *Philosophy of Right*

The young Marx's guilty verdict on Hegel's so-called 'doctrine of the state' in the *Philosophy of Right* is well known and within Marxist social and political thought it has long overshadowed access to the text. Marx maintained that Hegel concealed the forms of domination and violence characteristic of the modern state beneath a 'speculative' veneer of freedom and reason. The root of the problem, according to Marx, lay in Hegel's method: he reified the *predicate* of the modern state, the idea of universality, before deducing from this 'idea' the state's mundane institutional forms – the constitution, monarchy, legislature and executive (*MEW* 80). Once Hegel converted universality into the subject and the state into a mere moment of this 'mystical substance', the dogmatic character of the *Philosophy of Right* was set: Hegel's concern was 'simply to rediscover "the idea" in every sphere of the state that he depicted . . . to fasten on what lies nearest at hand and prove that it is an actual moment of the idea' (*MEW* 98). He acknowledged that Hegel gave a roughly accurate empirical account of power as it is exercised in a rather conservative form of constitutional monarchy, but he argued that his only philosophical contribution was to convert these empirical facts into the actualisation of freedom. The resemblance Marx saw between Hegel's 'rational state' and the actual Prussian state led Marx to despair of finding any critical edge in the substance of Hegel's politics. 'God help us all!' was his final, exasperated comment after he cited a passage in which Hegel seemingly attempted to deduce ministerial authority and the two houses of parliament, Commons and Lords, from the 'Idea' (*MEW* 198).

For Marx, the value of reading Hegel's *Philosophy of Right* lay in the mirror of reality it offered. He saw Hegel's idealist inversion of subject and predicate as the philosophical expression of the real inversion of subject and predicate in bourgeois society. He argued that it was not so much Hegel who inverted reality as reality that was itself inverted and reflected in Hegel's dialectic: '*uncritical mysticism* is the key both to the riddle of modern constitutions . . . and also to the mystery of Hegelian philosophy, above all the *Philosophy of Right*' (*MEW* 149). In bourgeois society real, subjective human beings are transformed into '*unreal*, objective moments of the Idea'; private property becomes the subject of the will and the will survives only as the predicate of private property (*MEW* 175); the state becomes the divine idea on earth and individuals survive only as moments of this higher reality (*MEW* 87). It is this upside-down reality which, according to Marx, Hegel's speculative philosophy mirrored and rationalised. Marx presented it as an idealised expression of the abstract forms of domination characteristic of the modern world. Its effect was to convert the everyday experience of alienation and domination into a semblance of reason.

Marx maintained that the rationality Hegel attributed to the state was contradicted at every point by its irrational reality. It is the *illusion* of the state that 'the affairs of the people are matters of universal concern'; the *truth* of the state is that 'the real interest of the people . . . is present only formally'. The state allows the people to appear only as 'idea, fantasy, illusion, representation', it offers no more than a 'ceremony' or 'spice' of popular existence; it expresses 'the lie that the state is in the interest of the people' (*MEW* 125). Both Hegel and the political world he represented must be 'turned on their head' if the people are to enter the political stage *in person* rather than through representation, in *body* rather than in name alone, in *actuality* rather than in mere form. This logic of inversion ran right through Marx's text. Its literary trope is that of chiasma. Thus Marx writes that Hegel's true interest was 'not to understand how thought can be embodied in political determinations, but to dissolve the existing political determinations into abstract ideas'; his true concern was 'not the logic of the subject matter but the subject matter of logic' (*MEW* 73); the task he set political philosophy was 'not to discover the truth of empirical existence but to discover the empirical existence of truth' (*MEW* 98); in his philosophy of right 'thought is not guided by the nature of the state, the state is guided by a pre-existing system of thought' (*MEW* 75); he 'does not provide us with the logic of the body politics . . . he provides his logic with a political body' (*MEW* 109). Marx presents himself, by contrast, as the one who put philosophy and the world back on their feet. Whereas in Hegel 'the condition is posited as the conditioned, the determinator as the determined, the producer as the product' (*MEW* 62), Marx according to his own account recognised that it is not the Idea that determines actuality but actuality that determines ideas; it is not the constitution that creates the people but people that create constitutions; it not the state that determines civil society but civil society that determines the state; or, as Marx and Engels put it most famously in *The German Ideology*, 'it is not consciousness that determines life; it is life that determines consciousness'.

This logic of inversion enters into almost every nook and cranny of Marx's critique of Hegel's theory of the state. According to Marx, Hegel 'does not say that the will of the monarch is the final decision, but that the final decision is the will of the monarch' (*MEW* 82). Hegel *idealises* the bureaucracy as the ultimate purpose of the state and the state as the ultimate purpose of the universal will, at the same time as he *empiricises* the 'real *empirical* state-mind, *public consciousness*' as if it were a 'mere hotchpotch made up of the thoughts and opinions of the Many' (*MEW* 124). Marx presents himself as the advocate of 'true democracy' in which 'matters of universal concern are *really* matters of universal public concern' and not the preserve of the class of officials; representatives of the people are delegates of the people and no longer a power over the people; the legislature is no longer subsumed to the bureaucracy (the power that makes all the 'petty . . . retrograde revolutions'), but the bureaucracy is subsumed to the legislature (the power that makes 'great, organic, universal revolutions'). While Hegel appears as the philosopher who 'proceeds from the state and conceives of man as the subjectivised state', Marx presents himself as the democrat who 'proceeds from man and conceives the state as objectified man' (*MEW* 87). In a democracy, he writes, 'man does not exist for the sake of the law, but the law exists for the sake of man' (*MEW* 88). Hegel merely interprets the world; Marx presents himself as changing it.

There is power and beauty in these inversions and reversals, but was Hegel in fact the 'Hegel' whom Marx imagined him to be: the alchemist who turned the grubby empirical existence of the modern state into the actualisation of the Idea? and was Marx in fact the 'Marx' whom he imagined himself to be: the relentless critic of all existing conditions who puts the world back on its feet? My contention is that Marx not only misconstrued what Hegel was doing in the *Philosophy of Right*, but in getting Hegel wrong he also misrepresented himself. In any event, too often we are left in contemporary Marxism with an essentially dogmatic acceptance of the truth and validity of the young Marx's critique. Let us, as it were, turn the tables and reconstruct Hegel's response.

Hegel's critique of representation

While the young Marx accused the older Hegel of being an uncritical apologist for modern representative government, even in its more backward and author-itarian forms, Hegel depicted his own work as an attempt to dispel the illusions of representation. In his *Lectures on the Philosophy of World History* (1975b) he summed up his own 'position' thus:

> it was a great advance when political life became the property of every-one through the advent of representative government . . . [but] to associate the so-called representative constitution with the idea of a free constitution is the *hardened prejudice* of our age.
>
> (*LPWH* 121)

The 'hardened prejudice of our age' – this is hardly the language of uncritical apolo-getics. Behind the illusions of a 'free constitution', Hegel writes, 'we encounter a definite constitution which is *not a matter of free choice* but invariably accords with the national spirit at a given stage of its development' (*LPWH* 123). If universal assent were the true basis of the state, then no law could be upheld unless everyone agreed to it; but people are *forced* to obey laws whether or not they agree. If the minority must submit to the majority, then this can 'no longer be described as freedom, for the will of the minority is no longer respected' (*LPWH* 122).

When we read the sections on representation in the *Philosophy of Right*, what we find is not an apology but rather an attempt to dispel the *aura* of representative government. This is why his analysis of the illusions of representation appeared so threatening to liberal commentators accustomed to associating representative government with the idea of a free constitution. Marx, however, had little awareness of his own *affinity* with Hegel when he too sought to dispel the mystique of liberal forms and question the 'hardened prejudice' of our age which associates modern representative government with the idea of a free constitution.

It was Hegel who first pointed to the manifold *guarantees* that restrict the principle of representation both as it is envisaged in republican thought and as it is practised in so-called 'representative government'. It is restricted to one part of the state, the legislature, or even to one House of the legislature, the Commons and not the Lords. Representatives are endowed with a privileged standing in relation to those they represent: they are not 'agents with a commission or specific instructions' but enjoy a relation of 'trust' with their electors which allows them to reach decisions on the basis of their own 'greater knowledge of public affairs' and 'the confidence felt in them'. The representatives are in any case answerable to the executive and it is one of the principal duties of the executive to curb what it sees as the 'excesses' of the popular assembly (*PR* §301R). The authority of representatives is restricted in relation to that of the constitutional monarch, who is endowed not only with formal powers of ultimate decision but also with certain substantial powers over the survival of the state. It is as if there were an unwritten rule that 'public freedom in general and a hereditary succession guarantee each other reciprocally' (*PR* §286R). The constitution allows representatives to make legislative changes, but only insofar as they are 'imperceptible' and 'tranquil in appearance'; and it demands that the constitution itself must not be regarded as something 'made even if it does have an origin in time', but rather as something 'divine and enduring . . . exalted above the sphere of all manufactured things' (*PR* §273R). The organisation of social and political interests in civil society is arranged in such a way as to 'prevent individuals from crystallising into a powerful bloc in opposition to the organised state' (*PR* §302) and to keep them under the 'higher supervision of the state' (*PR* §255A). Indeed, the key to modern representative government, in Hegel's account, is that everything is done to ensure that the people at no point become a 'formless mass' uncontrolled by the state. As Hegel puts it, the 'democratic element' is refused admission to the state unless it is first *mediated* by the representative system. Unmediated, the voice of the masses is treated as 'always for violence'. Hegel highlights the many *exclusions* from political participation practised by the state and justified by natural law theory. Kant, who was no democrat, had put forward a long list of exclusions: the labouring class, women, servants, criminals, children and foreigners. But, as Hegel observed, even what we call 'universal suffrage' means in effect the participation of the Many, never of All.

It was not Hegel's *opinion* that women ought to be excluded, nor that the democratic element ought to be supervised by state officials, nor that individuals ought to be prevented from forming an opposition to the state, nor that the monarch ought to have the power of ultimate decision, nor that the constitution ought be exalted above the sphere of social life, nor that the legislature ought to be policed by the executive, nor that representatives ought to be unaccountable to their electors, etc. This is just the way things are in certain forms of representative government once we view it stripped of its mystique. This is the reality of representation in the modern state. The real function of political representation, as Hegel presents it, is to admit the private interests of civil society into the organism of the state as *one of its several elements* – alongside the constitution, the monarchy, and the executive – and to serve as a *middle term* between civil society and the state. The role of representation is to embody the 'subjective moment in universal freedom' in order to prevent the isolation of the government which otherwise might become an arbitrary tyranny, and to prevent the isolation of civil society which might otherwise crystallise into a bloc in opposition to the state (*PR* §302). Hegel's account of the functions of representation in the modern state contrasts sharply with the homage paid to representative government by liberal philosophers like Kant, who identified it with 'the united will of all' and on this basis declared that 'every true republic is and can be nothing else than a representative system of the people'. And there is little that Marx said in his critique of representation that he did not draw from Hegel. He simply articulated in a more explicit way its critical content.

Although Marx misconstrued the nature of his difference form Hegel, he did not invent the fact of difference itself. The actual difference between them does not lie in the fact that one was a critic of representation and the other was an apologist, for they were both critics, but rather in the specific character of their respective critiques. This difference emerges most sharply in how they handled the *critique of representation*, first articulated by Rousseau, that has been coeval with the modern form of representation itself. Hegel combined his critique of representation with what we might call a *critique of the critique of representation* – and especially of the abstract ideal of 'true democracy' which Rousseau initiated and Marx later reconstructed. It was Hegel's critique of this 'abstract ideal' which Marx misread as conservative and doctrinal.

Hegel's critique of the critique of representation

Rousseau's critique of representation was expressed in two closely related propositions: one was the demand to abolish representation *as such* on the ground that I have a right to speak for myself and no one else has a right to speak on my behalf; the other was the demand to abolish the guarantees which restrict representation in the modern state and to make representation 'fully active and unrestricted'. When we read the *Philosophy of Right* we find both propositions analysed in detail.

Hegel observes that 'subjective opinion naturally enough finds superfluous and even perhaps offensive the demand for such guarantees, if the demand is made with reference to what is called the "people"' (*PR* §310R). In the name of the people, revolutionary thought puts forward the demand, 'all power to the assembly', and declares 'an essential opposition between the assembly and the state executive, as if the assembly were all good and the executive all bad'. To this opposition Hegel comments that it could equally be said that 'the representative assembly starts from private interests and is therefore inclined to devote itself to these at the expense of the general interest, and that the executive starts from the standpoint of the state and therefore devotes itself to the public interest'. Neither standpoint is more justified than the other. If representation is a middle term between civil society and the state and its role is to embody the 'subjective moment in universal freedom' as one of several elements of the state, then the appropriation of the *whole* state by the principle of representation cannot overcome the private point of view, it can only generalise it. Hegel argues that the legislature and executive should be seen for what they are, elements within the organism of the state as a whole, and that if an *essential* opposition is established between them (as there was in the aftermath of the French Revolution), this would be a sign only that the state was in the 'throes of destruction' (*PR* §300A). Hegel's discussion of Montesquieu's doctrine of the 'separation of powers' may serve to illustrate his criticism of the view that the legislature and executive are independent of one other. He writes:

> While the powers of the state must certainly be distinguished, each must form a whole in itself and contain the other moments within it. When we speak of the distinct activities of these powers, we must not fall into the monumental error of taking this to mean that each power should exist independently and in abstraction; on the contrary, the powers should be distinguished only as moments of the concept. On the other hand, if these differences do exist independently and in abstraction, it is plain to see that two self-sufficient entities cannot constitute a unity, but must certainly give rise to a conflict whereby either the whole is destroyed or unity is restored by force. Thus during the French Revolution, the legislative power at times engulfed the so-called executive and at other times the executive engulfed the legislature, so that it remains an absurdity in this context to raise . . . the moral demand for harmony.
>
> (*PR* §272A)

What Hegel is saying here is that we cannot take one element of the state, in this case the representative assembly, abstract it from its place within the whole, turn it into the totality and think that we have solved the problem of democracy. This would be equally true of any other element of the state – let us say, 'deliberation' – which contemporary theories of deliberative democracy also abstract from its place within the whole, idealise and extend into the totality.

An equally 'dangerous prejudice' Hegel identifies is one which sets the 'general will' of the people in opposition to the associations of civil society, either on the grounds that the factions and parties of civil society are self-interested, corrupted by money and incapable of subsuming their private point of view to the good of the whole, or on the opposite grounds that they are determined by the political system and incapable of representing the particular interests of civil society. Either way, the temptation arises to reject the alien institutions of representation in order that the people might appear in the assembly in person. At its limit Hegel argues that this attitude leads to the suppression of the associations of civil society – either because they put the private point of view before the universal or because they put the point of view of the state before the interests of civil society. Hegel's argument was that this particular type of radicalism threatens to introduce a new barbarity and provides a new mask beneath which the rule of the few and the indifference of the many remain firmly intact. Although Hegel recognised that the demand that *everyone* should participate in the business of the state arises naturally in opposition to the many formal and substantial exclusions established by representative government, he dismissed it as a 'ridiculous notion' – partly because it is based on the assumption that everyone is 'at home in this business' but more especially because it issues the instruction that everyone '*must* participate in this business' (*PR* §§301 and 301R). This 'must' was evidence of the *obligation* that lies behind this radical democratic demand.

Hegel maintained that a 'pure' form of representation, one in which citizens appear only as an atomised mass of individuals and the state is treated as the only legitimate association, would turn the state into a slave to public opinion and public opinion, as he put it, is by its nature not only a repository of 'true needs' and 'substantial principles of justice', but also suffers from 'all the contingencies of opinion, with its ignorance and perverseness, its false information and its errors of judgement' (*PR* §317). In public opinion 'truth and endless error are so closely united . . . that it cannot be genuinely *serious* about them both' (*PR* §317R). Hegel did not devalue the empirical consciousness of the people, as Marx thought he did, and he reaffirmed that public opinion deserves to be '*respected* as well as *despised*' (*PR* §318). However, he also insisted that to be independent of public opinion is 'the first formal condition of achieving anything great or rational either in actuality or in science' (*PR* §318), and that 'no one can achieve anything great unless he is able to despise public opinion as he here and there encounters it' (*PR* §318A). Hegel pointed out what is obscured by a certain type of democratic radicalism: that if we are not to turn *vox populi* into *vox dei*, then we have to go beyond 'subjective opinion and its self-confidence' and not take it as given that the people must always 'know best what is in their own interest' (*PR* §301R). In other words, critical thought must be prepared to be critical and when necessary to go against public opinion. In the end it all depends on substance – on *what* the people will. To translate this argument, as Marx did, into a statement of contempt for the people or reverence for the state is to miss the point of Hegel's determination to face up to the burden of judgement and not cloud it in democratic illusions.

Hegel's critique of Rousseau

Hegel's 'critique of the critique of representation' was based on a long engagement with Rousseau and Rousseauian ways of thinking. In his *Early Theological Writings* Hegel put himself on Rousseau's side when he wrote that, by posing the 'general will' as the principle of the modern state, Rousseau ushered in 'the revolution in the spirit of the age . . . the right to legislate for oneself, to be responsible to oneself alone for administering one's own law' (*ETW* 145). Rousseau's achievement was to rediscover the ancient political principle according to which citizens 'obeyed laws laid down by themselves, obeyed men whom they themselves had appointed to office, waged wars on which they themselves had decided, gave their property, exhausted their passions and sacrificed their lives by thousands for an end which was their own' (*ETW* 154). If Rousseau made the ancient *polis* (in the shape of Sparta) into a 'living example to mankind', the young Hegel added that the revival of this ideal (more in the shape of Athens) was 'the central task of the age' (Hegel 1984: 171).

It was especially in the context of the French Revolution that Hegel began to re-examine the foundations of this doctrine. In the *Phenomenology of Spirit* he formulated the Rousseauian principle thus:

> Neither by the mere idea of self-given laws . . . nor by its being represented in law-making . . . does self-consciousness let itself be cheated out of reality, the reality of itself making the law and accomplishing . . . the universal work . . . In the case where the self is merely represented and ideally presented, there it is not actual; where it is by proxy, it is not.
> (*PS* §588)

But the question Hegel addressed was this: why did this ideal culminate in the unity of 'absolute freedom and terror'. His answer was that 'only abstractions were used, the Idea was lacking'. The *abstraction* was the 'general will'; the *Idea* that was lacking was 'concrete freedom'. Why is the general will an abstraction? Hegel's answer had three aspects. First, the general will expresses the relation of the individual to society in a fantastical form. The illusion is that 'every personality . . . undivided from the whole, always does everything [that is done by the whole], and what appears as done by the whole is the direct and conscious deed of each'. Consequently, the real antagonisms which exist between individual consciousness and the general will are given no recognition within the 'universal work of absolute freedom' (*PS* §589). The general will permits no middle term between the universal and the individual so that individuals are instructed to see their only purpose as the general purpose and the significance of individual personality is thereby denied. It presents itself as the will of all individuals as such, but in reality it is the will of some *individuals* only insofar as they will the general will.

Second, Hegel argued that the general will presents the relations of 'man' to 'nature' in an equally illusory way by 'dissolving' the external world and re-presenting it as 'simply its own will'. It is as if the world is an empty vessel that can offer no resistance to what is willed by the general will. Since the general will recognises no natural limitations, it puts its faith in its own *omnipotence*. It believes it can move seas, but it ends up only with parched salt flats. Third, Hegel argues that the general will cannot create the positive condition of universal equality it espouses because its conception of freedom is essentially *negative* and it only experiences itself through the *annihilation of all particular and objective determinations*. Thus its relation to the individual becomes one of unmediated negation:

> The sole work and deed of universal freedom is therefore death, a death which has no inner significance . . . for what is negated is the empty point of the absolutely free self. It is thus the coldest and meanest of all deaths, with no more significance than cutting off a head of cabbage or swallowing a mouthful of water.
>
> (*PS* §590)

The general will can achieve nothing constructive by way of 'institutions of conscious freedom'. Government, which is supposed to be 'the individuality of the universal will', stands opposed to it as a specific will of its own and becomes in the eyes of other parties merely the victorious faction and a target for rival claims to power. All intermediate social groups and classes are abolished on the grounds that they represent merely partial interests and therefore oppose the general will. Suspicion and guilt rule supreme as the 'mask of virtue' is torn from the face of those suspected of secret intentions and being suspected takes the place of being guilty. In the end, Hegel argues, it is only through the fury and fanaticism of destruction that this negative will feels its own existence and power. Hegel did not blame Rousseau for what was done in his name, any more than Marx or Nietzsche are to be blamed for what has been done in theirs, but the terror marked for Hegel an event which, as it were, robbed Rousseau of his innocence. Representation was not in fact overcome; it was reproduced in a less rational form.

There were no fundamental 'breaks' in Hegel's critique of the revolutionary tradition from the *Phenomenology of Spirit* to the *Philosophy of Right*. In the latter Hegel again acknowledged the *democratic* aspect of the idea of the general will which he reformulated thus:

> *all* individuals ought to participate in deliberations and decisions on the universal concerns of the state – on the grounds that they are all members of the state and that the concerns of the state are the concerns of *everyone*, so that everyone has a *right* to share in them with his own knowledge and volition.
>
> (*PR* §308R)

He acknowledged that this idea 'afforded the tremendous spectacle, for the first time we know of in human history, of the overthrow of all existing and given conditions within an actual major state and the revision of its constitution from first principles and purely in terms of *thought*' (PR §258R), and that Rousseau was the first to put forward 'the *will* as the principle of the state, a principle which has thought not only as its form . . . but also as its content' (PR §258R). However, Hegel also registered the shadow that fell between the intention behind the idea and its unintended consequences:

> the *intention* behind this was to give it what was *supposed* to be a purely *rational* basis. On the other hand, since these were only abstractions divorced from the Idea, they turned the attempt into the most terrible and drastic event.
>
> (PR §258R)

Why did the Revolution degenerate into a 'most terrible and drastic event'? Hegel argues it was because it endeavoured to 'implant in the organism of the state a *democratic* element *devoid of rational form*'. If this seemed to be a plausible idea, it was only because it advanced an *abstract* determination of membership of the state and 'superficial thinking sticks to abstractions'. Having no notion of the 'will's rationality in and for itself', whether or not it was 'recognised by individuals' (PR §258R), it turned the union of individuals within the state into a *contract* based on their 'arbitrary will and opinions, and on their express consent given at their own discretion' (PR §258R). The general will demonstrated intolerance towards everything particular:

> Fanaticism wills only what is abstract, not what is articulated, so that whenever differences emerge, it finds them incompatible with its own indeterminacy and cancels them. This is why the people, during the French Revolution, destroyed once more the institutions they had themselves created, because all institutions are incompatible with the abstract self-consciousness of equality.
>
> (PR §5A)

The general will alone was 'free, infinite and absolute'. It alone was 'supreme in relation to things' and 'absolute in relation to everything else' (PR §44A).

In the *Philosophy of History* Hegel again took up the same thematic – though this time in a more historical mode. He celebrated the key idea which informed the Revolution, that of the free will as the principle of the state, and in a famous passage towards the end of the book commented:

> The principle of the Freedom of the Will . . . asserted itself against existing Right . . . The entire political system appeared as one mass of injustice. The change was necessarily violent because the work of trans-formation was not undertaken by the government . . . the idea of Right asserted its authority *all at once*, and the old framework of injustice could

offer no resistance to its onslaught. A constitution, therefore, was established in harmony with the conception of Right, and on this foundation all future legislation was to be based. Never since the sun had stood in the firmament and the planets revolved around him had it been perceived that *man's existence centres in his head, i.e. in thought*, inspired by which he builds up the world of reality . . . This was accordingly a glorious mental dawn. All thinking beings shared in the jubilation of this epoch . . . a spiritual enthusiasm . . . thrilled through the world, as if the reconciliation between the Divine and the Secular was now first accomplished.

(*PH* 447)

It seems clear to me that Hegel had not lost his enthusiasm for the Revolution, but neither did he become complacent over its results. In his analysis of the aftermath of the Revolution, he wrote of how the first constitutional form of government, based on a division between the monarch at the head of the executive and the legislature representing the people, collapsed – not least because of the absolute mistrust between them. There emerged in its place a government which theoretically proceeded from the people but in reality from the National Convention and its Committees. Now purely abstract philosophical principles were set up: Virtue in opposition to corruption and Terror in opposition to licence. Virtue distinguished the citizens into two classes – those who had it and those who did not, and Terror attained a terrible power. Virtue, Suspicion and Terror joined together to become the order of the day and exercised power without legal formalities. The punishment they inflicted was simple – death. The requirement that the general will had also to be *empirically* general, established the atomistic principle which insists on the sway of individual wills and which maintains that all government must emanate from them. The ruling party allowed no other political organisation to be set up, but the government itself was branded by its opponents as a particular will wielding arbitrary power in the name of the people. When it was expelled from power and the opposition filled the vacant places, they met with the same hostility and shared the same fate. Such tyranny could not last. An organised government was introduced in the shape of the Directory of Five, but under it suspicion was still in the ascendant and this constitution experienced the same fate as that of its predecessor. Then came the rise of one who knew how to rule by military means and who established himself as an individual will at the head of state. Under Napoleon great victories were gained but the sway of mistrust was exchanged for that of fear and 'never was the powerlessness of victory exhibited in a clearer light'. The religious and nationalistic dispositions of subject peoples brought about his ruin and an unstable constitutional monarchy was restored. This government was in turn overthrown and at length 'after forty years of war and confusion indescribable, a weary heart might fain congratulate itself on seeing a termination and tranquillisation of all these disturbances' (*PH* 449–51). Hegel died soon after writing these lines.[1]

Hegel and the French Revolution

Hegel's understanding of politics was, as it should have been, shaped and reshaped by the momentous political events of his day. Political philosophy cannot be isolated from *events* and in Hegel's writings we find an evolving relation between thought and actuality in which *experience* was the driving force. The conjunction of absolute freedom and terror provoked a major rethinking of the 'idea of freedom' that was actualised in the revolution and of its mimetic relation to the forces it overthrew. If Hegel's thinking had solidified into a static ideal, then this would have been indicative of a form of thought which had grown old and lost its life, but this was not the case. However, from the *Phenomenology of Spirit* through to the *Philosophy of Right* and thence to the *Philosophy of History* we also find a definite line of continuity in Hegel's analysis of the French Revolution.

In his seminal discussion of *Hegel and the French Revolution* (1982), Karl Ritter distinguished between three periods in Hegel's understanding of this event. The first, in the immediate aftermath, was characterised by positive support for the Revolution and its secular aims against the injustice of the old order and the dogmatics of positive Christianity (*The positivity of Christianity* 1795 and *The spirit of Christianity and its fate* 1799). At this time Hegel's attack was directed against a political and religious order that required blind obedience and sacrifice of intellect, and the experience of the Terror played only a minor role in this emplotment. In the second 'Jena period', disillusionment set in and the Terror became the nub of Hegel's reassessment. Enlightenment was now read through the lens of the Revolution, whereas before the Revolution was read through the lens of Enlightenment, and what it revealed was a madness within the dream of reason. In the third period, the violence of revolution was justified retrospectively by the 'cunning of reason' which redeemed the revolutionary Terror through its construction of the Napoleonic Code and its formation of a modern constitutional state. From this drama of affirmation, negation and finally reconciliation, Ritter drew the somewhat surprising conclusion that 'Hegel always affirmatively accepted the French revolution'. Ritter's conclusion, however, does not easily flow from this argument, and perhaps Jürgen Habermas came closer to its spirit when he concluded that the older Hegel accepted the Revolution's substantive achievements but dreaded the revolutionary process itself. According to Habermas, it was perhaps for this reason that Hegel was obliged to conceive the realisation of reason as an objective and necessary process of world history (Habermas 1974).

Neither of these formulations does justice to Hegel's texts. What I see in them is a determination not to philosophise away terror under the sign of historical progress, but rather the contrary: to look horror in the face. The darkness that followed the 'glorious mental dawn' impelled him beyond any faith in historical progress or in retrospective consolation. The idea of a final reconciliation attributed to Hegel belongs more rightfully to Kant, whose 'universal history' offered consolation for the violence of human history in the prospect of a future 'perpetual peace', as if providence and the plan of nature were destined to work out for the best. Kant's philosophy of history was no more designed to justify terror than was Hegel's, but he contemplated the modern exercise of violence 'philosophically' in a way that Hegel could not accept. The key to Hegel's investigation was the conviction that terror must not be left with the last word and that philosophy could not rest content either with a revolutionary *idealism* that rationalised violence or with a cynical *realism* that saw in history only a 'slaughter-bench on which all promises are broken and all ideals crushed'. The peace with the world which Hegel sought had more warmth and passion in it than this.

Ritter was right that Hegel never abandoned his enthusiasm for the French Revolution or for the idea of universal freedom which informed it. However, Hegel challenged the self-understanding of the Revolution shared by the Jacobins and Edmund Burke alike, namely that it represented a *novum*, the birth of something radically new, something which broke with all tradition. His contention was that the 'idea' of the Revolution reflected the power it opposed inasmuch as the idea of the general will, indicating the absolute and indivisible sovereignty of the people, was shaped and formed by the absolute and indivisible sovereignty of the absolutist monarch it resisted. It was not the revolutionary idea of freedom that Hegel turned against, but the fact that 'only abstractions were used'. On this basis there could be liberation from the old regime but no concrete freedom could be established.

It is important to be precise about the relation between the Revolution and its decline. If we follow Hegel's account, it is not just the case that the practices of the Revolution fell short of its concept, but rather that the concept itself was 'one-sided' and 'untrue'. Hegel understood the fate of the Revolution in terms neither of the corruption of an abstract ideal, nor in terms of the malpractice of the revolutionaries themselves, nor in terms of the backwardness of the people, nor because it was merely 'political' and not yet 'social'. For Hegel, the Revolution was not an abstract ideal impatient for its proper author, its proper context, its proper addressee and its proper epithet. It was a creature of its times, as 'bourgeois' as any other of the forms and shapes of right, possessed of the aura which only the system of right could generate. It replaced the indeterminate 'I' of the bourgeois property owner with the equally indeterminate 'we' of the people as if the world were a void waiting only to be filled with its soul, but when it discovered that the world was not a void, it could express its frustrated sense that 'everything was possible' only in a fury of destruction.

One final point concerns the way in which images of the past inform our collective imagination of the future – in this case how images of the ancient world informed the modern idea of revolution. Rousseau acknowledged the difficulty of adapting ancient principles of democracy to modern conditions: especially in relation to questions of *quantity* raised by the great size of modern nation-states and *equality* raised by modern idea of right. Hegel followed in Rousseau's footsteps when he wrote that such democratic constitutions as the Greeks possessed 'are possible only in small states' and that their necessary condition is that 'what among us is performed by free citizens – the work of daily life – should be done by slaves'

(*PH* 254–5). In Rousseau we find a melancholy note in the face of such difficulties: 'does the freedom of some entail the unfreedom of others?' he asks in *The Social Contract*, 'Perhaps. Extremes meet'. The older Hegel did not abandon his own youthful admiration for ancient democracy. It was a world in which citizens lived together in a common culture and on the basis of common interests and participated with their entire personality at critical stages of public business. He argued, however, that the principles of ancient democracy have quite another meaning when applied to modern times – now that the world of face-to-face, oral persuasion has been supplemented, if not replaced, by the world of writing. In a sociological mode he observed that in the Greek world

> that unity of opinion to which the whole community must be brought
> . . . must be produced in the individual members of the state by *oratorical
> suasion*. If this were attempted by *writing* – in an abstract, lifeless way –
> no general fervour would be excited among the social units; and the
> greater the number, the less weight would each individual vote have . . .
> A political existence of this kind is destitute of life, and the world is
> *ipso facto* broken into fragments and dissipated into a mere Paper-world.
> In the French revolution, therefore, the republican constitution never
> actually became a democracy: Tyranny, despotism, raised its voice under
> the mask of freedom and equality.
>
> (*PH* 255–6)

Hegel concluded that the architectonic of the modern state cannot be conceived in terms of the simplicity of the Greek temple and it is a mistake to look to the ancients for models of how constitutions ought to be organised in modern times. The modern system of right involves the complexity of a Gothic edifice of which 'the Ancients knew nothing, for it is an achievement of the Christian era' (*LPWH* 121). Its differentiated structure, consisting in the 'free development of its various moments', has principles distinct from those of the *polis* or its re-incarnations.

The limits of Marxist politics

Let us return to Marx. The young Marx's critique of Hegel's alleged 'doctrine of the state' prefigured many key tenets of the modern revolutionary tradition. Most contemporary Marxists have echoed Marx's critical analysis of parliamentarism and the modern representative principle; his conviction that sovereignty must no longer be transferred to government by the people but be retained by the people themselves; his appeal to a direct resumption on the part of society of the sovereignty which was alienated to the separate sphere of politics.

For example, in a collection of essays aptly entitled From *Rousseau to Lenin*, Lucio Colletti argued that Marx's political philosophy can be traced back to Rousseau's propositions that 'sovereignty does not admit of representation' and that 'every law the people has not ratified *in person* is null and void' (Rousseau

1973: 240).[2] Marx himself certainly declared his debt to Rousseau when he observed that 'the French' understood true democracy to mean that '*the political state disappears*' and the key question was how to adapt this Rousseauian principle to modern conditions (*MEW* 188). He argued that when Rousseau prescribed that '*all as individuals* should wish to share in the legislature', this prescription meant in effect that 'it is the will of *all* to be real active members of the state . . . to give reality to their existence as something *political*' (*MEW* 188). Marx accepted that Rousseau's treatment of the legislature as the '*sole* focus of universal participation' makes no sense in the modern age, not least for reasons of size, but he added that it is only because 'this single activity of legislation is the only political activity of civil society . . . that everyone both wishes and ought to share in it at once' (*MEW* 189). The solution, as the young Marx saw it, was to go beyond this 'abstract view of the state' and extend participation into *all* areas of the state and society until the point is reached at which the very distinction between civil society and the state is dissolved. In a shape of thought that goes back to the old European tradition of natural law and eventually to Aristotle, Marx declared that the 'true state' comprises both the political state and civil society in an undifferentiated unity.[3] This image of 'true democracy' was drawn most sharply in the shape of the Commune or Council: the 'simple machine' in which the 'haughteous masters' of the people are finally replaced by their 'removable servants' and 'mock responsibility' gives way to 'real responsibility'; the space in which the people take an independent part not merely in voting and elections but in the everyday running of the state; the form of rule in which the distinction between the rulers and the ruled is finally abolished and where instead 'all will govern in turn and will soon become accustomed to no one governing' (Colletti 1972: 221, quoting from Lenin's *State and Revolution* who in turn quotes from Marx's *Civil War in France*).[4]

The 'reply' to Marx which is implicit in Hegel's *Philosophy of Right* contains the proposition that the 'true democracy' which the young Marx contrasted to democracy of the state, ends up mirroring the unrealism of the society it seeks to overcome. The *real difference* between Marx and Hegel lies in the recognition we find in the latter that this form of opposition to power may not only mimic the forms of domination, mystification and abstraction which it most opposes, but may do so in irrational and destructive ways.

It should be noted, as Richard Hyland has done, that Marx's reading of the *Philosophy of Right* was rather conventional as far as the Young Hegelians were concerned (Hyland 1989). They generally understood Hegel's *Philosophy of Right* to be about the forms in which human freedom is exercised and agreed that the modern state represents a key political form for collective reflection, discussion and resolution of matters of universal concern. They disagreed, however, with what they read as the confusion of logic and history in Hegel's thought, the formalism of his notion of 'matters of universal concern', and his political conclusions. For example, Eduard Gans, who was a colleague of Hegel at the University of Berlin and probably taught Marx legal philosophy, criticised Hegel's 'justification' of Prussian constitutional monarchy from a liberal republican standpoint, and substituted for it the American Republic as a more appropriate exemplar. Against Hegel's doctrinalism, he affirmed the necessity of subjecting all forms of state to rational criticism. Arnold Ruge, who personified the revolutionary spirit of the 'Glorious Days' of 1830 and subsequently edited a radical journal with Marx, read the *Philosophy of Right* as a defence of the backward form of state currently existing in Prussia and criticised Hegel for abandoning political action in favour of a philosophy of eternal essences. The root of the problem for Ruge was Hegel's confusion of timeless logical categories with particular historical institutions. Marx's interpretation of Hegel was also close to that developed from the conservative side of the political spectrum by F. J. Stahl, who protested against what he saw as the *inversion* of subject and predicate in Hegel's theory of the state, the *deduction* of determinate institutions from abstract categories, and the *conversion* of irrationality and compulsion into the semblance of reason and freedom.[5] The young Marx pushed the Young Hegelian critique of the *Philosophy of Right* to a radical democratic conclusion, but he did not fundamentally reassess their reading of the text.

In any event, if Hegel were what the young Marx thought him to be, the idealist who interpreted a version of Prussian constitutional monarchy as the incarnation of the Idea, it is difficult to imagine why the inversion of such dogmatism should produce the rich pickings Marx ascribed to it. Marx himself never tired of criticising the 'Young Hegelians', and especially Feuerbach, for merely inverting Hegel and doing nothing to change either the terms inverted or the relation between them. In the *German Ideology* he and Engels argued that a self-proclaimed materialism that defines itself as the inversion of idealism, winds up determined by that idealism as its own determinate negation. They held, for instance, that Feuerbach's abstract materialism (with its ahistorical conception of 'man' and 'sensuous existence') did not overcome the abstract idealism of the Hegelian system but only offered a more naive, pre-critical idealism (Warminski 1998: 172 ff.). This is familiar ground among Marx-scholars, but can such criticism also be levelled at the young Marx himself? Was his own language of 'real life', 'sensuous man' and 'true democracy' *merely* an inversion of what he read as Hegel's idealism and no less abstract?

Below I shall pursue the suggestion put forward by Andrzej Warminski that if Marx was to be 'Marx' and not just another young Hegelian, then he had to move beyond this logic of inversion and the 'pre-critical, naive idealism' it propagated. If Hegel was not the absolute idealist that Marx thought he was, if there is another Hegel whose signature is legible in the text, then perhaps we can find another Marx: not the Marx who purported to put Hegel back on his feet and actually rekindled an older tradition of natural law, but a Marx who had to surpass the standpoint of the young Hegelians to become 'Marx'.

Notes

1 The lectures which Gans turned into the text of *Philosophy of History* were first delivered in 1822–3 and last delivered in the winter of 1830–1, just before his death and just after the three 'Glorious Days' of Parisian barricades which toppled the Bourbon dynasty and replaced it with the constitutional monarchy of the 'bourgeois king', Louis-Philippe. This was the first major breach of the system of restoration established by the Congress of Vienna and was described by Heinrich Heine as 'sunshine wrapped in newspaper'. It led to revolts among the Flemish and Walloon Catholics and among Polish nationalist troops, as well as exciting unrest in Italy, Spain, Portugal, Switzerland, England and Germany.

2 It is often argued that Marx's political thought should be understood as a *synthesis* of French political philosophy, Scottish political economy and German idealism, and that the Rousseauian thread is only part of a larger fabric. This is in part true. The French informed Marx's thinking about democracy; the Scottish informed Marx's thinking about the state as an instrument of bourgeois property; the Germans informed Marx's thinking about the formation of a rational state beyond the existing bourgeois state. But we should not assume that Marx wove these threads together into a unitary theory. What we find rather is a movement in Marx's texts from one source to another without synthesis. These different sources have subsequently provided the basis for conflicting varieties of Marxism: 'left Marxists' looking back to the anti-representational tradition of Rousseau; revisionist Marxism looking back to the constitutional theories of Smith and Kant; state socialism looking back to the idealism of the state present in Fichte and imagined in Hegel.

3 Marx's political thought was dominated by the thought of a new unity arising out of old divisions, which was to be accomplished not only by a transfer of power from one class to another, but by a transition from one form of power to another – from the alien form of the state in which the people are *only ideally* present, to a power that is directly into the hands of the people.

4 The spirit of Marx's critique of representation may be illustrated by the image of the Commune drawn by Guy Debord. Directing the critique of representation east and west, at a Leninism where 'the representation of the working class radically opposes itself to the working class', and at a parliamentarism where 'the people in miniature' opposes itself to the people themselves (Debord 1994: §§100–2), Debord depicted the representative principle as 'the quintessence of modern domination . . . the concrete inversion of life . . . the autonomous movement of the non-living . . . the heart of the unrealism of the real society' (§§2–3). He construed the Commune as the 'supersession' of the representative principle which puts democracy back on its feet and inverts the inversion. The Commune is presented as the form in which 'all prior divisions between rulers and ruled are finally reunited . . . the proletarian movement is its own product and this product is the producer himself . . . direct *active* communication is realised . . . specialisation, hierarchy and separation end'. It is the institution that is fundamentally anti-institutional; the form of representation which 'already knows that it does not represent the working class' but only actuates 'the generalisation of communication'; the organisation which recognises 'its own dissolution as a separate organisation'; the power which does 'not compromise with any form of separate power' and which 'cannot reproduce within itself the dominant society's conditions of separation and hierarchy'; the government which places no limit on participation and which 'can no longer combat alienation with alienated forms' (§119). In the Commune activity in the first person replaces mere contemplation of the actions of a party or leader: 'in the power of the workers' councils . . . the proletarian movement becomes its own product; this product is the producer himself' (§117). This crafted image of 'true democracy' is vulnerable, however,

both to the *realist criticism* that, viewed as an institutional system and bared of its revolutionary mystique, the Commune has its own tendencies toward hierarchy, centralisation and alienation, and to the *rationalist criticism* that, judged in terms of its capacity for rational decision-making, the face-to-face structures of the Commune fall victim to the vagaries of public opinion, the contingencies of the loudest voice, or the machinations of the best organised faction.

5   Stahl writes that Hegel's 'natural law can be truly understood only when one remembers that . . . everything is designed to obtain from human relationships a system in which each concept transcends itself, leads to its opposite, and by reunion creates a third . . . Whenever a rule of thought serves as the actual producer, as does the dialectic here, rigidity is unavoidable, and things only count in the sense in which the logical demonstration requires . . . Hegel reproached Kant that, from Kant's purely formal laws, collective ownership of property may be as easily deduced as private ownership, but the same is the case to an even higher degree in Hegel's formal movement . . . any deduction is purely a matter of whim . . . the essence of Hegel's philosophy consists in converting irrationality and compulsion, by means of speculative-dialectical deduction, into reason and freedom . . . But in social reality, wrong cannot thus be turned into right or compulsion into freedom . . . If thought determinations are declared to be all that exists, then personality has a derivative, subordinate existence; it is there only as a means to realise the relationships of mind . . . Freedom then is not the situation in which individuals may freely choose. Rather it consists of those circumstances in which they cannot . . . It is not the human being but the rules of mind that must be free . . . It is not the human beings who act in history . . . but rather the logical law of the three moments' (Richard Hyland's translations of F. Stahl, '*Hegels Naturrecht und Philosophie des Geistes*' in 1 *Materialien zu Hegels Rechtsphilosohie*, ed. M. Riedel, 1975).

5

RIGHT AND VALUE
Unity of Hegel and Marx

Marx's *doppelganger*

If there is one way we should *not* read the relation between Hegel and Marx, it is through Marx's own account of it! Not only does he give us a distorted and one-sided caricature of Hegel, but also a diminished view of himself. The ghost of Hegel haunted Marx's later writings. It arrived at once in the shape of a debt Marx wished to pay and a wrong he wished to rectify. On the one hand, he praised Hegel for having discovered the 'correct laws of the dialectic'; on the other, he criticised him for presenting the dialectic in an idealistic and mystifying form. In 1858 Marx wrote to Engels:

> In my method of working it has given me great service that by mere accident I had leafed through Hegel's *Logic* again and found much to assist me in the *method* of analysis. If I ever have the time for that kind of work again, I would find great pleasure in writing two or three pages on the *rationale which Hegel discovered* – but also mystified – to make it accessible for the common man.
>
> (*Letters* 50)

In March 1868 he wrote to Kugelman:

> my method of argument is *not* Hegelian, since I am a materialist, Hegel is an idealist. Hegel's dialectic is the basis of all dialectic, but only *after* the disposal of its mystical form.
>
> (*Letters* 126)

In his 1873 'Postface' to the second German edition of *Capital*, he recalled both aspects of his relation to Hegel:

> The *mystification* which the dialectic suffers in Hegel's hands by no means prevents him from being the first to present its general forms of motion in a comprehensive and conscious manner. With him it is standing on

79

its head. It must be inverted in order to discover the rational kernel within the mystical shell.

Marx emphasised that his own dialectic method was 'not only different from the Hegelian, but exactly opposite'. Just as he represented Hegel as a philosopher who transformed the process of thinking into an independent subject and the real world into the external appearance of the Idea, so too he presented himself as the social critic who recognises that 'the ideal is nothing but the material world reflected in the mind of man and translated into forms of thought'. Just as he represented Hegel's 'mystical form of the dialectic' as a philosophy of the state which only became the fashion in Germany because it functioned to 'glorify what exists', so too he presented his own 'rational form of the dialectic' as

> a scandal and an abomination to the bourgeoisie . . . because it includes in its positive understanding of what exists a simultaneous recognition of its negation, its inevitable destruction; because it regards every historically developed form as being a fluid state, in motion, and therefore grasps its transient aspects as well; and because it does not let itself be impressed by anything, being in its very essence critical and revolutionary.
>
> (*Capital* 1. 102–3)

Marx constructed 'Hegel' as the philosopher who transmuted historical into logical categories, the better to construct himself as the critic of all existing conditions who puts the dialectic back on its feet and revealed the 'historical specificity' both of the social forms of bourgeois society and of the social sciences which sought to comprehend them. Hegel was Marx's double or *doppelganger*. Yet when others dared to criticise him, Marx thundered against these 'pompous, pseudo-scientific professors' and 'ill-humoured, arrogant and mediocre epigones' who understood nothing of Hegel's method and treated him as a 'dead dog' no longer to be taken seriously (*Letters* 167–8). He saw himself as sitting on the shoulders of a giant and, thanks to this support, reaching higher and seeing further than all before him.

Most secondary discussions of Marx's writings have followed Marx's own presentation of his relation to Hegel. Lenin's daunting observation that 'it is impossible completely to understand Marx's *Capital* . . . without having thoroughly studied and understood the *whole* of Hegel's *Logic*', has been echoed in less exacting form by many contemporary commentators – especially since the republication of the *Grundrisse*, the 'Rough Draft' of *Capital*. Many commentators have observed how much Hegel's influence was manifest in this text. For example, in his introduction to the *Grundrisse* Martin Nicolaus comments (Marx 1973): 'If one considers not only the extensive use of Hegelian terminology in the *Grundrisse*, not only the many passages which reflect self-consciously on Hegel's method and the use of the method, but also the basic structure of the argument in the

Grundrisse, it becomes evident that the services rendered Marx by his study of the *Logic* were very great indeed.' In his seminal commentary on *The Making of Marx's Capital*, Roman Rosdolsky writes: 'If Hegel's influence on Marx's *Capital* can be seen explicitly in only a few footnotes, the *Rough Draft* must be designated as a massive reference to Hegel, in particular to his *Logic* . . . The publication of the *Grundrisse* means that the academic critics of Marx will no longer be able to write without first having studied his method and its relation to Hegel' (Rosdolsky 1980: xiii). David McLellan writes in a similar vein: 'The most striking passage of the *Grundrisse* in this respect is the draft plan for Marx's *Economics* which is couched in language (such as the distinction between essence and appearance) that might have come straight out of Hegel's *Logic*' (McLellan 1980: 13). Few Marxist commentators have challenged Marx's own view that Hegel's idealism hangs a 'shroud of mysticism over the leaping soul of his dialectic' or that it casts 'absolutist benedictions on the state' (Nicolaus in Marx 1973: 26–7). Rosdolsky introduces a slight note of scepticism about Marx's claims to exorcise the ghost of Hegel's idealism when he emphasises Marx's debt to Hegel 'irrespectively of how radically and materialistically Hegel was inverted!', but he regrets that he could only touch upon 'the most important and theoretically interesting problem presented by the "Rough Draft" – that of the relation of Marx's work to Hegel, in particular to the *Logic*'.

Recently, some Marxist scholars have began to challenge Marx's account of his relation to Hegel. David MacGregor speaks of 'the *myth* of Hegel as the idealist who had everything upside down' (MacGregor 1984: 3 and 1998: 2–4). Ian Fraser comments that 'Marx may not have seen this but his "own" dialectic clearly parallels that of Hegel . . . the dialectic of Hegel *is* the dialectic of Marx' (Fraser 1997: 103; see also Fraser 1998: 34). From another vantage point, Allen Wood acknowledges that 'there is a greater affinity between the Hegelian and Marxian theories of history than Marx usually acknowledges' (Wood 1993: 433). These revisionist accounts of the Hegel–Marx relation indicate a growing awareness that Marx was wrong about Hegel: that Hegel's dialectic was not mystical, did not confuse thought and reality, did not glorify what exists, did not turn the world upside down. However, they open up the debate on terms set by Marx himself. Hegel is presented as a Marxist *avant le nom* and Marx's mistake lay only in his failure to see that Hegel's dialectic was the same as his own. No consequence is seen to flow from this error of interpretation except in regard to Hegel's reputation. Hegel is incorporated into an already established Marxist canon. If we push this line of argument further, however, we have to confront the possibility that if Marx was wrong in his assessment of Hegel, this was a sign of some substantial limitation in his own understanding of political modernity.

Methodological affinity

In Marx's discussion of 'the method of political economy' with which he opens the *Grundrisse*, he characteristically presents himself as overcoming Hegel's confusion of the real and thought about the real. He claims to distinguish, in a way that Hegel did not, between the process by which the concrete comes into being and the way in which thought appropriates the concrete:

> The concrete is concrete because it is the concentration of many determinations . . . It appears in the process of thinking, therefore, as a process of concentration, as a result, not as a point of departure, even though it is the point of departure in reality . . . Hegel fell into the illusion of conceiving the real as the product of the thought concentrating itself, probing its own depths and unfolding itself out of itself, by itself, whereas the method of ascending from the abstract to the concrete is only the way in which thought appropriates the concrete, reproduces it as the spiritually concrete. But this is by no means the process by which the concrete itself comes into being.
>
> (*Grundrisse* 101)

According to this account, the rational kernel of Hegel's dialectic lies in its analysis of the movement of concepts and of the transition from one concept into another, but the mystical shell consists of its confusion of the movement of concepts with reality.[1] Hegel is accused of confusing 'the development of the moments of the notion' with the development of the concrete itself. Against this mystical form of the dialectic, Marx asserts that the dialectic is not logical but historical; that its driving force is not the 'notion' but the bourgeois economy; that it is not a self-affirming movement from one logical category to another, from 'identity to difference to opposition and on to contradiction', but a movement from one historical form to another – from commodity to money and on to capital. Hegel, according to Marx, assumes that the presupposition and the results of the dialectic continue indefinitely to form a logical circuit. Marx, according to Marx, recognises the historical character of bourgeois society – that it is not a closed system which ideal subjects indefinitely reproduce, but a transitory formation based upon historical presuppositions, torn apart by class struggles and open to revolutionary possibilities. In his 'Notes on Adolph Wagner' Marx makes explicit the contrast, as he sees it, between his own *historical* methodology and the merely *conceptual* character of Hegel's dialectic:

> I do not start out from 'concepts', hence I do not start out from 'the concept of value' and do not have to 'divide' these in any way. What I start out from is the simplest social form in which the labour-product is presented in contemporary society, and this is the 'commodity'. I analyse it and right from the beginning, in the form in which it appears.
>
> (Marx 1975: 198)

This is Marx's version of events. He makes Hegel merely conceptual and logical, and he makes himself historical and material. He identifies Hegel with the transmutation of social relations into timeless logical categories, and he identifies himself with recognition of the historically specific character of capitalist social relations. Against a Hegel who gets everything upside down, he puts himself forward as the one who finally put things right.

Marx was fighting against a ghost of his own making. The *historical* character of Hegel's analysis of the forms of right was no less pronounced than that of Marx's analysis of the forms of value – even if both are presented in the form of a logical construction. In the *Philosophy of Right* and in *Capital* the subject matter under consideration and the critical consciousness that attempts to grasp it are both conceived historically – as the forms and shapes of modern bourgeois society and as the cognition that is made possible by that society. When Marx wrote of the categories of political economy, that they express the 'forms of being, the characteristics of existence, and often only individual sides . . . of modern bourgeois society', this was but an echo of what Hegel had already said of the categories of political philosophy (*Grundrisse* 106).

Indeed, we find no better way of illuminating Hegel's methodological approach to the philosophy of right than to consider it in relation to Marx's critique of political economy. In the introduction to the *Grundrisse*, Marx points out that it may seem to be correct to begin with the 'real and the concrete, with the real precondition, thus to begin in economics with e.g. the population'. On closer examination, however, he argues that this proves false. Why is it false to begin with 'the real and the concrete'? Because the real and concrete is 'the concentration of many determinations'. Population, for instance, presupposes classes; classes presuppose wage labour and capital; wage labour and capital presuppose money; money presupposes exchange value and the commodity form. These are the *elements* which make up the 'chaotic conception of the whole'. Marx writes:

> If I were to begin with population, I would then . . . move analytically toward ever more simple *concepts* [Begriff] from the imagined concrete toward ever thinner *abstractions* until I had arrived at the simplest determinations. From there the journey would have to be retraced until I had finally arrived at the population again, but this time not as the chaotic conception of the whole but as a rich totality of many determinations.
>
> (*Grundrisse* 100)

Marx identifies the first path, which he calls the *analytic path*, with economics at the time of its origins, and the second path, which he calls the *genetic* or *dialectical path*, with economic systems which ascend from simple relations (value, exchange value, etc.) to the level of the concrete totality (the state, exchange between nations, the world market, etc.). The latter, Marx adds, 'is obviously the scientifically correct method'. Marx continues to follow closely in Hegel's footsteps when he asks:

do not these simpler categories also have an independent historical or natural existence predating the more concrete ones? That depends. Hegel, for example, correctly begins the *Philosophy of Right* with possession, this being the subject's simplest juridical relation'.

(*Grundrisse* 102)

Marx was not quite right. Hegel did not begin his *Philosophy of Right* with the idea of possession in general but rather with the idea of 'abstract right'. This error led Marx into some confusion. He admonished Hegel for saying that possession develops historically into the family, something which Hegel never said, and he argued that possession always presupposes some more concrete communal category, something which Hegel did say. Marx echoed Hegel's argument, however, when he observed that historically there are families in which there is possession but no private property and that to understand the modern form of family, we must see it in relation to private property. The point here is not to score points between Hegel and Marx but to recognise, as Marx put it, that the simpler category (say private property) *may* have an historical existence before the more concrete category (say the family), in which case the path of abstract thought, rising from the simple to the complex, would correspond with the real historical process, even if it achieves its full development only with the emergence of the more complex category. Marx followed Hegel, however, when he argued that it would be wrong

to let the economic categories follow one another in the same sequence as that in which they were historically decisive. Their sequence is determined, rather, by their relation to one another in modern bourgeois society . . . The point is not the historic position of the economic relations in the succession of different forms of society . . . Rather, their order within modern bourgeois society.'

(*Grundrisse* 107)

The order of presentation begins with the simple and the abstract and moves to the complex and the concrete. It is governed by logic, not by history. In beginning with the commodity form, Marx acknowledged that this starting point *may* correspond to some historical event – e.g. a barter between communities prior to all money relations – but the significance of this event lies not in its historical eventfulness but in its being the simplest economic form of the capitalist age.[2] Marx added a further comment on the illusions which may derive from the *mode of presentation* of this inquiry:

Of course, the mode of presentation must differ in form from that of inquiry. The latter has to appropriate the material in detail, to analyse its different forms of development and to track down their inner connection. Only after this work has been done, can the real movement be appropriately presented. If this is done successfully, if the life of the subject matter is now reflected in the ideas, then it may *appear* as if we have before us an *a priori* construction.

(*Capital* 1. 102)

In this passage Marx acknowledges that his own scientific analysis of the economic forms of bourgeois society, if done successfully, will *appear* as an *a priori* construction. He does not acknowledge, however, that this might be equally true of Hegel's *Philosophy of Right*. He cannot shake off the prejudice that the latter *must* be an *a priori* construction.

Marx did not realise quite how closely his own 'method' followed Hegel's approach in the *Philosophy of Right*. Having started with the simplest and most abstract form of their subject matter, both Hegel and Marx progress to more complex and concrete forms. In relation to the *political* forms of the modern age, Hegel argued that the simplest and most abstract element is abstract right and he analyses its self-division into 'person' and 'thing'. In relation to the *economic* forms of the modern age, Marx contended that the simplest and most abstract element is the commodity and he analysed its self-division into value and use value. For Hegel, the movement is from abstract right through contract and law to the state. For Marx, it is from value through exchange value and money to capital. Hegel and Marx both begin with the analysis of simple forms which permit them to explain other more developed forms and in their presentation they order the forms according to their increasing complexity, so that at every level the theory can be formulated in terms of concepts elaborated at the previous level. Neither in Hegel nor in Marx are we presented with the 'empirically existent', for both the forms of the state and the forms of capital abstract from all the contingencies, accidents and differences which they possess in actual political and economic systems. But in neither case are we given an *a priori* construction. If we ignore Marx's misleading comments about 'putting Hegel back on his feet', we find that there is no better practitioner of his scientific method. Their objects of investigation are different – Marx analyses the economic forms of modernity and Hegel analyses its legal and political forms – but their approach to scientific investigation is, roughly speaking, the same.

Marx's critique of 'right'

Marx's *Capital* was a *critique* of political economy. It was not an economics text but a study of a society dominated by the dull compulsion of economic forces, not an exercise in economic determinism but an analysis of a society in which economic determinism prevails. The subject matter of *Capital* comprises the inhuman, alienated, exploitative relations hidden behind the fetishised forms of modern economic rationality. To accuse Marx of *economism*, as many of his critics have done, is to miss the mark inasmuch as *Capital* was a critique of a society which actualises economism – that is, of a society in which the exchange of things is a primary condition of intersubjectivity, things appear as bearers of value, access to things is mediated by the ability to purchase them, and human activity is determined by the movement of things and the fluctuations of the market. It is a world in which everything has its price, even the capacities of our body and mind, and humanity has become the slave to the products of its own labour (Rubin 1972). It is misleading, therefore, to say that Marx treated the economy as the *base* on which legal, political and ideological superstructures rest. Marx was not consistent in his use of terminology but if we can still speak of a base, it is constituted in his work by *social relations of production and exchange* and not by the economic forms taken by the products of human labour. The imagery which informs *Capital*, however, is not that of base and superstructure but rather *form* and *content* – economic form and social content.

Marx maintained that the classical political economy of Smith and Ricardo had made considerable advances in understanding the economic forms of the modern age – value, exchange value, price, money, capital, interest, rent, profit, etc. – but he argued that it naturalised 'labour' as the origin of value without questioning under what circumstances labour takes this form. He argued that in analytical terms political economy was strong: it perceived, for example, that the magnitude of value was determined by the average amount of labour time that goes into the production of a commodity. But dialectically political economy was weak: it treated commodity form as a natural fact of life rather than as the product of historically determinate relations. Marx saw himself as the first to comprehend adequately the historical specificity of the value form and release it from the naturalistic framework in which it had previously been imprisoned.

Marx pushed the idea of 'the social' beyond anything conceived or conceivable within the natural law tradition. One weakness of Marx's approach, however, was that it could give the impression that the *economic* forms of capitalist social relations are their *only* forms, or at least that they are the *essential* forms of capitalist society, and that other non-economic forms – moral, legal, political, cultural, etc. – are in some sense epiphenomenal or inessential or even illusory. While we must recognise that Marx offered a critique of political economy, not an economics, there still remains something rather one-sided in the way he treated the economic as the privileged sphere of contemporary social life. This one-sided view of capitalist social relations is necessarily unconvincing to readers who seek recognition of the fact that modernity also conveys ideas of personality, free will, romantic love, moral agency, individual right, legal equality, collective self-regulation, etc. The individual is after all a juridical, moral, political, cultural and erotic subject as well as a 'bearer' of economic forces. The great difficulty that faced Marx's social theory was how to move, to use a phrase borrowed from Edward Thompson's *Poverty of Theory*, from the circuits of capital to capitalism as a whole. There is a sense in which Marx was in Thompson's words still 'trapped within the circuits of capital' and 'only partly sprung that trap in *Capital*', a sense in which he was sucked into the 'theoretical whirlpool of Political Economy' whose categories were interrogated and reinterrogated but whose main premise, the possibility of isolating the economic from other fields of social study, was left intact (Thompson 1978:

355). E. P. Thompson draws our attention to how far the structure of *Capital* is dominated by the categories of its antagonist, those of the economic sphere, and remains fixed within this order of things. Marx's failure to explore other subjects was symptomatic of a certain imprisonment within the economic categories whose social content he dedicated himself to uncovering. There is more to capitalism than the circuits of capital: there is Kant as well as Bentham, political philosophy as well as political economy, the fetish of the subject as well as the fetish of the commodity, the illusions of 'free creative practice' as well as those of economic determinism.

Marx himself was aware of the limitations of a critique in which 'the connection of political economy with the state, law, morality, civil life, etc. *is only dealt with in so far as Political Economy itself professes to deal with these subjects'*. He never abandoned the ambitious life-project of his youth: to 'present one after another a critique of law, of morality, politics, etc. . . . and then finally . . . to show the connection of the whole'. Although Marx's main concern in the *Grundrisse* and *Capital* was with the economic forms taken by the products of human labour, we find on the margins of these texts the beginnings of a critique of the idea and forms of right. The hypothesis at the margins of Marx's work is that the same social relations which transform the products of human labour into bearers of exchange value, also transform the producers themselves into bearers of right, and that the illusions of the commodity form are somehow paralleled by the illusions of free subjectivity. If we pull together the fragmented pieces of Marx's argument, we find something like this.

Marx maintained that in all societies there must be some form of possession but that it would be 'ridiculous' to make a leap from the general category of possession to the distinct social and historical form of private property. He contrasted modern private property with pre-capitalist forms of possession. For example, he wrote that in the ancient world

> the appropriation of land, tools, etc. is done on the basis of the individual's existence as a member of the community . . . an isolated individual could no more have property in land and soil than he could speak . . . the individual can never appear here in the dot-like isolation in which he appears as mere free worker.
>
> (*Grundrisse* 485)

Marx argued that the modern idea of private property, that individuals have a right to own and exchange the products of their own labour, would have been entirely alien to this world, but he no more romanticised the ancient world than did Hegel. He wrote that the ancient view according to which the good citizen rather than wealth was considered the aim of production, may appear 'very lofty when contrasted to the modern world where production appears as the aim of mankind and wealth as the aim of production'; but what is wealth, he asked, other than 'the universality of individual needs, capacities, pleasures, productive forces . . . the full development of human mastery over the forces of nature, those of so-called nature as well as humanity's own nature?' (*Grundrisse* 488). In any event, in antiquity those who did not belong to the community might appear among the 'objective conditions of production' as slaves, and in Roman law they were distinguished 'only as *instrumentum vocale* from an animal which is *instrumentum semi-vocale* and from a lifeless implement which is *instrumentum mutum*' (*Capital* 1. 303). There was no more nostalgia for the ancient world in the older Marx than there was in the older Hegel.

Marx argued that the kind of society which gives rise to modern forms of private ownership is the same as that which gives rise to the commodity form. They are merely two sides of the same medal. It is one based on production by *independent* producers whose contact with each other is mediated through the exchange of products on the market. Producers are *free* to produce what and how much they wish; they are *equal* in that no producer can force others to produce or expropriate their products against their will; they are *self-interested* in that they are all entitled to pursue their own private interests regardless of what others think or do. Their contact with other producers is left to their own *desires* and it takes the form of free and equal exchanges in which individuals alienate their own property in return for the property of another. This exchange of unneeded things in return for useful things is done for the *mutual benefit* of each party. The exchange relation makes no reference to the circumstances in which individuals seek to exchange, nor to the characteristics of the commodities offered for exchange. It appears as a self-sufficient relation, divorced from any particular mode of production and enjoyed among free and equal property owners who enter a *voluntary contract* in pursuit of their own mutual self-interests. In an exchange relation, Marx wrote:

> each confronts the other as owner of the object of the other's need, this proves that each of them reaches beyond his own particular need . . . as a human being and that they relate to each other as human beings . . . there enters in addition to the quality of equality, that of freedom. Although individual A feels a need for the commodity of individual B, he does not appropriate it by force, nor vice versa, but rather they recognise one another reciprocally as proprietors, as persons whose will penetrates their commodities. Accordingly, the juridical moment of the *Person* enters here. . . all inherent contradictions of bourgeois society appear extinguished . . . and bourgeois democracy even more than the bourgeois economists takes refuge in this aspect.
>
> (*Grundrisse* 243, 251)

It appears that the common interest that arises in exchange is not opposed to the particular interests of individuals but is based on their reciprocal development. The only compulsion which enters into the relation stems from the individual's own needs and drives. The parties to the exchange must place themselves in relation to one another as *persons* whose will resides in those objects and must behave in such a way that each does not appropriate the commodity of the other and alienate his own, except through an act to which both parties consent.

> The sphere of circulation of commodity exchange, within whose boundaries the sale and purchase of labour power goes on, is in fact a very Eden of the innate rights of man. It is the exclusive realm of Freedom, Equality, Property and Bentham. Freedom because both buyer and seller of a commodity, let us say labour-power, are determined only by their own free will . . . Equality because each enters into relations with the other as with a simple owner of commodities and they exchange equivalent with equivalent. Property because each disposes only what is his own. And Bentham because each looks only to his own advantage. The only force bringing them together is the selfishness, the gain and the private interest of each.
>
> (*Capital* 1. 280)

Marx describes the juridical relation between two wills as a 'mirror' of the economic relation. A mirror is an image, a reflection, it is not the real thing. It is the economic relation alone that is solid and substantial. He argues that the illusions of private property are soon dispelled once we relate exchange relations to production. The presupposition of exchange is the organisation of production which *forces* producers to exchange their products. Their actual interdependence means that individuals cannot survive except by exchanging the products of their labour and this interdependence determines both the form and content of their private interests:

> The private interest is itself a socially determined interest, which can be achieved only within the conditions laid down by society and with the means provided by society.
>
> (*Grundrisse* 156)

Both the form of their interconnections, that of a contract between two private parties based on the exchange of their property, and their content, the terms on which such contracts are made, are beyond the will of individuals and become a power over them. Individuals may appear to be independent but only if we abstract from these background conditions.

> These external relations are very far from being an abolition of 'relations of dependence'; they are rather the dissolution of these relations in a general form . . . *Individuals are now ruled by abstractions*, whereas earlier they depended upon one another. The abstraction is nothing more than the theoretical expression of those material relations which are their lord and master.
>
> (*Grundrisse* 163)

Individuals appear to be free and equal but are ruled by abstractions. Marx argued that the illusions of a free and equal relationship are dissolved once we explore the content of exchange: 'Equal right . . . is a right of inequality in its content like every right' (Marx 1968: 320). This becomes more evident when we consider the transition from commodity to capitalist production in the course of which 'the form and content [of equal right] are changed'.

Where commodity production is sporadic or peripheral and exchange takes the form of an occasional barter between communities, the terms of the exchange are determined by the producers themselves and each party has a right to defend its property by force of arms. With the generalisation of commodity production, competition between producers ensures that commodities exchange at or around their values, that is, according to the 'socially necessary labour time' that enters into their production. Since there is no guarantee that the actual labour-time taken by the producer corresponds with socially necessary labour-time for the goods in question, equal right in these circumstances entails that some producers exchange their commodities for more than their value and some for less. This necessarily leads to the impoverishment of some and enrichment of others: 'if one grows impoverished and the other grows wealthier then this is of their own free will . . . even inheritance does not prejudice this natural freedom and equality.' Under these circumstances producers must be 'forced to be free', that is, to recognise the rules governing the exchange of things. Logically the development of capital and wage labour is an extension of generalised commodity exchange, though historically this transition may be blocked or the order of development may be different. The new relation between capitalists and wage-labourers continues to take the form of free and equal exchanges but the form and content of this exchange have now changed. On the surface the relation between capitalist and worker is a simple exchange:

> a worker who buys a loaf of bread and a millionaire who does the same appear in this act as simple buyers . . . all other aspects are extinguished . . . the content of these purchases appears as completely irrelevant compared with the formal aspect.
>
> (*Grundrisse* 251)

The exchange between capitalist and worker *appears* like any other exchange, but it is in fact distinguished by the entry into the market of a new commodity, that of labour-power, whose historical presupposition lies in the 'double freedom' of individuals – their freedom to own their body, mind and capacity to work, and their freedom from other means of subsistence or production than their labour-power. The buyer of labour-power is no longer a simple buyer who wishes to use it as an object of personal consumption but rather a capitalist who uses it specifically for the production of surplus value. The secret behind the exchange between capital and labour is that workers receive in the form of wages a value equivalent to the value of their labour-power (i.e. the labour time socially necessary for the reproduction of the labourer) and not equivalent to the value of the products they produce on behalf of the capitalist. In this context, the appropriation of unpaid surplus labour becomes the *substance* of 'equal right'.

Turning to the reproduction of capitalist society, Marx argued that the social content of the exchange between capital and labour changes once more. Looked at individually, the exchange between capital and labour consists of the expropriation of part of the product of the workers' labour by the capitalist. The capitalist says that the capital which he exchanges for labour-power is his own private property – perhaps because he worked hard for it or because it is the product of his own earlier labour. This may be true of primitive accumulation, even if it ignores the role of robbery, terror and international pillage, but after several cycles of production the entire capital owned by the capitalist will consist only of capitalised surplus value, that is, of the product of the labour of workers expropriated by the capitalist and turned into capital. It is now revealed that the exchange between capital and labour is no exchange at all, since the total capital is but a transmuted form of the expropriated product of workers from a previous period. On the surface, free and equal exchange carries on. Beneath the surface, however, there is the appropriation of the property of one class by another without equivalent:

> Originally, the rights of property seemed to us to be grounded in man's own labour . . . Now, however, property turns out to be the right on the part of the capitalist to appropriate the unpaid labour of others or its product and the impossibility of the worker of appropriating his own product. The separation of property from labour thus becomes the necessary consequence of a law that apparently originated in their identity.
>
> (*Capital* 1. 729)

The law which presupposes that we own the products of our labour 'turns . . . through a necessary dialectic into an absolute divorce of property and appropriation of alien labour without exchange' (*Grundrisse* 514). Marx's argument reaches its climax in the conclusion that in this context abstract right is a 'mere semblance', a 'mere form . . . alien to the content of the transaction', a 'mystification', 'only a semblance and a deceptive semblance'.

Marx's social theory of right was developed in fragments, but its core proposition was that the same social relations of production which give rise to the 'commodity form' of the products of human labour also give rise to the 'right-form' of the producers themselves. Put at its very simplest, the imagery implicit within Marx's analysis goes something like that in Table 5.1. If we take this account seriously, then both economic and political categories, and the split between them, appear as consequences of determinate social relations of production. We might say that modernity is the separation of the political and the economic and that this separation expresses a deeper social phenomenon: the diremption of subject and

Table 5.1 Imagery in Marx's theory of right

Forms of the subject	Right	law	state
Social relations of production	SCP	GCP	CP
Forms of the object	Value	money	capital

(SCP = simple commodity production; GCP = generalised commodity production; CP = capitalist production)

object, person and thing, that occurs in modern society. This is a very fruitful thesis which Marx himself only touched on. The difficulty as far as Marx was concerned, and perhaps the reason why he did not pursue the idea, is that he 'neglected the formal side of political, juridical and other ideological notions – the way in which these notions come about – for the sake of their inner content' (Engels, Letter to Mehring, 1893). In principle this limitation could be addressed and remedied, but instead the parallel between Marx's critique of political economy and his critique of political philosophy broke down. Both are studies of illusion, but in the former the forms of value are understood as 'real appearances' and as substantial as their content; in the latter, if we stop where Marx ended his critique of right and give it a premature sense of completion, we are left with the presentation of right as a mere form, a semblance, an empty illusion. If the surface form of a thing is as real as its social content, and if neither can be equated with the thing in itself, so too the form of a person is as real as its social content and the person should be seen as the unity of form and content or as Hegel would have put it, the idea of the person is the unity of the concept and the actualisation of the concept.

The consequence of treating Marx's critique of right *as if it were complete* has been detrimental to Marxism in three main ways. First, there is little or no investigation of the *development* of the idea of right into the more complex forms of morality, law, civil society, the state, etc., such as we find both in Hegel's philosophy of right and in Marx's own analysis of the development of the value form into exchange value, money, capital, profit, etc. As a result, the idea of right is presented in a static, undialectical, non-developmental manner. Second, the equation of the idea of 'form' with that of mere semblance or illusion is used to negate the significance or validity of right itself. This encourages a nihilistic trend within Marxism in relation to the forms of bourgeois law (though it was one which Marx himself generally resisted). Third, least noticed but most important of all, Marx's focus on the *illusory* character of right leads to a neglect of its *fetishistic* aspect. This is important because it is the fetishism of the subject within the modern system of right that lies at the source of all totalitarian tendencies within the modern system of right. Marx's social theory of right goes some way towards addressing the one-sidedness of his critique of political economy and is extremely revealing about the connections between right and its economic content; but the question of the 'will' remains largely hidden from view. The theory of fetishism is not only a theory of illusion but a theory of power. The fetishism of the commodity is not only about the *illusions* of economic determinism but also about the real determination of people by the movement of things. Analogously, the fetishism of the subject is not only about *illusions* of free will but also about the abstract forms of domination created when the will becomes the triumphant organising principle of political life.

The opposition Marx set up between Hegel's 'logic' and his own 'historical' method, only heightens the difficulty. Hegel did not reduce history to logic, as Marx imagined, he did not transform the historically specific forms of bourgeois society into timeless logical categories. On the contrary, Hegel expressed the unity of the 'absolute' and the 'finite' in the shape of a struggle between two aspects of the self:

> I raise myself in thought to the Absolute . . . thus being infinite consciousness; yet at the same time I am finite consciousness . . . Both aspects seek each other and flee each other . . . I am the struggle between them.

Hegel had good reason to reaffirm the unity of history and logic. To grasp the fact that a particular social form is *historical* – that it came into being and that it can be surpassed – tells us little about what it is, what gives it life, how it functions, whether it *ought* to be surpassed, wherein lies its rationality, etc. To understand a social phenomenon, we need to keep both sides in mind: history and logic, the finite and the infinite. In practice, at least in their 'mature' writings, Hegel and Marx both affirm the unity of history and logic. However, in *imagining* that Hegel subsumes history to logic, Marx ends up merely *reversing* this order of priority. He turns the idea of 'historical specificity' itself into a *doctrine* which binds all truth to specific historical situations, except of course the truth of this doctrine itself. This idea of 'history' reveals the *transitoriness* of things, but nothing of their depth or weight. The rationalisation of historical categories and the historicisation of rational categories are two sides of the same coin.

For example, in an ambitious attempt to reconstruct critical theory for our own times, Moishe Postone goes further than Marx himself when he writes that not only are the economic forms of capitalist society 'historically specific' but so too are the categories Marx employs to analyse these forms, including that of labour. The charge Postone lays against 'traditional Marxism' is that it does not historicise enough: it mistreats aspects of Marx's theory, say the mode of production in contrast with the mode of distribution, as transhistorical. Against 'traditional Marxism', Postone insists that the commodity form is a historically specific form of social wealth, that industrial production is a historically specifical form of production, that the working class is a historically specific form of class organisation and interest, that the opposition between subject and object is a historically specific relation between people and things, that labour is a historically specific category of analysis, and that critical theory is itself a historically specific form of theorising. The term 'historical specificity' punctuates and pervades the text. It becomes in Postone a hallmark of critical theory.

For Postone, however, this idea of history (or historical specificity) is not associated with depth but rather with the possibility of 'transforming', 'over-coming', 'abolishing', 'superseding', 'transcending' and 'destroying' the actual forms of social life. Since even critical theory is itself historically specific, he argues that its final aim must be its own self-destruction: 'the historicity of the object . . . implies the historicity of the critical consciousness that grasps it: the historical overcoming of capitalism would also entail the negation of its dialectical critique' (Postone 1996: 143). The self-sacrifice of critical consciousness takes the idea of 'historical specificity' much further than Marx, who as far as I know expressed no desire to live in a society in which critical theory has abolished itself.

In *The Communist Manifesto* (1847–8: 243) Marx and Engels explicate the destructive character of this self-consuming idea of history in their representation of bourgeois culture. The image they drew from Shakespeare's *The Tempest* is now part of out political culture:

> The bourgeoisie cannot exist without constantly revolutionising the instruments of production and thereby the relations of production, and with them the whole relations of society . . . Constant revolutionising of production, everlasting uncertainty and agitation distinguish the bourgeois epoch from all earlier ones. All fixed, fast frozen relations, with their train of ancient and venerable prejudices and opinions, are swept away, all new formed ones become antiquated before they can ossify. All that is solid melts into air . . .
>
> (Marx and Engels 1998: 243)

Bourgeois society is portrayed as leaving no other nexus between man and man than naked self interest. It drowns religious fervour, chivalrous enthusiasm, philistine sentimentalism in the icy water of egotistical calculation. It resolves personal worth into exchange value. It strips of its halo every occupation hitherto honoured. It reduces the family to a mere money relation. It profanes all that is holy. It reduces freedom to the freedom of buying and selling. It reduces justice to the will the class raised to law. For exploitation cloaked by religious and political illusions it substitutes open, unashamed, direct, exploitation. For old complexities it substitutes the simplicity of the conflict between capital and labour. For everything that was permanent, fixed and certain it substitutes convulsive expansion and uncertainty. There is nothing that bourgeois society cannot destroy and surpass – even itself.

Marx and Engels welcome the revolutionary iconoclasm of the bourgeoisie and express no nostalgia for the annihilated past. Instead they endeavour to turn the destructive nihilism of the bourgeois into the affirmative nihilism of the

94

proletarian. If the bourgeois devalues all values, the workers are left like Nietzsche's 'last man' without name, individuality or place. Nothing can be taken from the worker because all has already been stripped: property, culture, family, marriage, childhood, education, country, religion, morality. For the worker all values appear as bourgeois prejudices, nothing is secure, the aim is to destroy all security. Workers are slaves to labour, appendages to the machine, mere commodities to be bought and sold on the market place. Communism *is* their movement. It has no interests apart from those of the proletariat as a whole. Its seeks to abolish property, family, independence, marriage, religion and nationality because capitalism has already abolished them for the great majority. It aims to abolish political life because political life is the organised power of one class for oppressing another. The workers have a world to win, not by restoring old values but by harnessing the nihilism of bourgeois culture. In *History and Class Consciousness* Lukacs (1971) captures the spirit of this manifesto when he states that the consciousness of the worker is the *'self-consciousness of the commodity'* (1971: 168) and that it is only when every human element has been taken away that it can reconstitute a world 'uncontaminated by any trace of reification' (1971: 184).

After the defeats of the 1848 revolutions, a crucial development in Marx's political thought lay in his recognition that the modern worker is *not* a commodity but the owner of commodities and therefore a subject of right, a person, a human being in the historical sense of the term. Workers have more to lose than their chains, which is just as well if they have a world to win. Their labour-power has become a commodity, but they themselves possess their own labour power as their property. It is this quality of personality that Marx now began to see as the beginning of their long and arduous journey in the development of self-consciousness.

After 1848 Marx moved towards Hegel. Before this meeting could occur, however, dogmatic Marxism fixed Marx's one-sidedness into a lifeless doctrine. It considered human beings merely as units in a chain of determined circumstances and evaporated the 'Hegelian', active side of human life – the fact that we are moral and intellectual beings capable of imagining and making our own history, confronting adversity and surmounting the limitations imposed by circumstances. It was this denial of human agency that Edward Thompson aptly dubbed Marxism's 'heresy against man'. One of the great difficulties facing Marxism has always been how to respond to this heresy.

The main tendency of critical theory has been to treat the commodity form as the ultimate determinant of all existing forms of social life, including the various forms and shapes of right. In *History and Class Consciousness* Lukacs illustrated or initiated this view when he declared that the chapter in *Capital* 'dealing with the fetish character of the commodity contains within itself the whole of historical materialism' (Lukacs 1971: 170), and that 'at this stage in the history of mankind there is no problem that does not ultimately lead back to that question, and there is no solution that could not be found in the solution to the riddle of the commodity structure' (1971: 83). Lukacs presented the commodity as the 'universal category' of the social totality (1971: 86) which determines the actual world in all its dimensions, including the very ways in which we understand it. According to Lukacs, the commodity form provides the key to the bourgeois negation of historical consciousness: 'the nature of history is precisely that every definition degenerates into an illusion: history is the history of the unceasing overthrow of the objective forms that shape the life of man' (1971: 186). According to Lukacs, the commodity form even explains the shape of modern epistemology – the contemplative manner in which we, as subjects, become in everyday life mere 'spectators' of a movement of commodities over which we have no control, and the positivistic manner in which science regards 'those "laws" which function in – objective – reality without the intervention of the subject' (1971: 128). Against this divorce of subject and object Lukacs looked to the construction of a critical theory which would reconstitute the unity of subject and object in a transformative rather than contemplative mode.

From this vantage point the idea of right appears essentially as a deviation from the commodity form, a *right over things* and endorsement of the instrumental manipulation of nature. It seems both to justify and to institutionalise a logic of disintegration based on the triumph of instrumental rationality. Small wonder, then, that in this image of a totally administered society the old school of critical theory tended either to ignore the extension of legal freedoms or to view it as an integral element in the reification of social life. Small wonder too that in elevating an essentially economic category, the commodity form, to a supreme status as the key structuring principle of modern society *as a whole*, critical theory can locate subjectivity only in the abstract ideal of 'free creative praxis' – free, that is, from all the 'commodified' social forms of subjectivity: right, law, the state, science, etc.[3] Far from addressing the fetishism of the subject, critical theory thereby repeats it in an abstract, disembodied form. A different relation both to the idea of right and to Hegel's *Philosophy of Right* must be conceived.

The case for reading Hegel and Marx together

I have argued that if there is one way we should *not* read the relation between Hegel and Marx, it is through Marx's own account of it. This is because Marx offers us a distorted and one-sided caricature of Hegel when he depicts him as an idealist who set the world upside down or rather mirrored an upside-down reality. What is more, in getting Hegel wrong Marx also gives us an illusory view of himself as one who put both Hegel and the world back on its feet. In other words, Marx's representation of Hegel and his presentation of self are intimately connected and both sides suffer.

And yet among all the commentators on Hegel, I think that Marx deserves pride of place – not by virtue of what he has to say about Hegel, which is misguided, but because he applied Hegel's 'method' to his own critique of modernity in ways that are extremely illuminating. Although Marx read Hegel in opposition to himself, we can no longer understand what Hegel was doing in the *Philosophy of Right* without reading *Capital*, nor can we reconstruct what Marx was doing in *Capital* without reading the *Philosophy of Right*. Although Marx always saw himself as putting Hegel and the world he represented back on their feet, he in fact followed Hegel's more original approach to the 'science of right' in his own approach to the critique of political economy. Their actual relation is one of close *resemblance*. Marx's approach to his subject matter was basically no different from Hegel's: both start from the simplest and most abstract elements of contemporary society; both work upwards toward the more complex and concrete.

It is their subject matter that is different. In the *Philosophy of Right* Hegel confronts the forms of *right* which constitute *political* modernity. In *Capital* Marx confronts the forms of *value* which constitute *economic* modernity. The subject matter of the *Philosophy of Right* comprises the forms taken by *subjects* or people in the modern age; these include abstract right, personality, ownership, contract, wrong, morality, family, civil society, the state, international relations, etc. The subject matter of *Capital* comprises the forms taken by *things* in modern capitalist society; these include value, exchange value, money, capital, profit, rent, interest, etc. We can make no assumption that one subject matter is more fundamental or essential than the other. With Hegel we address the *political* or *ideal* forms of modernity, with Marx its *economic* or *material* forms. Marx *complements* Hegel's analysis of the forms of right which constitute modern political life with his analysis of the forms of value which constitute modern economic life. Read together, they offer a more 'complete' image of modernity as a whole, one which includes both the social forms of the subject and the social forms of the object, than each offers in isolation from the other. Reading Hegel and Marx together, we are forced to concede that the modern age cannot be reduced either to its ideal or to its material aspects. An analysis which focuses on one rather than the other, or which treats one as essential and the other as merely epiphenomenal, mistakes the part for the whole and begs the question of how these aspects are related.

Each text also *supplements* the other by overcoming its actual or potential limitations. In the case of the *Philosophy of Right*, what is overcome is the *idealism* which flows from identifying modernity *exclusively* with the ideal forms of legal and political life. In the case of *Capital* what is overcome is the *materialism* which flows from identifying modernity equally *exclusively* with the material forms of economic life. Hegel is an *idealist* only to the extent that he focuses on the ideal forms of subjectivity which mark the modern age at the expense of the material forms taken by things. Marx is a *materialist* only to the extent that he focuses on the material forms taken by the products of labour at the expense of the ideal forms of the modern subject. Both Hegel's idealism and Marx's 'materialism' are wrong only inasmuch as they are one-sided; in their own spheres of investigation, they are equally valid. The tendencies to one-sidedness present in both Hegel and Marx have been accentuated in the two traditions of social theory derived from them. One, drawn from Hegel, concentrates on the forms of subjectivity which mark the modern age and is inclined to use the concept of 'modernity' to convey existing conditions. The other, drawn from Marx, concentrates on the commodification of social life and tends to use the term 'capitalism' to do the same. These categories have become theoretical icons of their respective one-sidedness. Rather than place ourselves in either camp, that of *Hegelianism* or *Marxism*, the perspective which starts from the unity of Hegel and Marx allows us to keep in mind both aspects of modernity/capitalism.

Recognition of the unity of Hegel and Marx also allows us to keep in mind the real, social dichotomies of the modern age: those of subject and object, person and thing, freedom and determination, politics and economics, right and value. These dichotomies are in the world and not merely the product of how we look at the world, and they are not reducible to general considerations of an ahistorical type. Reading Hegel and Marx together allows us to start from the substance of the social order rather than to proceed atomistically and end up only in the juxtaposition of these separate spheres.[4] Each sphere gives rise to its own illusions: illusions of free will in the case of the political and illusions of determination in the case of the economic. Each sphere also gives rise to its own abstract forms of domination: in one case, law and the state; in the other, money and capital. Hegel's concern was with processes of *personification* and the *fetishism of the subject* characteristic of the former; Marx's concern was with processes of *reification* and the *fetishism of the commodity* characteristic of the latter. When we draw these concerns together, we are in a better position to see that the supreme achievement of the modern age is to contain within itself and support these divisions and oppositions, and that the greatest danger arises when political will and economic rationality are cast adrift from one another. One manifestation, though not the only one, of this separation is to be found in the phenomenon of totalitarianism and it is to this that I now turn.

Notes

1 In the *Science of Logic* Hegel describes the process of becoming (*Werden*) of the notion as the process in which the 'idea' posits itself as reality. Marx describes this logic as 'the money of the spirit' and the 'becoming of the notion' as the reification of value relations in a closed and self-reproducing system.

2 The question of beginning, of where to start, was always a problem for Marx to which he readily admitted. For instance, in the introduction to the *Grundrisse* Marx says that the starting point must be 'the general, abstract determinants which obtain in more or less all forms of society' – namely labour (108); he actually begins the *Grundrisse* with a chapter on money ('the root of all evil'); in the published version of *Capital* he makes his starting point the commodity 'since the difficulty lies not in comprehending that money is a commodity but in discovering how, why and by what means a commodity becomes money' (*Capital* 1. 92). Isaak Rubin argues that in Marx's critique of political economy we should not take 'the concept of value as the starting point of the investigation, but the concept of labour' and that we should 'define the concept of labour in such a way that the concept of value also flows from it': that is, as abstract labour (Rubin 1978: 109–39).

3 The opposing tendency within critical theory was to conceive of human rights, the rule of law, morality, culture and/or love as belonging to entirely *different* logics from that of the commodity – perhaps corrupted or distorted by commodification but in

themselves representing independent values. For example, Franz Neumann and Otto Kirchheimer emphasised that aspect of 'rational law' which has to do with freedom rather than with the commodity. They criticised the legalism of Social Democracy in the 1920s and 1930s, and especially its reliance on a constitution which no longer had real guarantees behind it, but warned of the dangers of acceding to disillusionment over individual rights or to resignation in the face of their dissolution. They argued that rational law was necessary for the predictability of commodity exchange and for the legitimation of a competitive capitalist economy, and they explained the decline of rational law in monopoly stages of capitalism as the result of the fact that the market had become less important than planning and that capital had no further interest in maintaining legal norms. However, looking to Weber's analysis of rational law as an antidote to these historical trends, they argued that if the three major functions of formal-rational law in a modern society are to secure and conceal the dominance of the rulers, to make economic processes calculable and to guarantee the individual a minimum of security, equality and justice, the decline of the first two functions still leaves the third – the vinculum between right and freedom – intact. According to this line of argument, the independence of law from the commodity form derives partly from the formal qualities of law ('generality', 'specificity', 'non-retroactivity') and partly from the rights of subjective freedom it must to some extent guarantee (freedom of speech, thought, movement, religion, association, etc.). It might be interesting to note that Neumann and Kirchheimer held that even the most positivist conceptions of formal rational law positivise rather than abolish natural law, and that those who subsume natural law entirely to the sovereignty of state (who, as they put it, subsume *ratio* to *voluntas*), actually destroy the idea of the state and replace it with an irrational concept of force. They argued that under the cover of the absolute sovereignty of the state, totalitarian theorists were actually the most extreme critics of the state and that this was why they threw overboard doctrines of the state, such as that of Hegelianism. If the so-called 'totalitarian state' was no more than an instrument used by some elements of civil society to terrorise the rest, then in *this* context right and law really do become 'mere forms' (Neumann 1942: 69–73; 1986: 171–2).

4 Hegel writes: 'Either we start from the substance of the ethical order or else we proceed atomistically and build on the basis of single individuals. This second point of view excludes mind because it leads only to a juxtaposition. Mind, however, is not something single but is the unity of the single and the universal' (PR §156A). Adorno comments: 'Nothing can be understood in isolation, everything only as part of the whole, though it is of course also the case that the whole has life solely in its singular moments' (Adorno 1993).

6

TOTALITARIANISM AND
THE RATIONAL STATE
Arendt

> Comprehension ... does not mean denying the outrageous,
> deducing the unprecedented from precedents, or explaining
> phenomena by such analogies and generalities that the impact of
> reality and the shock of experience are no longer felt. It means
> rather examining and bearing consciously the burden that events
> have placed upon us – neither denying their existence nor submit-
> ting meekly to their weight as though everything that in fact
> happened could not have happened otherwise. Comprehension,
> in short, means the unpremeditated attentive facing up to, and
> resisting of, reality – whatever it may be or might have been.
>
> (OT xiv)

Writing under the shadow of totalitarianism, Hannah Arendt argued that nothing
could be more unjust or more dangerous than to put the blame for what happened
in the twentieth century on to any of the great nineteenth-century 'rebels against
tradition': Hegel, Marx or for that matter Nietzsche. She argued that totalitarianism was *illuminated* by these thinkers whom she described as the first to dare to
think 'without the guidance of any authority whatsoever'. It was not in any sense
'caused' by them. In *Between Past and Future* Arendt wrote as follows:

> The attempts of great thinkers after [and including] Hegel to break away
> from patterns of thought which had ruled the West for more than two
> thousand years may have foreshadowed this event [that of totalitarianism]
> and can certainly help to illuminate it, but they did not cause it. The
> event itself marks the division between the modern age ... and the world
> of the twentieth century which came into existence through the chain
> of catastrophes touched off by the First World War. To hold the thinkers
> of the modern age, especially the nineteenth century rebels against
> tradition, responsible for the structure and conditions of the twentieth
> century is even more dangerous than it is unjust. The implications
> apparent in the actual event of totalitarian domination go far beyond the
> most radical or most adventurous ideas of any of these thinkers. Their
> greatness lay in the fact that they perceived their world as one invaded

by new problems and perplexities which our tradition of thought was unable to cope with. . . . Neither the silence of the tradition nor the reaction of thinkers against it in the nineteenth century can ever explain what actually happened . . .

(BPF 26–7)

Arendt's own judgement on the legacy of Hegel and Marx was equivocal. She wrote of their reduction of 'the most divergent values, contradictory thoughts and conflicting authorities . . . into a unilinear and dialectically consistent thread of historical continuity', and her conclusion was that they were 'still held by the categorical framework of the great tradition' against which they rebelled (*BPF* 28). Her philosophical narrative went roughly along these lines: if the traditional form of philosophy, originating in Plato, viewed the sphere of human affairs in terms of 'darkness, confusion and deception' and pursued the search for Truth, Beauty and Justice beyond the mundane world of empirical need, to Hegel and Marx went the credit for relocating philosophy in *this* world and for reconnecting philosophy with the social and political life of human beings. She saw them as having rescued the concept of freedom from ancient Greece, a treasure lost when humanity abandoned the darkness of Plato's cave to gaze at the sun but whose recovery was now vital to save humanity from a godless world. According to Arendt, they were among the first to recognise that humanity had lived without the Absolute before and could learn to do so again – perhaps through an immortality built of deeds which shine in the public gaze and which reflect back an image of individual excellence sufficient to ward off the frailties of life. Before this politics of humanity could be retrieved, however, Arendt argued that *history* made its fateful appearance. Having rediscovered the lost treasure of ancient freedom, Hegel and Marx let it slip through their fingers: in one case hypostasising Freedom as the 'Idea' which advances over the heads of human beings, in the other inverting freedom into a doctrine of economic necessity (*BPF* 41 ff.). The problem with both Hegel and Marx, as Arendt saw it, was that ultimately their critique of tradition did not escape the traditional framework but replaced it with the idea of a single, continuous, unilinear and progressive world history. To this totalising Story of Humankind, endowed with its own march, rhythms, *telos* and laws, she counterposed a plurality of stories and their interplay. Arendt held that in the shadow of Auschwitz and the Gulag, the 'great thinkers after Hegel' could not be read in the same way again, but to hold them individually or collectively responsible for what was done, sometimes in their name, was an affront both to the 'horrible originality' of the totalitarian phenomenon and to the contribution of these writers to its understanding. In fact, her analysis of the origins of totalitarianism was more indebted to Hegel than she realised.

The difficulties of understanding

When Hannah Arendt subtitled her essay on *Understanding and Politics* 'the difficulties of understanding', she was referring to the difficulties of understanding a political world in which the phenomenon of totalitarian terror was not just a recent memory but a still existent reality.[1] Arendt was among the first to argue that totalitarianism signified a major rupture with all historical ideas of progress, all feelings of optimism, all engraved images of Europe as a civilised community. Her words still ring out:

> not only are all our political concepts and definitions insufficient for an understanding of totalitarian phenomena but also all our categories of thought and standards of judgement seem to explode in our hands the instant we try to apply them.
>
> (*EU* 302)

One of the questions she poses concerns the difficulty of understanding totalitarianism with the conventional tools of social theory. She resisted what she saw as the complacency of a social science which decides in advance that its categories are adequate to deal with events as original as Auschwitz and the Gulag and which proceeds as if nothing has happened to disturb its peace of mind.

Arendt objected in particular to what she saw as the prevailing assumption of rationality within social science and to its assumption that the phenomenon of totalitarian terror can be understood through a means–ends calculus. She argued that it was precisely this calculus that was missing in the case of totalitarianism. In the conventional exercise of violence, it is used as a *means* – perhaps of retaining power or intimidating enemies or forcing people to work. But where opposition has already become impossible, where it makes no difference what I *do* for my fate is already sealed, and where the exploitation of labour is at most only a secondary benefit subordinate to the main aim of extermination, the standards of instrumental rationality make little sense. What was most striking about totalitarian terror for Arendt is its lack of instrumental rationality. Violence ceases to be a means to an end; it is deprived of that element of rational calculation which governs its exercise even in the worst states; it becomes the very essence of rule and ends up in a 'frenzy of destruction' without political, economic or military utility.[2] The difficulty of understanding, as she saw it, was to comprehend whence arises this subsumption of instrumental standards.

Arendt argued that this difficulty was most apparent in dealing with the camps – the pivotal institution of totalitarian rule. She writes:

> It is not only the non-utilitarian character of the camps themselves – the senselessness of 'punishing' completely innocent people, the failure to keep them in a condition so that profitable work might be extorted from them, the superfluousness of frightening a completely subdued population – which gives them their distinctive and disturbing qualities, but their anti-utilitarian function, the fact that not even the supreme emergencies of military activities were allowed to interfere with these 'demographic policies'. It was as though the Nazis were convinced that

it was of greater importance to run extermination factories than to win the war.

(*EU* 233)

If the event is not governed by utilitarian criteria of power and profit, then any attempt on the part of the social sciences to situate totalitarian terror alongside other forms of organised violence, as something that has a definite purpose and benefits the ruler 'in the same way as an ordinary burglary benefits the burglar', necessarily falls short. Arendt wrote of the Nazi death camps in precisely this vein:

The gas chambers did not benefit anybody. The deportations themselves, during a period of acute shortage of rolling stock, the establishment of costly factories, the manpower employed and badly needed for the war effort, the general demoralising effect on the German military forces as well as on the population in the occupied territories – all this interfered disastrously with the war in the East, as the military authorities as well as Nazi officials . . . pointed out repeatedly . . . And the office of Himmler issued one order after another, warning the military commanders . . . that no economic or military considerations were to interfere with the extermination programme.

(*EU* 236)

The difficulty of understanding for Arendt was to resist the temptation to submerge the unfamiliar in a welter of familiarities, to reduce the unknown to something which is known, to recognise that in this case 'all parallels create confusion and distract attention from what is essential' (*OT* 444). In short, Arendt argued that we are dealing here with something new that does not fit within the rubric of instrumental rationality.

This was one side of Arendt's argument. The other was directed against the opposite tendency: to declare that totalitarian terror is ineffable, incomprehensible, beyond cognition. Arendt argued that because we can find no *rational* explanation for such phenomena, we are tempted to declare them 'beyond human understanding'. In reference to the camps she writes:

If we assume that most of our actions are of a utilitarian nature and that our evil deeds spring from some 'exaggeration' of self-interest, then we are forced to conclude that this particular institution of totalitarianism is *beyond human understanding*.

(*EU* 233)

Her contention is that we have to drop any assumption of instrumental or economic rationality if we are to begin to address the 'peculiar unreality and lack of credibility' of existence in the camps. The difficulty of understanding was evident among *survivors* who returned to the world of the living only to find themselves assailed by doubts with regard to their own truthfulness, as though they had 'mistaken a nightmare for reality'. It was faced by those of us with no experience of the camps in believing what we were told: 'What common sense and "normal people" refuse to believe is that everything is possible. We attempt to understand elements in present or recollected experience that simply surpass our powers of understanding.' It was faced by *eyewitnesses* in reporting what they had seen: 'they cannot supply anything more than a series of remembered occurrences that must seem just as incredible to those who relate them as to their audience.' Finally, perhaps, it was faced by social scientists like herself in making use of testimonies and eyewitness accounts for the purposes of political thought (*OT* 439–41). Difficulty is compounded upon difficulty. How can we understand a social process based on the mass manufacture of corpses? Why on earth did human beings construct this lunatic micro-world in which 'punishment is meted out without connection with crime . . . exploitation is practised without profit, and . . . work is performed without product'? (*OT* 443) Why did human beings fabricate these spaces in which 'the whole of life was thoroughly and systematically organised with a view to the greatest possible torment'? (*OT* 445). The only categories which seem to make sense of this world are those of senselessness, madness, unreality, insanity, lunacy.

In the face of such difficulties Arendt came to the defence of understanding itself. The concern she expresses is that the source from which answers should come – our quest for understanding itself – might dry up. The crux of her argument is that to give up on the need to understand is to surrender to the elements of totalitarian thinking which survive within our own society. Since totalitarianism suppresses the activity of understanding, the activity of understanding becomes itself a form of resistance. She characterises understanding as 'a profoundly *human* activity . . . a specifically human way of being alive; for every single person needs to be reconciled to a world into which he was born a stranger and in which, to the extent of his distinct uniqueness, he always remains a stranger (*EU* 308). Understanding is the opposite of indoctrination: its task is not to offer a premature sense of completion nor to engage in 'dialectical acrobatics' based on the superstition that something good might come from evil. Understanding is a political activity: it can only be done in concert with others, it must take into consideration the viewpoints of others, it must be prepared to share its conclusions in 'open and uncoerced discussion with others', it must be prepared like Penelope's weaving to 'undo every morning what it has finished the night before' (*LM* 1. 88). It should take as much pleasure, as Gotthold Lessing put it, in 'making clouds' as it does in clearing them (*MDT* 26).[3]

Nor is the activity of understanding opposed to political action. To those who say that one cannot fight totalitarianism without understanding it, Arendt replies; 'Fortunately this is not true; if it were, our case would be hopeless . . . We cannot delay our fight against totalitarianism until we have "understood" it, because we do not and cannot expect to understand it definitively as long as it has not definitively been defeated' (*EU* 307–9). Understanding is not opposed to moral

judgement. To understand totalitarian terror does not entail forgiving the perpetrators on the basis of the principle that '*tout comprendre, c'est tout pardonner*'
nor normalising their crimes on the basis of the argument that in everyone of us
there lurks a monster. We must not ignore what Arendt called 'the abyss that lies
between the acts of the perpetrator and the potentiality of what others might have
done' (Arendt 1994a: 278).[4] This commitment both to the politics of understanding and to the understanding of politics unites Arendt firmly to the tradition
initiated by Hegel.

The idea of totalitarianism

How are we to begin to understand such events as Auschwitz and the Gulag?
For Arendt, the key concept was that of 'totalitarianism'. This was by no means
a neutral starting point. Indeed, few concepts in political theory have come under
such sustained criticism. Let me offer one example. In his memoir *At the Mind's
Limits: Contemplations by a Survivor on Auschwitz and Its Realities* Jean Améry argued
that the concept of 'totalitarianism' was ill conceived because, as he put it (Améry
1989: 180), 'Stalin and Hitler were different in principle – the one still symbolises
an idea of man, the other hated the word "humanity" like the pious man hates
sin':

> I hear . . . it said that not Hitler embodied torture but rather something
> unclear, 'totalitarianism'. I hear especially the example of Communism
> being shouted at me. And didn't I myself just say that in the Soviet Union
> torture was practised for 34 years? And did not already Arthur Koestler
> . . . ? Oh yes, I know, I know.
>
> (Améry 1989: 179)

Rejection of the term 'totalitarianism' on the ground that it confuses two different
systems of rule was common among Marxists who refused to accept that the Soviet
Union was ever or could ever be 'like' Nazi Germany.[5] Under the register of
what Claude Lefort has called 'reformed totalitarianism', they maintained that
Communism holds universal values, only denounces democracy because it is
formal, endeavours at least in theory to establish a higher form of democracy,
justifies violence only if it serves as counter-violence, and has as its aim the good
of humanity. They held that Nazism by contrast glorifies nationalist passions, seeks
only to realise the particular destiny of the *Volk*, attributes absolute superiority to
a pure race summoned to subjugate or eliminate inferior races, puts antisemitism
and other forms of racism at the centre of its political programme and treats
violence as the highest expression of life. Communism refers to laws of history;
whereas Nazism refers only to mystical laws of nature. Communism is a political
order based on the overcoming of capitalist exploitation; Nazism is an ethnic order
in which capital profits from the slave labour of the subjugated 'races'. Such
objections to the concept of totalitarianism are not insignificant, but they are

ideologically driven and, in their failure to measure the difference between ideology and practice, remain on the surface of political life. No serious historian would deny, for example, that Stalinist terror in the 1930s vastly exceeded the scope of violence imposed by any instrumental necessity. What is as important as the manifest content of these rival ideologies is the comparable function they performed: in both cases, for instance, the dominant ideas were tied to the existence of a party-movement whose organisation and unity represented the untouchable ground on which the 'power of discourse and the discourse of power' became indistinguishable (Lefort 1998: 3–4). In this political context, the languages of class and race functioned in analogous ways. In any event, there is nothing wrong in principle in looking for the common features which unite these coeval regimes.

Améry's second reason for distrusting the concept of totalitarianism is that it replaces the 'event' as experienced by the victim with what he calls a 'codified abstraction'. Améry writes that only in rare moments of life do we truly stand 'face to face with the Event and with it reality' and that one such moment occurred to him when he stood face to face with his torturers:

> Gestapo men in leather coats, pistol pointed at their victim . . . then, almost amazingly, it dawns on one that the fellows not only have leather coats and pistols, but also faces . . . like anyone else's. Plain, ordinary faces . . . And the enormous perception . . . that *destroys all abstractive imagination*, makes clear to us how the plain, ordinary faces finally become Gestapo faces after all.
>
> (Améry 1989: 175)

Améry contrasts this unmediated experience of human cruelty with abstract concepts like that of 'totalitarianism':

> National Socialism . . . was stamped less with the seal of a hardly definable 'totalitarianism' than with that of sadism. Sadism as radical negation of the other, as the denial of the social principle as well as the reality principle. The sadist wants to nullify this world, and by negating his fellow man, who also in an entirely specific sense is 'hell' for him, he wants to realise his own total sovereignty . . . I have experienced the ineffable . . . thinking is almost nothing else but a great astonishment.
>
> (Améry 1989: 184–7)

Améry is saying that the use of a 'codified abstraction' like totalitarianism destroys the sense of astonishment which is the true source of thinking. It is true that experience of the particular must drive our use of universals, but we cannot escape from universals as such. 'Sadism' and 'torture' are themselves universalising concepts which link a particular experience with a multiplicity of others. No doubt they capture for Améry the experience he underwent, but they do not reveal what is distinctive and original about *totalitarian* sadism and torture nor do they explain why sadism and torture became principles of political rule.[6]

A concept can only be understood through its uses. To assess Arendt's use of the concept of 'totalitarianism' we have to distinguish between the use she put it to and its more conventional uses in political science. According to her own account, Arendt uses the term 'totalitarianism' to face up to the 'previously unthinkable reality' actualised in the camps. It makes sense not so much as a fixed and top-down *type* of political system that can be defined according to certain specifiable criteria, but rather in terms of the imaginary identity (found notably in Gentile) of total domination and total freedom. The crucial point is not to fall for the illusion that this conceptual hubris should be actualised but to see the consequences of its radical incompletion. It is perhaps not impossible in theory that the self-consciousness of the individual can be fully identified with the state, so that nothing is left over and there is no supplement. But the import of Arendt's argument is that it is not the success of totalitarianism that led to 'escalating orgies of destruction', but rather its repeated *failure*.[7] It is this thought that makes sense of Arendt's perceptive statement that 'until now the totalitarian belief that everything is possible seems to have proved only that everything can be destroyed' (*OT* 459). We are not speaking here of a structure of total domination, but of a movement which finds in the fact of something determinate a limit on its freedom that must therefore by destroyed. The substance of Arendt's use of the term 'totalitarianism' follows closely on the heels of Hegel's earlier insight.

Arendt was not, of course, the first or only political thinker to use the concept of totalitarianism after Gentile. In the 1930s it was used by number of writers to compare the terror practised in Stalinist Russia with that practised in Nazi Germany and there were some who believed that the whole world might be going down this path. After the war it was used by political philosophers to indict both Communism and Nazism and more broadly the whole tradition of utopian social engineering whose modern origins were traced back to Plato, Hegel and Marx. It was taken up by political scientists to denote illiberal political systems which annihilate all boundaries between the state, civil society and individual personality. During the cold war it was used in a blatantly ideological sense to indict twentieth-century Marxism and to contrast 'authoritarian' regimes on the right with 'totalitarian' regimes on the left on the ground that only the former were open to democratisation. The key to all these conventional uses of the concept is that it leaves liberalism intact as the innocent victim of external forces. No *intrinsic* relation between liberalism and the origins of totalitarianism is permitted.

Given the career of this concept, it may not be surprising that many critical theorists have wanted no part of it, but Arendt uses it precisely to reassess the role of liberalism in the origins of totalitarianism. She counts the failure of liberalism to live up to its own ideals and its inability to resist the rise of totalitarian movements to be 'among the historical facts of our century' (*EU* 282). For example, to former Communists who wanted to return after the war to the 'democratic way of life', Arendt declared with some contempt that it was 'the same world against whose complacency, injustice and hypocrisy these same men once raised a radical protest . . . where the elements which eventually crystallised . . . into totalitarianism are still to be found' (*EU* 281). Arendt warns of the 'great temptation to explain away the intrinsically incredible by means of liberal rationalisations' and comments that in each one of us 'there lurks such a liberal, wheedling us with the voice of common sense' (*OT* 439–40). The logic of her argument is that when liberalism presents totalitarianism as the Other of itself, it understands neither totalitarianism nor itself, for although totalitarianism reaches fruition only at limited times and in particular places, it has deep roots in the modern system of right. The spirit of Hegel permeates Arendt's argument. It points in two directions: first, the connection of totalitarianism with the system of right is immanent, intrinsic, not merely external; second, totalitarianism is inescapably original and cannot be understood as the 'culmination' or 'logical extension' or 'final result' of any preceding social process or intellectual tradition. Again, we need to keep both sides in mind. She writes:

> An event belongs to the past, marks an end, insofar as elements with their origins in the past are gathered in its sudden crystallisation; but an event belongs to the future, marks a beginning, insofar as this crystallisation itself can never be deduced from its own elements, but is caused invariably by some factor which lies in the realm of human freedom.
>
> (*EU* 326)

What makes totalitarianism an *event* is the unexpected landscape of possibilities which transcends the 'sum total of all willed intentions and the significance of all origins' (*EU* 320). It is one thing to detect *elements* of the system of right in the origins of totalitarianism, be they reason, science, technology, bureaucracy, law, the state, the police, instrumental rationality, etc. It is another to tar them all with an overstretched brush of totalising thought. In other words, we must resist the tendency to totalise totalitarianism.

The critique of instrumental rationality

We may elucidate Arendt's analysis of totalitarianism by comparing it with that put forward by the sociologist, Zygmunt Bauman, in his *Modernity and the Holocaust*. Bauman's central argument is that the Holocaust should not be seen as a failure of modernity but as its product. The most 'shocking' of the conclusions he reaches concerns what he calls 'the rationality of evil' and the 'evil of rationality'. The idea of instrumental rationality dominates his understanding both of the conception and execution of the Holocaust. In terms of conception, Bauman portrays the dominance of instrumental rationality through the metaphor of a 'garden culture' in which the extermination of weeds is the destructive aspect of the gardener's productive vision. A gardener has an image of how he wants his garden to be: well ordered and in conformity with his own dreams of beauty and serenity. He likes certain plants and breeds them to fit in with his plan; he designates others as weeds and poisons or incinerates them. The gardener sees nature instrumentally, in terms of how it affects him and may be affected by him, rather than as a world endowed with an intrinsic value of which he is guardian. In modernity, human beings too are stripped of intrinsic value: some are defined as weeds, others are selectively bred. Genocide is an extreme kind of social weeding and Hitler and Stalin but 'the most consistent, uninhibited expressions of the spirit of modernity' (Bauman 1990: 93).

Bauman also holds instrumental rationality responsible for the *execution* of the Holocaust. He argues that the Final Solution was accomplished through the normal functioning of the bureaucracy and that even the political master, Hitler, found himself in the position of the dilettante next to the trained expert and official.[8] He depicts the choice of extermination as 'an effect of the earnest effort to find *rational* solutions to successive "problems"' and maintains that at no stage did it clash with the '*rational* pursuit of efficient, optimal goal-implementation'. He argues that it 'arose out of a genuinely *rational* concern, and it was generated by bureaucracy true to its form and purpose' (Bauman 1990: 16), and he sees in Max Weber's exposition of *rational* bureaucracy 'no mechanism . . . capable of excluding the possibility of Nazi excesses' (1990: 10 *my emphases throughout*). Auschwitz appears as a product of 'routine bureaucratic procedures' generated by bureaucracy 'true to its form and purpose' (1990: 17). For Bauman, the cardinal sin of instrumental rationality is to put a narrowly conceived self-interest on the one hand and the imperatives of technical efficiency on the other before all considerations of morality. In a vivid use of phrases, he describes the bureaucracy as a machine for the 'silencing of morality' or as a 'moral sleeping pill' (1990: 22).

Rationality is the villain of the piece. It explains the behaviour of those who conceived the genocide, those who organised it, those who perpetrated it, those who stood indifferently by, and even the behaviour of the victims. When Jewish administrators and police in the Ghettos were enticed to co-operate with the Nazis in the deportation of Jews, Bauman argues that the Nazis merely had to rely on the Jews to act rationally. In the world of Auschwitz, 'obedience was rational; rationality was obedience . . . Rational people will go quietly, meekly, joyously into a gas chamber, if only they are allowed to believe it is a bathroom' (Bauman 1990: 203). The rational individual would play his part in gassing millions if it meant holding on to a good job. He would look the other way if intervention were not in his job description. Most scientists are no different: they would be prepared in exchange for research grants 'to make do with the sudden disappearance of some of their colleagues with the wrong shape of nose or biographical entry' (Bauman 1990: 109).

What makes this theory plausible is that it expresses a wider hostility to reason, legal-rational administration and science, but it is this very hostility that is also its undoing. For Arendt, the distinguishing mark of the camps was their own *lack* of or even *hostility to* instrumental rationality. Nothing was to get in the way of the destruction. If norms of instrumental rationality were considered, then they would have acted as an inhibition on what was done. Arendt refers to the 'so-called totalitarian state' because it is not properly speaking a state at all and she offers an altogether more equivocal picture of the relation of totalitarian rule to the 'rational architectonic' of the modern state. For example, she writes:

> Totalitarian rule exploded the very alternative on which all definitions of the essence of governments have been based in political philosophy . . . that is the alternative between lawful and lawless government . . . totalitarian rule confronts us with a totally different kind of government.
>
> (OT 462)

Totalitarian rule defies all natural right and positive law but it is not lawless. It appeals to a kind of natural law, the 'laws' of Nature and History that were personified in the Leader whose word was law. It objects to 'petty legality' in order to establish the rule of justice on earth – something which, Arendt adds, 'the legality of positive law admittedly can never attain' (OT 463). It denies all fixed standards of right on the premise that nothing can be accepted as it is. It identifies its own rule with historical and natural necessity and resists any framework of stability which might inhibit its mobility of action. Even its administration is based not so much on rational bureaucracy, but on the intermeshing of multiple state and party institutions and the proliferation of police apparatuses of whom all were 'equal with respect to each other and no one belonging to one group owed obedience to a superior officer of another' (EJ 71).[9] To be sure, elements of legal-rational authority existed in the Third Reich: people were sometimes numbered, processed by bureaucratic-type machines, placed under systems of surveillance; there were papers, form filling, official stamps and files of information kept on individuals. But there was no bureaucratic hierarchy of command or system of rules that would be recognisable to a student of Hegel or Weber. Officials who were technically in positions of authority could be denounced and replaced by their juniors; one apparatus was liable to be liquidated in favour of another; the stability and hierarchy of genuine bureaucracy were absent. What we find is a simulacrum of bureaucratic efficiency, not to be confused with the real thing.[10]

Neither can the Holocaust easily be characterised in terms of the *rationalisation* of murder. The Holocaust used methods of its time, including modern management, but the industrial image of Auschwitz should not be allowed to overtake our understanding of the Holocaust as a whole. The Nazis devised two basic strategies for the annihilation of Jews: mass shooting and mass gassing. Special duty troops of the SS's Security Service and the security police of the *Einsatzgruppen* were assigned to each of the German armies invading the Soviet Union and given the task, alongside various other 'military' and 'police' forces, of rounding up Jews and killing them through crude and primitive methods of shooting. These methods were the antithesis of Bauman's image of clean and dispassionate white-coated technicians introducing gas into gas-chambers. The killers were confronted with the faces as well as blood of the victims. It is estimated that some two million Jews were murdered in this way. To murder the rest of European Jewry the Nazis built some camps with large-scale gassing and sometimes crematorium facilities (Auschwitz, Belzec, Chelmo, Majdanek, Sobibor and Treblinka) and other camps designed to work and starve their inmates to death. The technology used here was often barely more sophisticated than the brute violence of the *Einsatzgruppen* and it was only when death camps were combined with labour camps (such as at Auschwitz and Majdanek) that any significant architectural relics of industrial killing were left behind. All in all about three and a half million Jews were murdered in this way. A further half a million Jews or so were killed through hunger, disease and exhaustion in the ghettos or as victims of random terror and reprisal. To understand the Holocaust, we must be wary of a synecdoche which substitutes the industrial image of Auschwitz for the whole.

The relation between rationality and 'morality' is not contained in the notion that 'morality' was the suppressed party in the conception and execution of the Holocaust. Arendt's own answer is not without its own ambiguities. She writes that totalitarian terror indicated the 'collapse of all existing moral standards' and doubtless its exercise was rendered possible by the skilful use of 'moral sleeping pills' made available by modern technology. But it was also due to the skilful use of moral imperatives to overcome the natural resistance of 'ordinary men' to slaughtering entirely innocent human beings. Following Hegel, we should say that the 'moral point of view' was an integral aspect of the whole grisly business. The picture of *modernity* as the triumph of instrumental rationality over the moral point of view offers a one-sided view of modernity itself. Morality is one sphere of right within the system of right as a whole, and even in Weber's conception of legal-rational authority, officials are held morally responsible for their actions. Indeed part of the immense power of bureaucracy is based on a responsibility for decision-making and rule interpretation which is distributed throughout the hierarchy. The process of following a rule is always mediated through consciousness and rules are nothing without interpretation: 'a system of rationally debatable "reasons" stands behind every act of bureaucratic administration, that is, either subsumption under norms or a weighing of ends and means' (Weber 1991: 219). Rational authority is not the same as brute force. People choose to defer to authority. To be sure, their choices are never completely free; they are made within the limits of what is possible and what alternatives are available; yet rarely are those constraints so rigid that there is no choice and rarely is the structure so dominating as to remove all moral agency.

If the totalitarian form of organisation had been rigidly bureaucratic, it would not have annulled all idea of morality. But it was not rigidly bureaucratic in any sense that Hegel or Weber would have recognised. It is at least arguable that the actual forms of administration that were involved in the exercise of totalitarian terror augmented the moral point of view. For example, the so-called 'leader principle' worked through the will of every member to know and act in accordance with the will of the leader and take responsibility for all the decisions taken in their field of operation. Every holder of position was respon-sible for all the activities of his subordinates, even when they disobeyed or failed to execute commands, and wide latitude was given to sub-leaders for the execution of policies. It took zeal and creativity to grasp the will of the *Führer* far in excess of the old-fashioned plodding bureaucrat. Moral incentives were given to 'ordinary men' to become 'extraordinary' by committing vile deeds. These perpetrators were not generally forced into the formations which implemented the Holocaust. Adolf Eichmann, for example, was keen to win promotion on his particular 'front line' and the members of the murderous police battalions (the *Einsatzgruppen*) were given the opportunity to withdraw from the killing actions (Browning 1993).

One of the propositions Arendt puts forward is that the exercise of totalitarian terror marked the emergence of a new type of bourgeois: no longer the Kantian citizen who combines public virtue with moral responsibility, but the 'mass man' who renounces his claim to personality, does his duty at the expense of his own inclinations, and kills without passion or enmity – simply as a job and in the service of the state. The force of Arendt's argument, however, is that the perpetrators were not simply 'cogs in a machine' but only conceived of themselves *as if* they were and as if they made no moral choices. She wants to explode this illusion of 'thingness'. For example, she quotes Adolf Eichmann as having declared at his trial that he lived his whole life *prior* to his assumption of responsibility for the Final Solution according to a Kantian definition of moral duty, but that from the moment he was charged with carrying out the Final Solution he knowingly ceased to live according to Kantian principles and instead put blind obedience to the Leader before any moral concerns. This was Eichmann's version of events, or the version he presented in court, but Arendt's comment on this presentation of self is highly pertinent. It is that Eichmann did not so much abandon the Kantian moral imperative when he acted in line with the Leader principle, as adapt it to an absolute morality which declares that duty is duty, law is law, and Jews must perish – with no exceptions, not even for his own friends.[11]

Arendt writes that the rapid adaptation of ordinary people to Nazi terror before the war and then the equally rapid adaptation of former Nazis to the democratic way of life after the war, may serve to indicate that what we call 'morality' is no more than 'a set of *mores*, customs and manners which could be exchanged for another set with hardly more trouble than it would take to change the table manners of an individual or a people' (*LM* 5). Yet she also recognises that some individuals made reflective judgements on what is right and wrong quite independently of established norms. She cites the case of Anton Schmidt, the German soldier executed in 1942 for helping Jews, and comments how utterly different everything would have been 'if only more such stories could have been told' (*EJ* 231).

The faculty of judgement, for Arendt, is a human faculty which in conditions of terror most people will surrender 'but *some people will not*' (*EJ* 233), and she finds a certain cause for hope in the fact that the conscience of the individual can still find another voice than that of society – even when all around them conform.

In a 'post-traditional age' there are no *absolute* moral standards but this is not to say that there are no moral standards at all, or that they can all be changed at will, or that the border police of a particular society can always bar the entry of universal moral standards from without. The idea that we do not accept anything as right which we do not ourselves judge to be right according to universal criteria, is as much a product of our age as is that of instrumental rationality. The difficulty, then, is to recognise the ambiguities of 'morality'. The conclusion I think we should draw from her work is that the connections that tie totalitarian terror to 'modernity' do not depend simply on the suppression of the moral point of view by the forces of instrumental rationality. The demonisation of 'rationality' on one side and the idealisation of a pre-social 'morality' on the other do not help us understand this event. Rather we need to recognise, in the spirit of Hegel, that morality itself is implicated.

Spiritless radicalism

Arendt describes totalitarian terror as an organised attempt to 'eradicate the concept of the human being' (A&J: 69), to 'obliterate the idea of humanity (OT 459) and to introduce into politics the principle of 'all or nothing – all, and that is an undetermined infinity of forms of human living together, or nothing, for a victory of the concentration camp system would mean the same inexorable doom for human beings as the use of the hydrogen bomb would mean the doom of the human race' (OT 443). She describes the camps as an attempt to eliminate 'under scientifically controlled conditions spontaneity itself as an expression of human behaviour', to transform the human personality into a mere 'thing', to treat all human beings as 'equally superfluous', to destroy all sign of 'human plurality', etc. (OT 438–9). The camps were the laboratories in which the experiment of total domination, impossible to accomplish under normal circumstances, could be actualised. The process of admitting people into the camps was a process of stripping people of any notion of personality or possession of right: first rights of political participation, then rights of property, then even rights of survival. The camps were the visible proof that human beings could be turned into inanimate and expendable *things* and that murder could be made as impersonal as the squashing of a gnat. Their achievement, as Arendt saw it, lay not in *making* anything, but in 'robbing man of his nature . . . under the *pretext* of changing it' (OT 443). If the idea of personality, as Hegel put it, is the achievement of the modern age, then totalitarian terror was the attempt to undo it.

If it is the case, as Arendt argued, that the totalitarian imagination has as its primary aim the destruction of the idea of 'humanity', the question this raises is why did the idea of humanity cause offence? What is it that the totalitarian consciousness objected to? Why does the idea of humanity have to be destroyed? To address this question, Arendt draws on Nietzsche's depiction of destructive nihilism. In *The Will to Power* he writes: 'What does nihilism mean? That the highest values devaluate themselves. The aim is lacking; "why?" finds no answer'

(Nietzsche 1969: 9). In a passage from *Untimely Meditations* Nietzsche captures this experience thus:

> Now how does the philosopher see the culture of our time? Naturally quite differently than those philosophy professors who are satisfied with their state. When he thinks of the universal haste and the increasing speed with which things are falling, of the cessation of all contemplativeness and simplicity, it almost seems to him as if he were seeing the symptoms of a total extermination and uprooting of culture. The waters of religion are ebbing and they are leaving behind swamps or ponds; the nations are again separating from one another in the most hostile manner and they are trying to rip each other to shreds. The sciences, without any measure and pursued in the blindest spirit of *laisser faire*, are breaking apart and dissolving everything which is firmly believed; the edified classes and states are being swept along by a money economy which is enormously contemptible. Never was the world more a world, never was it poorer in love and good. The educated classes are no longer lighthouses or sanctuaries in the midst of all this turbulent secularisation; they themselves become more turbulent by the day, more thoughtless and loveless. Everything, contemporary art and science included, serves the coming barbarism.
>
> (Nietzsche 1983: 148–9)

Nietzsche prefigured the *fin-de-siècle* mood of irredeemable decline when the values and beliefs that were taken as the highest manifestation of the spirit of the West lost their validity and when this loss of values bred a destructive and spiritless radicalism, full of hostility to culture and images of destruction. The barbarism Nietzsche anticipated, however, was but a pale image of the barbarism to come.

What Arendt seeks to demonstrate is that the rise of European nihilism was an expression of *justified* disgust with the fake world of bourgeois values, and if these values remain as fake as they were, then the ground is still fallow. Arendt argued that nihilism was the spectre haunting Europe after the Great War because all thinking beings shared a sense of revulsion at the gulf between the values which society espoused and the mechanised murder which the 'front generation' had experienced in the war:

> simply to brand as outbursts of nihilism this violent dissatisfaction with the pre-war age . . . is to overlook how justified disgust can be in a society wholly permeated with the ideological outlook and moral standards of the bourgeoisie.
>
> (OT 328)

It was this sense of justified disgust with all existing standards and with every power that be that was transmuted into the hope that the whole culture and texture of life might go down in 'storms of steel' (Ernst Junger): 'destruction without mitigation, chaos and ruin as such assumed the dignity of supreme values' (*OT* 330). War appeared to be the progenitor of the new world, a means of chastisement and purification in a corrupt age (Thomas Mann), the great equaliser in class-ridden societies (Lenin), the arena in which selflessness obliterates bourgeois egoism (Bakunin), the site of the doomed man with no personal interest, no affairs, no sentiments, attachments, property, not even a name of his own (Nechaev), the ruined ground on which philosophies of action enunciate the dream of ordinary men that they might escape from society and do something quite extraordinary, something heroic or criminal, something undetermined. War fed the 'anti-humanist, anti-liberal, anti-individualist and anti-cultural instincts' of the front generation. It elevated violence, power and cruelty as the 'supreme capacities of humankind', and it provoked many of the front generation to become 'completely absorbed by their desire to see the ruin of this whole world of fake security, fake culture and fake life' (*OT* 330).

Arendt maintained that the critique of parliamentary democracy developed both by 'left' and 'right' revolutionaries (Lenin on one side and Carl Schmitt on the other) was based on the fact that the practices and institutions of representative government knew nothing of 'action and participation' and left the 'masses' unintegrated in political forms of organisation. Behind all the conventional political parties she discerned 'slumbering majorities' who played no active part in public life. The enforced marginality of the masses under representative systems of government caused little problem as long as they remained invisible and as long as the focus stayed on the representatives themselves. At a time of social and political crisis, however, the underlying deficiencies of representative government came to the surface and the masses emerged from obscurity not as a revolutionary force for freedom and justice, but rather as 'one great unorganised, structureless mass of furious individuals' (*OT* 315). At least one of the reasons why totalitarian movements were the beneficiaries of the crisis of parliamentary democracy was that the ground was prepared for them by a representative system which left people atomised, malleable, at best politically indifferent, or worse, brimming with resentment at the invisibility of their sufferings. Totalitarian movements channelled this contempt for representative institutions into a doctrine of 'movements' which obscured the very distinction between inner-party elites and the people with whom they claimed identity. What this meant in practice was that all forms of representation were suppressed except that of the totalitarian movement itself: representation was not overcome, it was monopolised.

Arendt argued that the key source of this reactive politics lay in the double standards and hypocrisy of the bourgeoisie, who wore the mask of humanity the better to conceal their actual appetite for power:

> Since the bourgeoisie claimed to be the guardian of Western traditions and confounded all moral issues by parading publicly virtues which it not

only did not possess in private and business life, but actually held in contempt, it seemed revolutionary to admit cruelty, disregard of human values, and general amorality, because this at least destroyed the duplicity upon which the existing society seemed to rest.

(OT 334)

In the twilight of double moral standards, it seemed radical to flaunt extreme attitudes: 'to wear publicly the mask of cruelty if everybody . . . pretended to be gentle'. Arendt cited the case of Celine's *Bagatelles pour un Massacre* in which he proposed the massacre of all Jews, and the welcome which André Gide gave to it, 'not of course because he wanted to kill the Jews . . . but because he rejoiced in the blunt admission of such a desire and in the fascinating contradiction between Celine's bluntness and the hypocritical politeness which surrounded the Jewish question in all respectable quarters' (OT 335). This radicalism attacked the separation of public and private life in the name of the wholeness of man. It exposed the false trust on which representative institutions were based, but only to promote a philosophy of universal distrust. It exposed the untruths of the existing system of right only to repudiate the very distinction between truth and falsehood and to declare its contempt for facts as such. It expressed contempt for political parties only to grant a political monopoly to the 'movement' itself.

The further argument we find in Arendt is that such blunt admission of desire as we find in this 'spiritless radicalism' was often welcome to a bourgeoisie tired of managing the tension between words and deeds and prepared to remove their masks and reveal a more naked brutality. The key precipitant of this new celebration of violence was imperialism: the form in which she argued the political rule of the bourgeoisie was finally consolidated and expansion for expansion's sake became for the first time the political credo of the age:

> Expansion as a permanent and supreme aim of politics is the central political idea of imperialism . . . it is an entirely new concept in the long history of political thought and action . . . this concept is not really political at all, but has its origin in the realm of business speculation.

(OT 125)

Drawing on the writings of Rosa Luxemburg, Arendt held that the imperialist principle of politics mirrored the bourgeois principle of economics: unlimited accumulation of power mirrored the unlimited accumulation of capital. What was new was not, of course, violence as such but the fact that violence was becoming the very aim of the body politic and was incapable of rest until there was 'nothing left to violate' (OT 137). It was in the age of imperialism that Arendt saw the 'will to power' becoming emancipated from all traditional restraints, moral and political, and the ground laid for a power which 'left to itself can achieve nothing but more power'. Nihilism in this sense became the practical spirit of the bourgeois age.

Arendt recognised that the imperialist ambition of power for power's sake came up against the obstacles, such as those imposed by nation-states at home and national movements in the colonies. However, these opponents of imperialist expansion were often weak in relation to the imperialist powers or they too became invested with the standards of the powers they opposed. In her exploration of the response of nationalist movements to the post-war collapse of the great multinational empires which had dominated central and eastern Europe, Arendt argued that the disappearance of these central despotic bureaucracies deprived the formerly subject nations of a common focus for their anger and led to the evaporation of the last remnants of solidarity between them. Now everybody was against everybody else and most of all against their closest neighbours: Slovaks against Czechs, Croats against Serbs, Ukrainians against Poles, all against Jews. Inside every political community internal divisions arose between those who belonged to the 'nation' and those who fell outside its boundaries: between *state-peoples* who won the right to their 'own' state, *minorities* (like Jews, Roma and Armenians) who were given special status, and *stateless* or *displaced persons* recognised by no one. Even the treaties guaranteeing the rights of minorities had the effect of declaring that only 'nationals' could be full citizens and that the rest needed some law of exception. Everyone became convinced, as Arendt put it, that 'true freedom, true emancipation, and true popular sovereignty could be attained only with full national emancipation, that people without their own national government were deprived of human rights' (OT 272). This conviction was made all the stronger by the fact that the two most powerful representatives of universal human values – Woodrow Wilson and Lenin – both advocated a 'right of nations to self-determination' which had the unintended consequence of inverting the idea of the nation-state from a rational principle based on the determination of the nation by the state, to an 'ethnic' principle based on the determination of the state by the nation.

What Arendt observed is that when Europe was confronted by large numbers of stateless persons, deprived of the right to have rights, it was but a short step to ascribe their rightlessness to their own natural deficiencies. The victims themselves found little consolation in appeals to the 'rights of man' and found hope mainly in the thought of acquiring their 'own' national state. The idea of human rights, which in theory referred to the inalienable dignity of every individual human being that no power on earth could deny, became a mere abstraction since everything depended on practices of the state. And the readiness with which those who belonged to a political community came to justify the denial of the 'right to have rights' to those who did not, became another of the established facts of twentieth century politics. Totalitarian movements exploited this fact to declare hostility to the idea of 'right' as such.

Totalitarian movements were not, in any conventional sense, nationalist movements. They represented a revolt against the existing order of nation-states and against the various nationalisms that were its ideological expression. Arendt opens her discussion of the origins of totalitarianism on precisely this point, when she argues against the identification of modern, political antisemitism with rampant nationalism and its xenophobic outbursts:

> Unfortunately, the fact is that modern antisemitism grew in proportion as traditional nationalism declined, and reached its climax at the exact moment when the European system of nation-states and its precarious balance of power crashed . . . The Nazis were not simple nationalists. Their nationalist propaganda was directed toward their fellow-travellers and not their convinced members; the latter, on the contrary, were never allowed to lose sight of a consistently supranational approach to politics . . . The Nazis had a genuine and never revoked contempt for the narrowness of nationalism, the provincialism of the nation-state, and they repeated time and again that their 'movement', international in scope like the Bolshevik movement, was more important to them than any state, which would necessarily be bound to a specific territory . . . The antisemitic parties in the last decades of the nineteenth century were also among the first that banded together internationally.
>
> (OT 4–5)

Antisemitic propaganda was directed at the 'supranational Jews' as a supposedly rival international movement and used the 'Protocols of the Elders of Zion' as 'evidence' of the Jewish quest for 'world empire'. Arendt emphasised that Nazism and Stalinism 'owed more to Pan-Germanism and Pan-Slavism (respectively) than to any other ideology or political movement' and shared with overseas imperialism the 'contempt for the narrowness of the nation-state' (OT 222–3). She quotes Hitler's promise that the Nazi movement would 'transcend the narrow limits of modern nationalism' (OT 359), and she describes the totalitarian movement as 'international in its organisation, all-comprehensive in its ideological scope and global in its political aspiration' (OT 389). Nationalism would simply frustrate its exterior expansion. In Arendt's view, the recourse of totalitarian movements to an old-fashioned nationalism – the Nazi claim, for example that its ambitions would be satisfied when the traditional demands of a nationalistic German foreign policy were fulfilled, or the Stalinist claim that it would restrict its sphere of operation to 'socialism in one country' – were basically lies designed to assuage certain public opinions at home and abroad. The ideas of 'race' and 'class' both cut across the unity of the nation and both were the grounds for alliances beyond the nation.

Following Hegel, Arendt pointed to the equivocations and perplexities inherent in the idea of right. If the modern idea of right was from the eighteenth century attached to the nation state as its author, provider and enforcer, the decline of the nation state signified the end of the rights of man. When certain groups of people were denied the right to have rights by virtue of their statelessness, it was a small step to attribute to such people certain natural characteristics (such as their 'Jewishness') to account for and justify the expropriation of their rights.

Rightlessness became the mark of Cain. Not only was the idea of right no longer conceived through a universalistic lens, but the idea of the right to have rights was itself denounced. The thought which Arendt pursued is that the 'spiritless radicalism' whose hostility to the whole rational architectonic of right, law, nation and state proved so violent and destructive, was itself the product of the system of right broken down under the weight of its own contradictions and partial reconfigurations. Perhaps the moral of the story is one that Arendt took from Kafka's K: 'that human rights are [despite all] worth fighting for and the rule of the castle is not divine law' (cited in Bernstein 1996: 76).

Notes

1 It was published in *Partisan Review* 20(4) (1954). Arendt originally called it 'The difficulties of understanding'.

2 In the report of the war crimes Branch of the Judge Advocate's Section of the Third US Army, dated 21 June 1945, the conditions at the Flossenburg concentration camp were investigated, and one passage may be quoted: 'Flossenburg concentration camp can best be described as a factory dealing in death. Although this camp had in view the primary object of putting to work the mass slave labor, another of its primary objects was the elimination of human lives by the methods employed in handling the prisoners. Hunger and starvation rations, sadism, inadequate clothing, medical neglect, disease, beatings, hangings, freezing, forced suicides, shooting, etc. all played a major role in obtaining their object. Prisoners were murdered at random; spite killings against Jews were common, injections of poison and shooting in the neck were everyday occurrences; epidemics of typhus and spotted fever were permitted to run rampant as a means of eliminating prisoners; life in this camp meant nothing. Killing became a common thing, so common that a quick death was welcomed by the unfortunate ones.' The report states that a certain number of the concentration camps were equipped with gas chambers for the wholesale destruction of the inmates, and with furnaces for the burning of the bodies. Some of them were in fact used for the extermination of Jews as part of the 'final solution' of the Jewish problem. Most of the non-Jewish inmates were used for labour, although the conditions under which they worked made labour and death almost synonymous terms. Those inmates who became ill and were unable to work were either destroyed in the gas chambers or sent to special infirmaries, where they were given entirely inadequate medical treatment, worse food if possible than the working inmates, and left to die. See *EU* 316.

3 Lessing wrote: 'I am not duty-bound to resolve the difficulties I create. May my ideas always be somewhat disjunct, or even appear to contradict one another, if only they are ideas in which readers will find material that stirs them to think for themselves.' Arendt commented: 'Lessing not only wanted no one to coerce him, but he also wanted to coerce no one, either by force or by proofs. He regarded the tyranny of those who attempt to dominate thinking by reasoning and sophistries, by compelling argumentation, as more dangerous to freedom than orthodoxy.' Later Arendt approves Lessing's sentiment that human society is in no way harmed by those 'who take more trouble to make clouds than to scatter them' (Arendt 'On humanity in dark times: Thoughts about Lessing', *MDT* 8 and 26).

4 There may arise moments of tension between understanding and judgement. The Auschwitz 'survivor', Primo Levi, wrote of his desire to understand the Germans, but he still recounts how he refused to meet Dr Muller, the German chemist at Auschwitz, because he ran 'the risk of believing him' and because this human encounter might

119

prevent him from making 'the correct judgement' (Levi 1986a: 218). Levi declares his failure: 'I cannot say I understand the Germans' (Levi 1997a: 396); and he expresses his fear of the consequences of understanding the Germans: 'Perhaps one cannot, what is more one must not, understand what happened, because to understand is almost to justify . . . there is no rationality in the Nazi hatred: it is a hate that is not in us; it is outside man; it is a poison fruit sprung from the deadly trunk of Fascism, but it is outside and beyond Fascism itself. We cannot understand it, but we can and must understand from where it springs, and we must be on our guard. If understanding is impossible, knowing is imperative, because what happened could happen again' (Levi 1997a: 395–6). Repeatedly Levi declares that he has not forgiven and that he is not inclined to forgive, but fears that understanding the Germans might lead to identification, thence to justification and finally to forgiveness.

5 Leon Trotsky was a notable exception. In his later writings Leon Trotsky had no trouble in likening the Soviet Union to Nazi Germany, except for the greater barbarism of the former, and characterising both as 'totalitarian'. Trotsky faced up to the conjunction of socialism *and* barbarism in a way that has been largely absent in a Marxist tradition which has either denied or downplayed the *barbarism* of Soviet socialism or has denied or downplayed the *socialism* of Soviet barbarism.

6 In his highly perceptive but largely forgotten article, 'Ideas toward a sociology of the concentration camp' (*The American Journal of Sociology* 63(5) (1958), 513–22), H. G. Adler writes of the camps: 'If cruelty is a mental attitude with which society is often burdened and which sometimes determines the very social existence of a community, so are depersonalisation and its modern expression – reduction to a mass – essentially social phenomena. Strictly speaking, the mass is a fiction, since no individual is a member of the mass or of any one mass but is always an individual in a group of men . . . But the mass can be defined in the following way: mass is the elimination of personality' (p. 521). Adler goes on to discuss two ways in which this can occur: 'men who renounce claim to personality and men who are forced to tolerate not being recognised a individuals . . . The subjection is completed in the concentration camps . . . Only this makes the concentration camp the place of utter human degradation' (p. 522).

7 We are accustomed to the argument that the way people present themselves should not be confused with who they are, but we are inclined to forget that this holds not only when people present themselves as all-good but also when they present themselves as all-powerful. An analogy might be drawn with Michel Foucault's error when he turned the advertising slogans of Jeremy Bentham's *panopticon* – that it would be all-seeing, all-knowing, all-powerful, a perfect machine for 'grinding rogues honest', etc. – into the actuality of disciplinary power. Foucault was ready to use Bentham to devalue the claims of penal reformers who presented their reforms in the language of the 'rights of man' or as advances in humanitarian practice, but he did not apply the same sceptical consciousness to those like Bentham who claimed in an equally illusory fashion that they had finally discovered the means of achieving a rational, complete, pervasive, gapless and seamless power. Somehow, when it came to power rather than to humanism, he missed the shadow that lies between the image and the act. See Fine (1985: 189–202). The *lebensraum* theory of the Holocaust, that it can be explained in terms of the positive ambition of the Nazis to 'Germanise' the East, forgets that it was the abject failure of the ambition that preceded the extermination of Jews.

8 Compare with Alan Bullock: '[Hitler] had a particular and inveterate distrust of experts. He refused to be impressed by the complexity of problems, insisting until it became monotonous that if only the will was there any problem could be solved' (Bullock 1983: 381).

9 See also Bullock 1983: 381: 'There was always more than one office operating in

any field. A dozen different agencies quarreled over the direction of propaganda, of economic policy, and the intelligence services. Before 1938 Hitler continually went behind the back of the Foreign Office to make use of Ribbentrop's special bureau or to get information through Party channels. The dualism of Party and State organizations, each with one or more divisions for the same function, was deliberate. In the end this reduced efficiency, but it strengthened Hitler's position by allowing him to play off one department against another.' In September 1939, the Security Service of the SS, a party organisation, was fused with the regular Security Police of the State, which included the Gestapo, to form the Head Office for Reich Security (RSHA), commanded by Heydrich. The RSHA was one of twelve Head Offices in the SS, two others of which were the Head Office of the Order Police, which was responsible for rounding up Jews, and the Head Office for Administration and Economy (WVHA) which ran concentration camps and later the 'economic' side of extermination. The RSHA contained Section IV, the Gestapo, divided into Section IV-A, dealing with 'opponents' and Section IV-B, dealing with 'sects'. The Higher SS and Police Leaders were in a different command structure to the twelve offices of the RSHA, while the *Einsatzgruppen* were under the command of the RSHA, but were not one of the twelve offices (Arendt 1994a: 70). In this context, not even a thorough knowledge of Nazi ideology can help in predicting what the will of the Führer will be on any given day. Hitler summed this up as follows, in relation to the interpretation of law by judges: 'The legislator cannot possibly catalogue or prescribe for every conceivable crime. It is the duty of the judge to pass sentence on the merits of the case. The Body Judicial must be recruited from the best elements of the nation. The Judge must possess a keen sensitivity which permits him to grasp the intentions of the legislature . . . It is essential that a judge have the clearest possible picture of the intentions of the legislature and the goal which this latter pursues' (*Hitler's Table Talk*, London: Weidenfeld and Nicolson, 1953, 641, quoted in Allen Lane, *Nuremberg – A Nation on Trial*, London: Penguin, 1979, 271). This restatement of an ordinary liberal analysis of the relationship between the judiciary and the legislature gains a whole new meaning when it comes out of the mouth of Adolph Hitler. The *only* law was the 'intentions of the legislature'. This is quite opposite to a bureaucracy which is organised on the basis of formal rules which must be interpreted and carried out on every level of the hierarchy.

10 According to Arendt the view that National Socialism represented an extreme form of nationalism suppresses the memory of its 'genuine and never revoked contempt for the narrowness of nationalism' and the 'provincialism of the nation state'. Both the Nazi and the Bolshevik movements inherited the mantle of the pan-national movements of an earlier era which declared that 'the movement, international in scope, was more important . . . than any state which would necessarily be bound to a specific territory' (*OT* 4).

11 This episode also exposes the inversion of reason and passion that occurs in Bauman's reformulation of Kant. Kant identifies 'practical reason' with larger moral concerns and 'passion' with self-interest, self-advancement and self-preservation. Bauman reverses this order of association: reason is now identified with self-interest, self-advancement, self-preservation, etc. and morality is identified with the subject's emotional response to the face of the Other. In Kant's hierarchy of reason and passion, passion is subordinated to the demands of reason but it is not annulled. Bauman's hierarchy is more severe: he degrades 'reason' (which Kant called 'passion') in favour of 'morality' (which Kant calls 'reason'). The effect of this inversion is to disconnect ethics from any conception of instrumental rationality.

7

STATE AND REVOLUTION REVISITED

Arendt

The critique of representation

In many contemporary commentaries, Arendt is acclaimed for her theory of political *action* and critique of *representation*. Bonnie Honig, to take one example, welcomes Arendt's unwillingness to 'allow political action to be a site of representation' and her determination to 'reclaim the practice of politics from representative, state-centred and state-centring institutions' (Honig 1993: 124–5). This is true as far as it goes and captures one side of Arendt's politics. Arendt followed a line of argument drawn from Hegel and Marx when she identified the source of the defects of representative government in the modern separation of formal legal equality and substantive social inequality which leaves political community deeply vulnerable: 'The fundamental contradiction between a political body based on equality before the law and a society based on the inequality of the class system prevented the development of functioning republics as well as the birth of a new political hierarchy' (OT 12). When she wrote *On Revolution* over a decade later, Arendt had lost none of her old radicalism. She writes:

> What we today call democracy is a form of government where the few rule, at least supposedly in the interest of the many . . . and public happiness and public freedom . . . become the privilege of the few.
>
> (OR 269)

In a representative democracy, she wrote, only the representatives, not the people themselves, have the opportunity to engage in those activities of 'expressing, discussing and deciding which in a positive sense are the activities of freedom' (OR 235). The political parties are instruments through which 'the power of the people is curtailed and controlled'. Their programmes are 'ready-made formulas which demand not action but execution' (OR 264). Their function is to exclude the masses from public life and their effect is to create widespread indifference to public affairs.[1]

In her analysis of the American Revolution of 1776, however, Arendt acknowledged the revolutionary origins of representative government and the 'forgotten' links forged between representation and revolution. The achievement of the American Revolution was to construct a representative form of government based on the consent of the people, a constitutional framework in which power was balanced against power in a manner first formulated by Montesquieu, and a Bill of Rights that succeeded in guaranteeing the private rights and property of individuals. And yet she also argues that the American revolutionaries *mirrored* in their own self-conception the shapes and forms of the limited monarchy they opposed, when they presented the revolution in the illusory light of a *restoration* of ancient liberties. The result, as Arendt viewed it, was a combination of public atrophy and private hypertrophy. The Bill of Rights was exemplary in this respect. It defended the private realm against public power, but in a society whose main defect derived not from the colonisation of private interests by public power but rather from the colonisation of the public realm by private interests, it was the public realm which was most in need of guarantees. To remedy this lack, Arendt argued that a quite different solution would have been required: an institutional and constitutional framework designed to guarantee the rights of *public* life as well as private rights. She argued that this alternative was in fact proposed on the margins of the revolution, particularly by Jefferson, but the prevailing decision to place all guarantees on the side of private right and the consequent failure to consolidate institutions of popular participation meant that public life was inexorably subsumed to private interest. The freedom which the revolutionaries themselves had enjoyed in the *act* of constitution was a freedom no longer available once the constitution became an inviolable framework to which all (except perhaps those with the money or power to buy themselves out) became subject.

The critique of the critique of representation

This critique of representation, however, reveals only half the picture. Arendt's originality lay in combining the critique of representation with what I have called the critique of the critique of representation. The 'bourgeois' quality of the American Revolution drove successive generations of revolutionary thought to the French Revolution of 1789 as a more radical model. For example, in the same year as Arendt wrote *On Revolution*, 1963, Jürgen Habermas wrote an essay on *Natural Law and Revolution* in which he elevated the Rousseauian spirit of modern natural law infusing the French Revolution, over the Lockeian spirit of traditional natural law on which the American Revolution was based (Habermas 1974). According to Habermas, the American Revolution was limited both in respect of its traditional form (the restoration of an imaginary past) and its bourgeois content (the protection of private wealth); the French Revolution, by contrast, was premised on 'a fundamentally new system of rights' (Habermas 1974: 87) and a strong sense of 'participation in . . . political public life' (Habermas 1974: 116). Habermas endorsed what he read as the principles of the Rousseauian mandate – that every individual has the right to participate *in person* in the making of laws, that mere *representation* robs individuals of this right of participation in public life, that no private right is valid that is not first validated by the people, and that a political order ought to correspond with the idea of right itself.

Arendt's critique of the Rousseauian idea, by contrast, follows closely that of Hegel. She argued that the general will does not refer to what individuals actually will, but to what they *would will* if they acted as rational and virtuous citizens. Indivisible and dedicated to unanimity, the general will expresses the will of the people only as a singular entity. It conceives the people as a 'multi-headed monster, a mass that moves as one body and acts as though possessed by one will' (*OR* 94). It presents itself as always right. It not only holds that the particular interests of individuals are subordinate to the interest of the whole but that the value of individuals should be judged by the extent to which they act against their own interest and for the good of all. It tears the mask of hypocrisy off 'society' and celebrates 'the unspoilt, honest face of *le peuple*' (*OR* 106); but by pinning its faith on the natural goodness of the people it prepares the ground for abolishing all legal and institutional guarantees. It hears in the voice of the people only an echo of its own voice, and the appeal to the people becomes a mask behind which a new class of political representatives sets itself up in opposition to the people. In the general will representation is not in fact overcome, it is reconfigured in a less rational form. It becomes the enemy of all genuine public life. It inaugurates a world of universal suspicion and denunciation. And it mirrors the absolute, exclusive and indivisible sovereignty of the monarch it once opposed.

Arendt distinguished between two moments of liberation in the French Revolution: the first is political and aims at liberation from the old regime; the second is social and looks to liberation from material want. In the first, there is a natural solidarity between leaders and the people in a shared project; in the second, solidarity has to be produced artificially through an effort of solidarisation. In the first people have and exchange many opinions; in the second the 'voice of the people' is identified with the unanimous cry for bread. It is in the second revolution that the Rousseauian general will prevails. Arendt's response was equivocal. On the one hand, she declares that 'every attempt to solve the social question *with political means* leads to terror' (*OR* 112) and that nothing could be more 'obsolete . . . futile . . . dangerous' than to 'attempt to liberate mankind from poverty by political means' (*OR* 114, my emphasis). On the other hand, she recognises that 'liberation from necessity because of its urgency will always take precedence over the building of freedom' (*OR* 112), that nothing deprives people more effectively of the 'light of public happiness' more than poverty, that in America the question of poverty was not really resolved but merely hidden from sight (particularly in the case of slavery), and that in the final analysis 'no revolution was possible . . . where the masses were loaded down with misery' (*OR* 222). She refers to the 'compassionate zeal' of the revolutionary 'spokesmen for the poor' who attempt to transform the *malheureux* into the *enragés* by inviting 'the rage of naked misfortune' to pit itself against 'the rage of unmasked corruption'. It is this *misuse* of destitution in the struggle against tyranny that Arendt sees as most destructive of the idea of right and most conducive to terror.[2]

The third road to which Arendt looked is neither the American nor the French Revolutions but what she calls 'the lost treasure of the revolutionary heritage' (*OR* 215 ff.). In America she finds it in the town-hall meetings which Emerson dubbed the 'units of the Republic' and 'schools of the people' and which she saw as embodying the true spirit of modern revolution: 'the constitution of a public space where freedom could be realised' (*OR* 255). In France she finds it in the *sociétés révolutionaires* and the *sections* of the Paris Commune which originated in the election of representatives to the National Assembly and then turned to the formation of an autonomous Commune. In the revolutions of the twentieth century, right up to Hungary 1956, she finds it in the councils, communes and soviets of modern working-class history: 'spaces of freedom' based on 'the direct participation of every citizen in the public affairs of the country' (*OR* 264). She sees the councils not as temporary institutions of struggle but as foundations, created from below, for an entirely new form of government. The fact that they are always suppressed either by the forces of the old order or by new revolutionary governments testifies only to the freedom they embody. For a moment Arendt places her hopes and expectations here, in a revolutionary tradition which has no convergence with the inner tendencies of totalitarianism.

Even as Arendt made this claim, she acknowledges that this 'lost heritage' is beset by its own internal contradictions. The councils may be ideally suited to their *political* function of 'satisfying the human appetite for participation in public life', but not to their *social* functions of administration and management which require more bureaucratic and hierarchical structures. Drawn into the social domain, the council system is either destroyed by its own excess or, if it divests itself of its social functions, this means that the first rule of these 'spaces of freedom' is to forbid their occupants from speaking about the social conditions which lead them to participate in the first place.[3] The attempt to abstract politics from society mirrors what it most opposes: the Rousseauian demand that when citizens enter the assembly, they *must* leave behind their social existence and speak only for the good of the whole. Arendt acknowledges too that the councils are an 'aristocratic' form of government, in the sense that they are run by those who are politically 'the best' and who show 'a taste and capacity for speaking and being heard' (*OR* 279). As for the rest, they can find consolation only in the notion that they are exercising the most important negative liberty which the modern world adds to the classical heritage: that of freedom from politics. The councils may change the way in which political elites are selected, but not the fact of selection itself.

Arendt reaches an impasse. Having argued that Rousseau's critique of representation serves to reinstate representation in an irrational form, she seeks to *perfect* the critique of representation. From the American Revolution comes the idea of rights; from the French the idea of a 'beginning'; from the councils the idea of public life. There is, however, no end to this journey. Clouds are made, not cleared.

Arendt draws inspiration from the Greeks – Athens rather than Rousseau's Sparta – and takes from the *polis* the idea of politics as a 'space of freedom' to which citizens rise from their private lives.[4] It is a space in which citizens participate in person in deliberation on public affairs, express and exchange their opinions in the company of others, recognise their differences without violence or coercion, and claim public recognition of their own special qualities. Politics signifies a special sphere of human intercourse, distinguished from everyday life by 'the gulf that the ancients had to cross daily to transcend the narrow realm of the household and "rise" into the realm of politics' (HC 33). Arendt is tempted by the myth of a 'fall' – from ancient politics where thought and action are united and the function of politics is, as Socrates put it, to establish a 'common world, built on the understanding of friendship, where no rulership is needed' (Arendt 1990: 81); to the rise of modern distinctions, first expressed by Plato, between thought and action, politics and philosophy, rulers and ruled. The *polis* is a benchmark against which the modern reduction of workers to machines, action to labour, can be denatured; a place where public happiness is an end in itself, the essential ingredient of a good life and not merely an instrument for private purposes. By contrast, modern political life appears a tawdry and dangerous business: passive, non-participative, merely representative, beset by unresolved conflicts, and marked by the decline of both private and public life before the 'levelling demands of the social' (HC 39).[5] Arendt acknowledges, however, the contradictions of the *polis*: women, foreigners, slaves, craftsmen, etc. are excluded; the freedom of citizens exists only in contrast to the unfreedom of others; the time available to citizens to act freely depends on the labour performed by others. Even for the citizens themselves freedom is deficient:

> The perfect elimination of the pain of labour would . . . deprive the specifically human life of its very liveliness and vitality . . . for mortals the easy life of the gods would be a lifeless life . . . vitality and liveliness can only be conserved to the extent that men are willing to take the burden, the toil and trouble of life upon themselves.
>
> (HC 120–1)

Neither the *polis* nor its modern reincarnations can remedy the exclusion from the 'light of public life' which is the scandal of the modern state; nor can they meet the demands of a philosophy of natality in which beginning was held as the 'supreme capacity of *every* man' and 'guaranteed by *each* new birth' (OT 479). Ultimately, Arendt does not contrast the harmony of Greece with the conflicts of the modern world, but the conflicts of the one with the conflicts of the other.

Antinomies in the idea of revolution

For Arendt, the essential idea of the modern revolutionary tradition is the constitution of freedom (*constitutio libertatis*). The idea of freedom and the experience
of a 'new beginning' are said to coincide. Liberation from oppression aims at the
constitution of freedom; the constitution of freedom entails the constitution of a
republic; and the republic is identified not only with constitutional government
guaranteeing private rights but with the admission of everyone to the public realm.
Its aim is not 'government' but a form of political organisation in which the citizens
live together without any division between rulers and ruled – a condition Arendt
calls *anarche* or *isonomia* (*OR* 30). The difficulty has been well analysed by Miguel
Vatter (1998): if freedom is 'the spontaneity of beginning something new', then
it is impossible for it also to be 'a stable, tangible reality' (*LM* 203) or to acquire
the fixed form of a constitution.

Vatter's argument goes as follows: if freedom is a repeatable event out of which
political forms emerge and into which they can always be revoked, then the
'something new' loses its authority and we are left only with the spontaneity of
beginning as such.[6] But the idea of revolution contains both moments at once:
that of constituting a form of government and that of being a repeatable political
event, the spontaneity of new beginning and the founding of a 'permanent, lasting
enduring body politic' (*OR* 36). The strength of the idea lies in holding on to both
poles of this antithesis.

Arendt argues that political freedom can be realised in the form of a republic
without introducing the violence with which she charges the earlier revolutionary
thinking of Machiavelli, Robespierre and Marx. But if the 'beginning' (1789, 1776,
1917 . . .) is fetishised as the founding moment of all subsequent authority, then
we are back where we started: at an abstract freedom which only imagines its
separation from violence. The unconditional beginning turns into the condition
of all beginning. Machiavelli acknowledges that the revolutionary event is
inescapably violent and that every attempt to turn its emancipatory force into
a permanent and necessary state of affairs is doomed to failure because it is self-
refuting. It amounts to providing a necessary form for freedom from necessity.

Arendt distinguishes between rebellion and revolution on the ground that 'the
end of rebellion is liberation, while the end of revolution is the foundation
of freedom' (*OR* 142). She makes an analogous distinction between a legal government that safeguards negative liberties and a republic where citizens are endowed
with positive liberty and participate in public affairs. The revolutionary act *par
excellence* is that of giving oneself a constitution – an act that creates power rather
than simply delimits it (*OR* 145). Arendt means by the constitution of freedom
something more than constitutional government. If the latter is defined in terms
of the ability of law to delimit the rule of the government, the former entails
the empowerment of political subjects. At the same time, Arendt endows her
conception of freedom with those qualities that only constitutional government
can provide, the stability and endurance of a system of law. She argues that one

of the things that distinguishes the American Revolution from the French is that it did not ground law upon the will of the people but on the authority of the Constitution. Without this precaution political freedom would not have found its stability, for popular power, based merely on promises made among equals in a moment of 'no-rule', is an inherently evanescent phenomenon. The law cannot be founded on the basis of the power and freedom of the people, rather the power and freedom of the people finds its stability in the law. In the act of political constitution, therefore, there emerges what Vatter identifies as 'the problem of law': from where is the Constitution, understood as the 'fundamental law' that gives authority to all other laws, to receive its own authority?

Some interpreters ascribe to Arendt the belief that 'power' and 'authority' have the same root simply because they are both non-violent. But for Arendt, as Vatter argues, power is not only antithetical to violence but also to rule, while authority is by contrast the non-violent ground for rule. Hence the crucial question is what happens to power when it is given a legal form, i.e. when it is constituted as authority. For Arendt, political life stands in tension with authority: the former is about freedom as 'no-rule', the latter is about the capacity to rule. Arendt tries to resolve this problem by turning freedom ('no-rule') into the ground of rule, that is, into the source of authority which grants freedom its 'stable, tangible reality'. Her thesis is that the Constitution, as the fundamental law, derives its authority from the fact that the act of foundation is itself an absolute beginning:

> From this [possibility] it follows that it is futile to search for an absolute
> to break the vicious circle in which all beginning is inevitably caught,
> because this 'absolute' lies in the very act of beginning itself.
>
> (OR 204)

But in what sense is a beginning absolute? and what relation does 'absolute beginning' have to the possibility of authority? How can 'no-rule' become a source for rule? Arendt does not provide an argument for why a beginning, once posited as an act of foundation, is in itself authoritative. She merely claims that 'the very concept of Roman authority suggests that the act of foundation inevitably develops its own stability and permanence' and that in this context authority is nothing more or less than an 'augmentation' by virtue of which innovations and changes remain tied back to the foundation which at the same time they augment. Thus amendments to the Constitution 'augment' the original foundation of the American Republic and the authority of the American Constitution resides in its capacity to be so 'augmented' (OR 203). The beginning is authoritative only because of an institution (*religio*) which takes it upon itself to bind all political action back to this beginning and to rehearse its 'spirit of foundation' in a continuous process of constitution-making (OR 201). *Auctoritas* means 'to augment, to increase and enlarge the foundations as they had been laid down by the ancestors', by keeping the act of foundation 'present' through history in what amounts to the repetition of the beginning itself.

The beginning functions as a principle of authority because it conditions the repetition of itself. The *repetition*, though, does not begin anything radically new and that is why 'augmentation' is recognisable as falling under a law. This is what Arendt means when she says that the repetition of the revolutionary beginning amounts to 'a coincidence of foundation and preservation by virtue of augmentation' (OR 202). This beginning is absolute because it is absolved from being 'just another beginning' and is posited as the 'first beginning'. Its repetition by other beginnings simply reinforces its primacy. Augmentation turns out to be a process of 'continuous foundation' whose continuity disallows other beginnings. The politicisation of the citizen that is supposed to occur in the moment of augmentation is always limited by the structure given by the founders. Augmentation necessarily falls short of revolution, understood as the *suspension of every* form of political rule and the opening of a space of 'no-rule'. It amounts to the *reform* of a given political system. The system of authority does not and cannot permit the occurrence of new beginnings, that is, of republican events or revolutionary discontinuities, but maintains the state in its capacity to rule without violence. The system of authority sketched by Arendt is the negation of the act of revolution, understood as the emergence of the new, since change could only mean 'enlargement of the old' (OR 201).

This uninterrupted presence of beginning gives the second sense in which the system of authority constructs an absolute concept of beginning which undermines the idea of new beginnings. Authority absolutises the 'beginning' by abstracting it from its own eventfulness. The need to keep the 'beginning always present' undermines the attempt to keep alive 'the republic and its revolutionary spirit'. The freedom of beginnings is not something that can be 'always present' without denying itself: its character as an event stands opposed to its ground-like presence. Arendt claims that 'what saves the act of beginning from its own arbitrariness is that it carries its own principle with itself' (OR 212). If this is taken to mean that each beginning is a principle *only* unto itself, this limitation is what frees the possibility for other beginnings. Each beginning is just another beginning and cannot be posited as unique or absolute. Such a claim presupposes a proliferation of beginnings and an absence of originals to be imitated or examples to be followed. But then all that is begun is beginning itself. The authority of beginning, by contrast, is intended to prohibit just this proliferation of beginnings, but at the cost of giving it a quasi-*religious* sanction. If freedom as beginning is a ground, then every subsequent political change has to assume the shape of a reform and political life is inevitably closed off from republican events of 'no-rule'. Freedom can only be a beginning if it somehow subverts the fetishism of beginnings in favour of their dissemination, but then political freedom has to pay a price for this plurality, for it can no longer claim to be authoritative. It cannot set itself up as an absolute foundation, for to do so would be to give up on its proper self-understanding as the power to changes the times.

Faced with these contradictions, which he analyses so precisely, Miguel Vatter comes to a definite conclusion: namely, that freedom is an event and must remain open to its own historicity. Let me quote:

Hannah Arendt in the end accepts that freedom exists without ground but she cannot articulate this lack in positive terms, as freedom's internal relation to its historicity, whose structure is that of originary repetition. In this case, Arendt did not follow her distant cousin Walter Benjamin's *Theses on the concept of history*, where revolutionary praxis is explicitly understood in terms of active historical repetition. The politics of historical repetition, in all its possible variants, remains a promising, yet barely trodden, path for thought.

(Vatter 1998: 83)

The conclusion Arendt draws is different. The problem with plumping for one side of this contradiction against the other, for freedom as a repeatable event rather than as ground, is that it might appear from one angle to be 'anti-authoritarian' and from another to convey the destruction of all that is determinate. If we plump for freedom as ground rather than repeatable event, then from one angle it might appear to guarantee lasting institutions but from another to deny freedom beyond the augmentation of the constitution. The aporia of revolution which Arendt analysed, signifies that we have to stop thinking that the concept of revolution can be actualised in some ideal form, if only we can find or think it, and revive Hegel's recognition that revolution itself is a form of right that is relative to other forms, and is not free of the contradictions which beset the system of right as a whole. This is not to abandon or to reject the idea of revolution, which is our only resource against the continuation of injustice, but rather to bring it down to earth, to recognise its mystique and acknowledge that it is not above the equivocations of modern political life.

Notes

1 Arendt is not indifferent to different forms of representation. Her discussion of whether representatives are to act according to instructions received from their electors (a *mandat imperatif*) or to be independent of those who elected them until the next election, may appear irresolvable: if representatives are bound by instruction, they become mere messengers or experts, paid agents of those unable or unwilling to attend public business; if they are independent, the idea that all power resides in the people is true only for the day of the election, after which the distinction between rulers and the ruled reasserts itself and public business becomes again the privilege of the few. Arendt also distinguishes between the relative stability of the 'British' two-party system in contrast to the relative instability of the multi-party systems operating on the Continent. The difference between them, as Arendt sees it, is that in multi-party systems there is a separation of state and party, such that the state stands above the disparate parties and claims to represent the nation as a whole; while in the two-party system state and party are unified in the sense that the ruling party is both representative and governmental. Since multi-party government is formed through party alliances, no one party can take responsibility for government. The parties, therefore, never transcend the particular interests which they represent to become parties of government managing the public affairs of the people as a whole (*OT* 250–66).

2 Arendt writes: 'The direction of the American Revolution remained committed to the foundation of freedom and the establishment of lasting institutions, and to those who acted in this direction nothing was permitted that would have been outside the range of civil law. The direction of the French Revolution was deflected almost from its beginning from this course of foundation through the immediacy of suffering; it was determined by the exigencies of liberation not from tyranny but from necessity, and it was actuated by the limitless immensity of both the people's misery and the pity this misery inspired. The lawlessness of the "all is permitted" sprang here still from the sentiments of the heart whose very boundlessness helped in the unleashing of a stream of boundless violence' (OR 92).

3 Sheldon Wolin, among many others, argues that Arendt's circumscribed notion of politics left the councils void of substance. What else were people to talk about but their social concerns? He writes: 'Arendt's indifference, to put it blandly, to the culture of ordinary and poor citizens produced a severely impoverished notion of the historical meaning of the political' (Wolin 1994: 300).

4 In The Human Condition Arendt writes of what she calls 'the space of appearance' which 'comes into being wherever men are together in the manner of speech and action, and therefore predates and precedes all formal constitution of the public realm and forms of government' (HC 199). The peculiarity of this public space is that it does not survive the actuality of the movement which brought it into being but 'disappears not only with the dispersal of men . . . but with the arrest of the activities themselves' (HC 199). Arendt explores the potentiality of beginning something genuinely new that lies in the simple fact of being, acting and speaking together, but she does not consider in this work the problems tied to the political foundations of such a concept of free action. In On Revolution this space of free political action is explicitly identified with that in which revolutionary action occurs.

5 The notion that violence in the ancient world was pre-political and that only 'finding the right words at the right moment' was political, does not make us forget that 'great words' are themselves a preamble to military force. Similarly, the notion that in the modern age 'action' is opposed to the forces of commodity fetishism does not make us forget that great deeds, as every publicist knows, may be sponsored and sold.

6 Miguel Vatter makes the point that the aporetic character of Arendt's discourse on political freedom is not easily granted by those interpreters who seek to extract from her texts a positive political project tied to action rather than representation. As Bonnie Honig has it, for Arendt 'the problem of politics in modernity is, how do we establish lasting foundations without appealing to gods, a foundationalist ground, or an absolute? In short, is it possible to have a politics of foundation in a world devoid of traditional (foundational) guarantees of stability, legitimacy and authority?' (Honig 1993: 97). From this perspective, it seems that Arendt sets out to resolve the 'legitimacy crisis' tied to the downfall of traditional or metaphysical sources of authority by seeking new, post-metaphysical sources for authority. But this reading conceals how far a 'politics of foundation' is a contradiction in terms, since the very project of establishing 'lasting foundations' for freedom is part and parcel of what extinguishes freedom.

8

KANT'S COSMOPOLITAN
IDEAL AND HEGEL'S CRITIQUE

Kant's magnificent endeavour to develop a theory of cosmopolitanism was pursued in a series of essays spanning a twelve-year period before and after the French Revolution.[1] These essays have become a focus for contemporary study among those who see the need to revive the idea of cosmopolitanism for our own age, and they are widely seen as a philosophical origin of contemporary ideas of cosmopolitan democracy (Bohman and Lutz-Bachmann 1997; Habermas 1998; Apel 1997; Honneth 1997; Archibugi, Held and Kohler 1998; Held 1995; Held 1997). Kant's work expresses the fact that the modern idea of cosmopolitanism is coeval with the rise of nationalism and presents itself as an antidote to the wrongs of nationalism. Among contemporary supporters of the Kantian idea of cosmopolitanism, criticisms of Kant's approach take the form of ironing out inconsistencies in his theory (especially concerning the relation between his philosophy of history and his metaphysics of morals), developing further his critique of absolutist notions of national sovereignty, adapting his theory to modern conditions, and endorsing his essential insight. In the words of Karl-Otto Apel, they seek to 'think with Kant against Kant' and reserve their real criticisms for the 'scurrilous' and 'contemptuous' dismissals of the alleged formalism, hypocrisy and false universalism of the cosmopolitan idea – such as is to be found in Carl Schmitt's anti-humanistic observation that the concept of humanity either 'excludes the possibility of a foe' or turns the foe into an 'inhuman monster . . . who must be definitively annihilated' (Habermas 1997: 146). They criticise Hegel for his allegedly regressive, bellicose and nationalistic critique of Kant which Habermas describes as 'close' to that of Schmitt. This view – that, as Adorno put it, Hegel's nationalistic doctrine of the 'popular spirit' was reactionary in relation both to Kant's idea of a cosmopolitan order and his own earlier idea of the 'world spirit' (Adorno 1990) – has become a kind of orthodoxy. I want to suggest, however, that this version of Hegel's critique of Kant's cosmopolitan ideal seriously misreads what Hegel was doing and in misreading Hegel loses sight of the substance of his objections.

Kant's cosmopolitanism

In his *Idea for a Universal History from a Cosmopolitan Point of View*, written in 1785, Kant posed the attainment of a cosmopolitan order as the greatest problem facing the human race – even greater than the achievement of republican civic constitutions within particular nation-states. Kant recognised that it was a 'fantastical' idea, without precedent in world history, but he also argued that it was a 'necessity' if the human race was not to consume itself in wars between nations and if the power of nation-states was not to overwhelm the freedom of individuals. By a 'cosmopolitan order', Kant meant an order in which there are established 'a lawful external relation among states' and a 'universal civic society'. The idea of 'lawful external relations among states' was a reference to the development of international law and institutions which would treat states as legal subjects with rights and obligations vis-à-vis other states and which would aim to create peaceful relations among them. The idea of a 'universal civic society' was a reference to the development of 'cosmopolitan law', that is, a law which would guarantee the fundamental rights of every individual, by virtue of his or her humanity, whether or not such rights were respected by individual nation-states. Kant argued that the idea of a cosmopolitan order required the institution of a league or federation of nations which would guarantee with its 'united power' the security and justice of even the smallest states as well as the basic rights of even the most downtrodden individuals. This global authority would not be a world government but a federation in which the autonomy of nations and differences of language, religion, culture, etc. would be respected. It would act only in accordance with decisions reached under the laws of the nations which composed it. Kant recognised that there was little overt sign of a cosmopolitan order of this sort coming into being, but he argued that its establishment was nonetheless a rational necessity and a moral imperative.

This, roughly speaking, was Kant's view prior to the French Revolution. In *Perpetual Peace* (1795), written ten years later, Kant acknowledged that his idea looked no less fantastical since European states related to one another ever more like individuals in a Hobbesian state of nature. They exploited newly discovered colonies as if they were 'lands without owners', and they treated foreigners coming to their lands more like enemies than guests. This view was doubtless reinforced by the collapse of cosmopolitan ideals following the French Revolution. For a brief period of time at the start of the Revolution, something that looked like a cosmopolitan policy was developed by its leaders. Decrees were passed offering French citizenship to all foreigners who had resided in France for five years and who had means of subsistence; societies and newspapers for foreigners were encouraged; the use of force against other nations was disavowed; support was given to revolutionaries from other countries to rid themselves of despotic rulers; and certain 'benefactors of humankind' (including Tom Paine, Mary Wollstonecraft, Jeremy Bentham and William Wilberforce) were awarded honorary French citizenship. This new dawn was not to last. After the launching of the so-called 'revolutionary wars', xenophobia became an active political force: foreigners were held responsible for all that went wrong – military defeats, economic difficulties, political crises, foreign clubs and newspapers were disbanded, and revolutionary terror was often directed against foreigners. Even Tom Paine, 'citizen of the world', the man who signed himself *Humanus*, was impoverished, imprisoned and then expelled (Kristeva 1991). The immediate occasion for the writing of this essay was an event that was hardly portentous for Kant's cosmopolitan idea: it was the signing of the Treaty of Basel in which Prussia agreed to hand over to France all territories west of the Rhine in exchange for being allowed to join Russia and Austria in the east in partitioning Poland. It was precisely the sort of *realpolitik* treaty that Kant condemned as a mere 'suspension of hostilities' and as the enemy of true peace.

Kant's great merit was not to surrender to the prevailing nationalistic currents. He saw an analogy between the Hobbesian 'state of nature', characterised by the war of all individuals against all individuals, and current relations between states:

> each state sees its own majesty . . . precisely in not having to submit to any external legal constraint, and the glory of its ruler consists in his power to order thousands of people to immolate themselves for a cause which does not truly concern them, while he need not himself incur any danger whatsoever.
>
> (KPW 103)

This state of affairs was, according to Kant, as insupportable in relations between states as it was in relations between individuals. Either it displayed 'the depravity of human nature without disguise', or it diminished the concept of international right by interpreting it in a 'meaningless' way as the right to go to war:

> There is only one rational way in which states coexisting with other states can emerge from the lawless condition of pure warfare. Just like individual men, they must renounce their savage and lawless freedom, adapting themselves to public coercive laws, and thus form an international state (*civitas gentium*), which would necessarily grow until it embraced all the peoples of the earth.
>
> (KPW 105)

In such an order, he wrote, standing armies would be abolished, no national debt would be incurred in connection with the external affairs of state, no state would forcibly interfere in the constitution and government of other states, and no acts of warfare would be allowed which would 'make mutual confidence impossible during a future time of peace' (KPW 125). The right of 'universal hospitality' would mean that foreigners would not to be treated with hostility when they arrived on another territory and the indigenous inhabitants of newly conquered countries would not to be 'counted as nothing' (KPW 106). Out of the 'unsocial sociability of man' there would arise a true community of nations. Once established, there could be no return to a state of nature between states but neither would the cosmopolitan order be equated with the domination of one country. A federation of free states, such as Kant envisaged, would not be an amalgamation of separate nations under a single power (France) which rules over the rest; it would not be a 'universal despotism which saps all man's energies and ends in the graveyard of freedom'; it would rather entail the separate existence of many independent states and the peace it created would be guaranteed by an equilibrium of national forces and by a vigorous rivalry between them.

Kant put forward a beautiful utopian vision of perpetual peace, but he also looked to certain underlying historical trends to support its validity and viability. First, he argued that it was a kind of realism since it recognised the fact that 'the peoples of the earth have entered in varying degrees into a universal community and it has developed to the point where a violation of rights in one part of the world is felt everywhere' (KPW 107–8). Second, he argued that it corresponded with the necessities of economic life in an age of commerce when peaceful exchange was generally more profitable than the pursuit of war. Third, he argued that it corresponded with the interests of the states themselves which had been forced to arm themselves in order to encounter other nations as armed powers but which were now burdened by the increasing costs and risks of war. Fourth, he argued that the spread of republican governments – based on the example set by one 'powerful and enlightened nation', France – meant that rulers could no longer declare war without consulting their citizens and that the 'moral maturity' of citizens was higher than in monarchical states. Kant acknowledged that even in advanced European countries people were 'civilised' mainly in respect of 'courtesies and proprieties' and remained a long way from being 'morally mature'. He also acknowledged that as long as nation-states applied their resources to violent schemes of expansion, no progress could be expected on this front since nothing more obstructs the efforts of people to 'cultivate their minds' than militarism. But behind the scenes he insisted that 'providence' or 'the plan of nature' or the 'hidden hand' of history or the 'cunning of reason' – call it what you will – was working toward a universal end: 'a perfect civil union of humankind'. Beneath the appalling violence of modern warfare, he argued that 'the germ of enlightenment always survived, developing further with each revolution, and prepared the way for a subsequent higher level of improvement'. The costs, risks and horrors of war, the growing maturity of the masses, the expansion of commerce, the interests of the rulers – all these factors were combining to impel the human species to regulate the hostility which prevailed among states. Thus the eventual achievement of a cosmopolitan order was in Kant's view guaranteed 'by no less an authority than the great artist Nature herself' (KPW 114).[2]

Over and above any such historical arguments, Kant maintained that the idea of cosmopolitan right was a postulate of practical reason – a pure idea derived from the principles of right and a duty which every human being had to observe whether or not it accorded with their inclinations:

the rights of man must be held sacred, however great a sacrifice the ruling
power may have to make . . . All politics must bend the knee before right.

(KPW 125)

The less true to immediate life the idea of a cosmopolitan order became, the more
Kant abstracted this idea from experience. This abstraction reached its highpoint
in the *Metaphysics of Morals*, where Kant argued that we have a duty to act in
accordance with the idea of perpetual peace, even if there is not the slightest
possibility of its realisation. Kant held that the proposition that there shall be
no war is a categorical imperative and that we must act as if it could really come
about, even if its fulfilment were forever to remain an 'empty piety'. Kant declared
that reason 'absolutely condemns war', and makes the achievement of peace into
an 'immediate duty'; it proclaims that 'there shall be no war', that the 'disastrous
practice of war' must end forever. This, he writes, is the 'irresistible veto' of the
'moral, practical reason within us' (KPW 164–74). The rule that we must make it
our maxim to work unceasingly toward perpetual peace, Kant writes, cannot be
derived from experience; if it were, then those who fared best under present
arrangements would set these arrangements up as a norm for others to follow. It
has to be based on metaphysics and metaphysics, for Kant, becomes all the more
important in dark times.

Kant accepted that *provisionally*, that is, prior to the attainment of perpetual
peace, wars may be justified but argued that there must be instituted certain rules
of war to limit how it is inaugurated and conducted. For example, the traditional
right of sovereigns to declare war and then to send subjects to fight on their behalf
must be abolished. This so-called 'right' was 'an obvious consequence of the right
to do what one wishes with ones own property', but it is impermissible to apply
it to the relation of rulers to citizens who are 'co-legislative members of the
state' and must therefore give their free consent through their representatives to
'every particular declaration of war' (KPW 166). Once war is declared, it must
be conducted in accord with principles that leave states with the possibility of still
entering a 'state of right'. This means that there can be no merely punitive wars,
no wars of extermination or enslavement, no means of defence which would render
subjects unfit to be citizens, no demands of compensation for the costs of war,
no ransom of prisoners, etc. Every nation has the right to have commerce with
other nations, every individual to visit other countries, and if colonisation may
be justified in terms of 'bringing culture to uncivilised peoples' and purging the
home-country of 'depraved characters', Kant argued that it cannot wash away
the stain of injustice caused by plunder, slavery or extermination.

Kant and contemporary social theory

The greatness of spirit which Kant exhibited was to stand up to the rising
nationalism of his times and defend the best traditions of enlightenment universalism. By combining a metaphysics of justice with a teleological philosophy of

history, he lifted the cosmopolitan ideal both above a dispiriting *positivism* which declares that the way things are is the way they have to be, and above a superficial *empiricism* which declares that the ways things look on the surface is the totality of what those things are. Kant did not simply abstract his cosmopolitan ideal from history, as is sometimes alleged, but rather fought against a view of history which cannot see beyond what already exists and which cannot reach for another form of life. Kant's 'abstract ideal' was his attempt to stem the growing tide of nationalism and to harmonise the principle on which the world revolution was turning, the individuality and sovereignty of the state, with the universalism of enlightened thought. The virtue of this approach is still apparent in recent attempts to apply Kant's cosmopolitan way of thinking to contemporary social theory.

For example, the idea of France as a 'nation without nationalism' put forward by Julia Kristeva (1993) in her book *Nations without Nationalism*, is a good case in point. Kristeva draws on Montesquieu to argue that the French concept of the nation permits us to live with different people while retaining our own moral codes; it expresses a paradoxical community of foreigners reconciled to their foreignness; it puts the national and the cosmopolitan in the right order – humanity first and the nation second; it forces everyone to take into account both their own values and their opposite; it constructs a polymorphic and perverse culture which returns everyone to their otherness. If it is not always able to withstand the attempts of 'disappointed souls' to restore their own battered identity by rejecting others, she presents such dogmatism as a violation or betrayal of French nationhood – or at least as a loss of republican spirit. Kristeva echoes Kant when she dissociates the idea of republicanism from nationalism. However, the idea of the French nation constructed after the Revolution also proffered a new and arguably more dangerous form of nationalism – the nationalism of a 'universal nation' whose own particular interests are held to accord with the interests of humanity as a whole. When Kant maintained that the proliferation of republicanism was the condition of cosmopolitan progress, he obscured the existence of its own global ambitions, its own attachments to war and conquest, and its own notions of a natural, fundamental and given 'Frenchness' or 'Englishness' or 'Jewishness' or 'Germanness'. It is perhaps in this very conception of a 'universal nation', a nation without nationalism whose particular interests are identical to the universal interest, that the roots of modern nationalism are most deeply and firmly embedded.[3]

At the same time as Kristeva depicts 'French' republicanism as fundamentally cosmopolitan, she associates the rise of nationalism with the 'German' roman-ticism of the likes of Johann Gottfried Herder (1744–1803) whose ideal of the *Volkgeist* is said to express a mystical concept of the nation, rooted in soil, blood and language rather than in right, law and civil society. Following Kant, Kristeva contrasts the universalistic and differentiated political community of Montesquieu's *esprit générale* with the cultural notions of national community that appear as the basis of Herder's idea of the *volk*. Herder himself, however, hardly fits the role allocated to him. His love of national peculiarities, differentiated on the basis of their languages, transcends official national boundaries and narrow chauvinism. Herder wrote: 'How the dickens did the Germans, who were ordinarily praised for showing a manly modesty . . . and appreciating the merits of foreigners, come to be so unjustly and crudely scornful of other nations, and precisely of those they have imitated, from which they have borrowed?' Herder warned that 'the historian of mankind should be careful not to choose a given people exclusively as a favourite of his, thus diminishing the importance of lineages'. Herder's polemics against 'cosmopolitan despotism' did not express an unenlightened nationalism but cautioned against the overweening pretensions of the most advanced nations. He remained true to enlightenment cosmopolitanism but unlike Kant, who maintained that to interpret history philosophically we must assume a goal to which it is progressing, Herder insisted that every period must be valued for its own sake rather than be seen simply as a precursor to later periods; and unlike Kant, who always insisted on the need for a state to coerce people into obeying the law, he criticised both Kant's view and the national principle that people need a master and that master should be the state (*KPW* 195–7).

Perhaps the real culprit as far as the intellectual rise of nationalism is concerned, should be Fichte rather than Herder. But Fichte did not cease to be an enthusiast for the French Revolution when he became an ultra-nationalist. His nationalism was implicated in, if not inseparable from, his republicanism. Fichte reveals that the diremption of nationalism and republicanism is forced. Even the Declaration of the Rights of Man and Citizen declares that 'the source of all sovereignty resides essentially in the Nation' and that there is no right that does not derive from the nation. Elie Kedouvie explores how far this mix of republicanism and nationalism, whose premise is that the self-determination of the will consists in the absorption of the individual consciousness in the whole, pervades Fichte's political writings. In *Foundations of Natural Law* (1796) he writes:

> I want to be a human being . . . it is the aim of the state fully to procure this right for man . . . Between the isolated man and the citizen, there is the same relation as between raw and organised matter . . . In an organised body each part continuously maintains the whole, and in maintaining it, maintains itself also. Similarly the citizen with regard to the state.
>
> (Kedourie 1993: 30–2)

In *The Closed Commercial State* (1800) Fichte argues that true individuality can be secured only in a state which regulates to the minutest detail the lives of citizens. In *The Characteristics of the Present Age* (1806) he writes that 'a state which constantly seeks to increase its internal strength is . . . forced to desire the gradual abolition of all favouritisms and the establishment of equal rights for all people, in order that it, the state itself, may enter upon its own true right' (Kedourie 1993:

35). In *Addresses to the German Nation* (1807–8) he rejects a state which merely maintains 'internal peace' or satisfies 'the needs of material existence', and insists that this is only preparation for 'what love of fatherland really wants to bring about, namely, that the eternal and the divine may blossom in the world' (Kedourie 1993: 39). Hegel rejected Fichte's political philosophy but saw that its significance lay in demonstrating the origins of nationalism within the modern system of right – embodied in the right of a people to determine their own future, to learn from their own experience, to create and change constitutions according to their own needs and circumstances, and to think for themselves what constitution is best.

Jürgen Habermas also follows in Kant's footsteps when he argues that nationalism once provided certain 'moral resources' for anti-imperialist struggles and for the building of welfare states, but that it can no longer meet the needs of the modern age. He endorses Kant's realist argument that there is no state any more that does not contain a mix of nationalities, cultures and traditions and that is not itself inserted in a larger international set of associations. If this was beginning to be true in Kant's time, Habermas rightly says that it is all the more true in our own global society. Habermas repudiates the central principle of all nationalism – that national identity should be converted into a principle of political cohesion and that the boundaries of the state should be identified with those of the nation – and advances in its place what he calls a 'post-nationalism'. This is conceived as a cosmopolitan consciousness that relativises one's own way of life, grants strangers with all their idiosyncrasies the same rights as oneself, enlarges tolerance, shows respect for others, and replaces the conventional law-and-order orientation based on fixed rules, unreflective duty and respect for authority with a mature, reflective, self-scrutinising attitude toward identity formation. Cosmopolitanism signifies for Habermas the capacity to evaluate moral authority critically in terms of general ethical maxims and thus to surpass the 'sociocentrism' of a traditional order. It is hard to disagree with these sentiments but Habermas's identification of post-nationalism with 'constitutional patriotism' reveals a link with nationalism that is not so easily severed. He concedes that there always lurks the danger that the universalistic elements of republicanism may be swamped by the particularistic self-assertions of one nation against another, but he insists that the 'abstract viewpoints of legality, morality and sovereignty under whose aegis bourgeois society developed' are 'best suited to the identity of world citizens, not to that of citizens of a particular state that has to maintain itself against other states' (Habermas 1991: 165). He concedes also that the principle of constitutional patriotism might be turned into a demand for unthinking obedience to the law – an 'authoritarian legalism' which Kant may have suffered from – but the more fundamental principle he finds both in Kant and in the idea of constitutional patriotism is one which distinguishes between law and right in such a way that all positive laws must be evaluated in the light of universal precepts drawn from the idea of right and embodied in the constitution.[4]

Habermas proffers a cosmopolitan post-nationalism as an antidote to the wrongs of nationalism, but the substance of post-nationalism retains an affinity to patriotism – to faith in the state or at least in its constitution. Habermas reserves the term 'nationalism' for the kind of regressive credo which unreflectively celebrates the history, destiny, culture or blood of a nation – 'a terrible, horrific regression Western Europe only surmounted . . . in 1945' (Habermas 1991: 102) From this perspective, nationalism appears as a sign of personal and political immaturity, as the enemy of the republican tradition, as that which has at all costs to be overcome. It is a conception, however, which conceals the presence of nationalism in the republican tradition itself and, even in the very presentation of 'nationalism' as its enemy (see Fine 1994b). It is this 'neo-Kantian' way of thinking – a way of thinking that is now widely disseminated in contemporary social theory – that Hegel explores, confronts and criticises, and it is in part 'our' own attachment to this way of thinking that, I think, makes his ideas on this question so difficult for us to assimilate.

Hegel's critique of Kant's cosmopolitan ideal

Nowhere does Hegel say that Kant was wrong to oppose the growth of nationalism or to provide a cosmopolitan alternative to it. On the contrary, he recognised that the elaboration of the cosmopolitan idea was one of the great achievements of Kant's political writings. Hegel's critique was based on other grounds – it had to do with the merely formal and legal conception of cosmopolitanism which Kant put forward.

One issue concerns Kant's analysis of nationalism and more especially his belief that nationalism is in principle opposed to 'genuine principles of right'. Kant viewed nationalism as a kind of enslavement to the passions, an error, something alien to the free spirit of republicanism; and as nationalism gained ascendancy in the wake of the French Revolution, he could only console himself with the thought that cosmopolitanism was the inevitable end of all this violence. Hegel argued, by contrast, that nationalism, far from being opposed to the modern republican spirit, was in fact its faithful companion. If for Kant nationalism was a sign of human immaturity, at best a stepping stone on the road to the enlightenment to come, for Hegel the roots of nationalism may be traced back to the idea of right itself. He writes:

> Patriotism in general is certainly based on truth . . . As such, it is merely a consequence of the institutions within the state, a consequence in which rationality is *actually* present, just as rationality receives its practical application through action in conformity with the state's institutions . . . This disposition is in general one of trust . . . or the consciousness that my substantial and particular interest is preserved and contained in the interest and end of another (in this case, the state) and in the latter's relation to me as an individual. As a result, this other (the state)

immediately ceases to be an other for me, and in my consciousness of this I am free.

(PR §268)

Here Hegel is not *advocating* patriotism on the ground that my interest is preserved in the interest of the state (a 'truth' that only holds within fixed limits); rather he is drawing our attention to the *rational* character of patriotism in the modern system of right:

Patriotism is frequently understood to mean only a willingness to perform *extraordinary* sacrifices and actions. But in essence, it is that disposition which in the normal conditions and circumstances of life habitually knows that the community is the substantial basis and end . . . Human beings . . . convince themselves that they possess this extraordinary patriotism in order to exempt themselves from the genuine disposition, or to excuse their lack of it.

(PR §268R)

On the one hand, Hegel declares that there is nothing wrong in 'feeling', or as he puts it in his introduction to the *Philosophy of History* 'nothing great in history can be achieved without passion'. On the other hand, patriotism in the modern sense of the term has little to do with extraordinary and passionate acts. If Kant had the insight to warn of the dangers of nationalism as a wild and destructive passion, and to construct a rational cosmopolitan opposition to it, Hegel argued that his separation of nationalism from reason, right, law and the state is artificial and forced – and not true to Kant's own analysis of right.

From the point of view of the citizen Hegel argues that when 'the state as such and its independence are at risk', all citizens are required not only to rally to the state's defence but also to sacrifice their individuality to the 'individuality of the state'. When standing armies are formed, their ethos is not so much that of individual courage and valour as that of 'sacrifice in the service of the state' and 'integration with the universal' (PR §327A). Here the individual counts merely as 'one among many'.[5] Individuality falls before the demands of discipline. Hegel argues that the ultimate end of valour in the modern state is not the attainment of individual virtue but the sovereignty of the state itself, and that for the individuals who are caught up as cogs in the military machine, this entails the 'harshness of extreme opposites':

alienation as the existence of freedom . . . supreme self-sufficiency which at the same time exists in the mechanical service of an external order . . . total obedience and renunciation of personal opinion and reasoning, and hence personal absence of mind, alongside the most intense and comprehensive presence of mind . . . the most hostile and hence most personal action against individuals along with a completely indifferent or even benevolent attitude toward them as individuals . . .

(PR §328)

In the modern army the expression of valour appears more mechanical than it does in other ways of risking one's life: it is 'not so much the deed of a particular person as that of a member of a whole . . . directed not against individual persons, but against a hostile whole in general' (PR §328R).

Hegel wishes to reveal what Kant denies: the ties that bind the republicanism he endorses to the nationalism he opposes. Hegel was clearly referring to Kant when he wrote that 'perpetual peace is often demanded as an ideal to which mankind should approximate' and that a 'league of sovereigns' is proposed to settle disputes between states (PR §324A). Hegel responds that even when modern states combine in a voluntary federation, the outcome does not necessarily have anything to do with peace. The nexus between modern states and war is not so easily broken. Hegel writes:

> Kant proposed a league of sovereigns to settle disputes between states, and the Holy Alliance was meant to be an institution more or less of this kind. But the state is an individual and negation is an essential component of individuality. Thus even if a number of states join together as a family, this league in its individuality must generate opposition and create an enemy.
>
> (PR §324A)

From the point of view of the state Hegel argues that the benefits and costs of war are not so easily counted as Kant assumes:

> Successful wars have averted internal unrest and consolidated the internal power of the state . . . Not only do peoples emerge from wars with added strength, but nations troubled by civil dissension gain internal peace as a result of wars with their external enemies. Admittedly, war makes property insecure, but this *real* insecurity is no more than a necessary movement . . . wars will occur whenever they lie in the nature of the case. . . . In peace, the bounds of civil life are extended, all its spheres become firmly established, and in the long run people become stuck in their ways. Their particular characteristics become increasingly rigid and ossified . . . the result is death . . .
>
> (PR §§324R and A)

Hegel's pronouncements about the 'ethical' significance of war and peace are usually interpreted as an advocacy of war and distrust of peace, and judged accordingly. They are read as if they were statements of Hegel's belief that

142

unrelieved peace is bad, because it leads to social stagnation, and that war is good because it stirs things up and injects health into the body politic; or that peace fosters individualism and exclusive concern with private enrichment and security, while war has the advantage of putting a higher aim before us – the good of the community as a whole (see e.g. Walsh 1998: 50–1). But if we treat Hegel's own opinion with the indifference he demands, we find in the *Philosophy of Right* not an advocacy of war but the beginnings – perhaps no more – of a far more interesting analysis of the relation between war and the modern state.

Hegel points out that in the modern state, even as Kant conceives it, responsibility for the command of the armed forces and for making war and peace lies with the 'sovereign' – the supreme commander. Normally the consent of parliament or other representative institutions is required, particularly in relation to the provision of financial means, and Hegel observes that in England no unpopular war could be waged. However, he argues that, far from the consent of the people being a guarantee against rash and intemperate wars, whole nations are often more prone to enthusiasms and more subject to passion than their rulers. Hegel illustrates the point with the observation that in England 'the entire people has pressed for war on several occasions and has in a sense compelled the ministers to wage it . . . Only later when emotions had cooled, did people realise that the war was useless and unnecessary and that it had been entered into without calculating the cost' (*PR* §329A). Whatever the truth of this concrete historical example – Hegel was referring to the wars of coalition waged against France 'by' William Pitt the Younger – the point remains that 'republicanism' may be no less bellicose than other forms of rule. The question is at least open and subject to further inquiry.

In any event, if perpetual peace is an abstract ideal which Kant derives from the postulates of practical reason, republicanism introduces another principle – namely that the people themselves should determine what the relation of their state to other states ought to be. They may determine that perpetual peace is of supreme value, but they may not – particularly if the condition which perpetual peace consolidates is seen as an unjust condition or one which confirms an inequality in the international division of power. Kant argues that 'reason . . . absolutely condemns war' and sees the achievement of peace as an 'immediate duty' (*KPW* 104), but for Kant this is ultimately not an empirical judgement based on the horrors of war, or on the burdens of debt to which it gives rise, or on the loss of liberty that ensues for the vanquished, or on the moral decline that ensues for the victors. Perpetual peace is presented rather as an *a priori* deduction from the postulates of practical reason. First, in its form this categorical imperative is lacking inasmuch as it has no deliberative dimension in its own constitution; Kant instructs rulers and people in what they must do but does not involve them in the process of deciding what must or must not be done. His idea of reason takes the form of legislative prescriptions that ultimately pay no heed to the lessons of experience or to the consequences of following a certain course of action. Second, in its content Kant's categorical imperative is also lacking because it fails to relativise perpetual peace in relation to other demands of 'international right'. He takes it as read that the primary evil is war and that the primary goal is peace, and that the other issues which are at stake in people's lives – questions of justice, poverty, famine, inequality, etc. – are subordinate to that of perpetual peace. It tells people that perpetual peace *must* be their highest priority and it treats the positing of alternative ends as a sign of unreason. In short, the identification of cosmopolitanism with perpetual peace offers a restrictive and ultimately rather conservative view of what is involved in the development of a cosmopolitan consciousness.

Kant treats states as if they are private persons who relate to one another on the basis of private right and morality. But the question Hegel raises is in what sense are states 'like' private individuals. He argues that the position of private persons in relation to civil society – that they are subject to the authority of a court which establishes and implements what is right in itself – does not apply in the same way to states. When it comes to relations between states, there is no power present to decide what is right in itself or to actualise such decisions. Every state is a sovereign and independent entity in relation to other states, and the legitimacy of the state is treated as a purely internal matter based on the principle that no state should interfere in the internal affairs of another. However, the state cannot be a subject of right without relations to other states, any more than an individual can be a person without a relation to other individuals. It is essential, therefore, that its legitimacy is *supplemented* by recognition on the part of other states. But 'this recognition requires a guarantee that the state will likewise recognise those other states which are supposed to recognise it', i.e. that it will respect their independence. Accordingly, Hegel adds, 'these other states cannot be indifferent to its internal affairs' (*PR* §331R). Relations between states cannot in fact be based on absolute and exclusive notions of sovereignty or on the principle of mutual indifference to what rulers do to the people who live under their jurisdiction. Relations between states typically take the form of a contract or treaty and the basic principle of international law is that contracts and treaties must be observed. But since the sovereignty of states is the principle governing their mutual relations, they exist in a state of nature in relation to one another and their rights are actualised not in a universal will with constitutional powers over them, but in their own particular wills. There is in other words no 'praetor' to adjudicate between them. At most there are arbitrators or mediators. On to this situation Kant sought to impose the idea of a federation or league of nations which would settle all disputes and resolves all disagreements without the use of force, but Hegel argues that such a federation presupposes an agreement between states which is dependent on their particular sovereign wills; if no agreement is reached, then conflict between states may only be settled by war – and there is plenty of scope for a particular state to feel that it has suffered an injury, that this injury represents a danger from another state, and that its own welfare is at stake. In short, Hegel argues that, by identifying political states with private individuals, Kant downplays the actual nexus between war and the modern state.

If war does break out, a condition which Hegel describes as one of 'rightlessness, force and contingency', the force of international law is to declare that states must continue to recognise one another reciprocally as states: they must wage war in such a way as to preserve the possibility of peace; they must fight in a humane manner; individuals must not confront one another in hatred; they must not wage war on internal civic institutions or on family life or on private individuals. Hegel was not, of course, opposed to such laws; he was not in favour of some military free-for-all. But when Kant spoke of an opposition between morality and politics and demanded that the latter conform to the former, Hegel described this confusion of the state and the individual as a superficial notion. He argued further that the attachment of the state to the moral point of view might introduce into wars between states the fanaticism that is characteristic of the moral point of view in general when it is turned into the supreme value, and lead to the portrayal of the enemy as an 'inhuman monster'. As Arendt was later to confirm on the basis of experience, Hegel's concerns were well grounded.

Methodologically, Kant could not bridge the gap between a philosophy of history with the connotation of natural necessity and a metaphysics of morals with the connotation of *a priori* right. Substantively, he could not bridge the gap between absolute and exclusive national sovereignty on the one hand and a cosmopolitan law which offers recognition to the rights of subjects persecuted by their own rulers on the other, for the latter has to transgress any principle of non-interference in the internal affairs of another nation. Historically, Kant obfuscated relations between modern states when he wrote that they were 'naturally' leading to a universal cosmopolitan end. Kant's faith, that 'the germ of enlightenment always survived, developing further with each revolution and preparing the way for a subsequent higher level of improvement', indicated that he kept his eyes firmly on the future. In this philosophy of history, progress toward perpetual peace could be discerned taking its course behind the backs or over the heads of the actors themselves, and Kant maintained that the eventual achievement of a cosmopolitan order was guaranteed 'by no less an authority than the great artist Nature herself'. This 'hidden plan of nature' may have offered some consolation for the organised political violence of existing states, but it also served according to Hegel to give meaning and purpose to the evils of war.

Doubtless, Kant could not foresee the abuse to which this philosophy of history was to be put: to justify political violence on the ground that violence is required to achieve a new world order of peace – popularised in the hoary old chestnut beloved of totalitarian movements 'you cannot make an omelette without breaking eggs'. Nor could he envisage the incredible depths of inhumanity to which humanity from time to time sinks – in the extermination of indigenous peoples or of innocent civilians deemed to belong to the wrong race or class. He could not appreciate the thinness of all future-oriented consolations after events like Auschwitz and the Gulag have happened. At its limit, in the case of total destruction caused by nuclear war, Kant could not be expected to see that the term 'perpetual peace' might have another, more eerie meaning when used to refer to the death not only of the idea of humanity but of humanity itself. Perpetual peace is in this case what we have when we die. Kant's philosophy of history offers the consolation of philosophy for the suffering of the present-day world by looking to a future world. He says: we know terrible things are taking place but the good news is that the laws of history are bringing them to an end. Keep your eyes on what is to come, for the future is beautiful. When the worst that can happen is that people are killed in war, perhaps this perspective makes a certain sense; but when what is at issue is the fate of humankind itself, what possible good can be distilled from the fury of destruction? By its own dialectic Kant's optimism is only maintained by converting unspeakable horror into the march of reason.

The world's court of judgement

We find in Hegel's critique of Kant an injunction we also find in Arendt: look horror in the face. Hegel's 'angel of history' is different from Kant's and perhaps more like that immortalised by Walter Benjamin in his discussion of Klee's painting, the *Angelus Novus*:

> His face is turned toward the past. Where we perceive a chain of events, he sees one single catastrophe which keeps piling wreckage upon wreckage, and hurls it in front of his feet. The angel would like to stay, awaken the dead, and make whole what has been smashed. But a storm is blowing from Paradise; it has got caught in his wings with such violence that the angel can no longer close them. This storm irresistibly propels him into the future to which his back is turned, while the pile of debris before him grows skyward. This storm is what we call progress.
>
> (Benjamin 1968: 257–8)

When Kant advances cosmopolitanism as an abstract ideal, his historicism also leaves us with a sadness whose source is not at first easy to discern. Benjamin puts it thus:

> The nature of this sadness stands out more clearly if one asks with whom the adherents of historicism actually empathise. The answer is inevitable: with the victor . . . empathy with the victor invariably benefits the rulers . . . Whoever has emerged victorious participates to this day in the triumphal procession in which the present rulers step over those who are lying prostate. According to traditional practice, the spoils are carried along in the procession. They are called cultural treasures . . . they owe their existence not only to the efforts of the great minds and talents who have created them but also to the anonymous toil of their contemporaries. There is no document of civilisation which is not at the same time a document of barbarism . . .
>
> (Benjamin 1968: 256)

Is Kant's perpetual peace the final spoils of victory? Is it the sign of a triumphal procession of those who have emerged victorious? This is certainly not the whole story, but it is part.

At the end of his essay 'Is the human race continually improving?', the second part of 'The Contest of the Faculties' (1798), Kant states that humanity is 'by its very nature capable of constant progress and improvement without forfeiting its strength' (*KPW* 189). The cosmopolitan ideal is not conceived by him as a fixed 'end of history' but as a constant progress and improvement, presumably without end. Kant makes this case more explicitly in *The Critique of Pure Reason* where he states that 'no one can or ought to decide what the highest degree may be at which mankind may have to stop progressing, and hence how wide a gap may still of necessity remain between the idea and its execution. For this will depend on freedom, which can transcend any limit we care to impose' (*KPW* 191). For Kant, however, this constant process was always bound to the condition that it must be based on 'genuine principles of right' and accordingly on the institutional framework which these principles of right require for their actualisation. Within his promise of a 'universal history', the forms of right and law always remain as categorical imperatives to be worked upon and within – but not as forms which can in any sense be 'overcome'.

Hegel argues that Kant's inadequacy lies in his abstraction of right from need. He enjoins us not to forget that 'right comes into existence only because it is useful in relation to needs', even if we cannot stay 'confined to the merely sensuous realm' (*PR* §209A). Kant was not wrong to advance a cosmopolitan ideal nor did Hegel think he was wrong. Hegel fully acknowledged that those like Kant who have proclaimed the perfectibility of the human race have 'some inkling of the nature of spirit . . . to assume a higher shape than that in which its being originally consisted'; and that for those who reject this thought, spirit remains an 'empty word' and history remains a 'superficial play of contingent . . . human aspirations and passions' (*PR* §343R). Kant was wrong only to 'adopt a fixed position – for example, cosmopolitanism – in opposition to the concrete life of the state' (*PR* §209R). Hegel was no less committed to the 'universal' than was Kant. He writes, for example:

> it is part of education . . . that I am apprehended as a *universal* person, in which respect *all* are identical. *A human being counts as such because he is a human being*, not because he is a Jew, Catholic, Protestant, German, Italian, etc. . . . this consciousness is of infinite importance . . .
>
> (*PR* §209)

But Hegel wishes to show that the idea of cosmopolitan right contains its own equivocations: it is *not a resolution* of all prior antagonisms but a *sublation of contradictions* present within the less developed forms of right. As such, it cannot help but reproduce the violence which it also transcends. This is not to invalidate the cosmopolitan idea but it is to recognise that its translation into a *pure idea* of reason or into an *end of history* takes it out of the world of human conflict, conquest, loss and mourning of which it is part.

Cosmopolitan right is a form and shape of right within the system of right as a whole; it is one element of the whole – a '*finite* spirit in world history' as the old man put it. Hegel points the way not to any denunciation of cosmopolitanism but rather to the avoidance of a premature celebration of cosmopolitanism as justice. Hegel offers a conceptualisation of justice that lies in its refusal to turn *any* form of right into the absolute, a recognition of the perplexities of a universal law which has to recognise the particularity of concrete and singular needs, an affirmation of a sense of incompletion which opens out to the future *without* rationalising the past, an acknowledgement of the *impossibility* of making whole what has been smashed, and an understanding of the 'ceaseless turmoil of . . . passions, interests, ends, talents and virtues, violence, wrongdoing and vices' which mark what we call political life (*PR* §340).[6] It is through this dialectic, Hegel writes, that the

> *spirit of the world* produces itself in its freedom from all limits, and it is this spirit which exercises its right – which is the highest right of all – over finite spirits in *world history* as the *world's court of judgement*.
>
> (*PR* §340)

There is no form of *right* that is absolute – only world history. Kant posits the idea of cosmopolitanism conceptually and legally – as an abstract ideal. His utopian universalism attempts in an eschatological way to reconcile all conflicts through the establishment of a new law and institution. But this 'easy way' (Rose 1995: 115) forgets the limitations inherent in any such juridical exercise.[7] Hegel's 'ethical' philosophy takes a more difficult way: it refuses to make any leap of faith – be it faith in the state or faith in the cosmopolis; it refuses to stop time by predetermining the structure of what has not yet come into being; it refuses to establish any political code premised on unquestionable assumptions of what is right; it warns against philosophy's 'pride of *Sollen*' – against any imposition by philosophy of abstract ideals or imaginary communities or progressive narratives of history; it instructs us to break from the idea of ultimate breakage and acknowledges a constant reconfiguration of elements; it overcomes the limits of 'what is' in a way that confronts the indeterminate messiness, risk and violence of political action. Ethical philosophy necessarily puts reason before power as the author of judgement in world history. Hegel puts it thus:

> it is not just the *power* of spirit which passes judgement in world history – i.e. it is not the abstract and irrational necessity of a blind fate. On the contrary, since spirit in and for itself is *reason*, and since the being-for-itself of reason in spirit is *knowledge*, world history is the necessary development, from the *concept* of the freedom of spirit alone, of the *moments* of reason and hence of spirit's self consciousness and freedom.
>
> (*PR* §342)

This is the problematique of a politics which we might call 'critical cosmopolitanism'. It was Arendt above all who recognised that its development remains the most important political task of our age. And it is to her critical cosmopolitanism that I now turn.

Notes

1 The key essays are collected in Reiss (1991). They are 'Idea for a universal history from a cosmopolitan point of view' (1785), 'Reviews of Herder's *Ideas on the Philosophy of the History of Mankind*' (1784–85); 'On the common saying "This may be true in theory but it does not apply in practice"' (1793), 'Toward perpetual peace: a philosophical sketch' (published 1795, revised 1796), 'International Right' in *The Metaphysics of Morals* (1797); 'The contest of the faculties' (1798).

2 In the section on 'International Right' in the Metaphysics of Justice Kant reiterated his well-tested Hobbesian analogy. In existing external relationships with one another states act like lawless savages in a condition 'devoid of right' – a condition of war. States are bound, however, to abandon such a condition and establish a federation of peoples in accordance with the idea of an original social contract, so that they will protect one another against external aggression while refraining from interference in one another's internal disagreements. This federation must not embody a sovereign power as in a civil constitution but only a partnership or confederation of independent states which can be terminated at any time.

3 If the concept of *la patrie* inaugurated the modern conception of the 'universal nation', Russia arguably proved to be its greatest twentieth-century heir when its rulers identified the particular interests of Russia with the universal interests of the proletariat throughout the world, and then identified the universal interests of the proletariat with the interests of humanity. Thus for every Communist militant, from South Africa to England, the first duty was always to Russia and only through Russia to the idea of humanity. This is why strategic 'lines' and 'periods' could change with such temporal suddenness and worldwide uniformity.

4 In theory Habermas offers a somewhat restrictive justification of civil disobedience in terms of 'valid constitutional principles'. In *Between Facts and Norms* he writes: 'These acts of nonviolent symbolic rule violation are meant as expressions of protest against binding decisions that, their legality notwithstanding, the actors consider illegitimate in the light of valid constitutional principles . . . The justification of civil disobedience relies on a *dynamic understanding* of the constitution as an unfinished project . . . the constitutional state does not represent a finished structure but a . . . fallible and revisable enterprise whose purpose is to realise the system of rights *anew* in changing circumstances, that is, to interpret the system of rights better, to institutionalise it more appropriately, and to draw out its contents more radically. This is the perspective of citizens who are actively engaged in realising the system of rights' (Habermas 1997: 383–4, emphasis in original). Any modern constitution is conceived as fallible and revisable, that is, as susceptible to augmentation, but the status of moral justifications which are not valid constitutional principles (for example, Habermas's own justification of the civil disobedience practised by nuclear protesters) remains unclear.

5 Hegel adds by way of illustration: 'In India, five hundred men defeated twenty thousand who were not cowards, but who simply lacked the disposition to act in close association with others' (*PR* §327A).

6 It seems to me that Hegel's philosophy of right contains the deconstructive moment within its dialectic: between the generality of the legal norm and the uniqueness of

interpretation in any single case; between the 'madness' and 'violence' involved at the moment of decision and the constant deferment of the problem of justice; between the idea that 'justice exceeds law and calculation' and that it 'should not serve as an alibi for staying out of juridico-political battles' (Derrida 1992: 28). The unstable relation of justice to law leads Derrida on the one hand to denounce the irresponsibility of prematurely declaring our own justice, for justice like democracy is always 'to come', and on the other hand to make the statement that 'deconstruction is justice'! Perhaps Richard Beardsworth inadvertently points to the limit of Derrida's deconstruction when he describes it as a 'transformation of the "formal" criteria of democracy . . . which avoids at the same time a "substantial" understanding of justice' (Beardsworth 1998: 48). For Hegel this avoidance is precisely the problem. In the end 'everything is substance'.

7 In his book *Cosmopolis* Danilo Zolo writes that 'if it is recognised that within the international legal order the legal equality of states is nothing more than a myth, and if it is admitted that *de facto* situations and the logic of power cannot fail to influence the normative structure of international institutions . . . then even cosmopolitanism risks appearing no better than wishful thinking, an escape into the pure world of what ought to be' (Zolo 1997: 102).

9

ARENDT'S CRITICAL COSMOPOLITANISM

Arendt and the Nuremberg debates

The juridical concept of 'crimes against humanity' was devised in 1945 as a supplement to crimes already existing under international law, 'war crimes' and 'crimes against peace', and was instituted by the Allied Powers at Nuremberg to address the atrocities committed by the Nazis against Jews, Roma and many other innocent civilians. To Arendt's friend, Karl Jaspers, the institution of 'crimes against humanity' marked the dawn of a new cosmopolitan order in which individuals, as well as states, would be held accountable to international law. Individuals acting within the legality of their own state would be tried as criminals. Service to the state would no longer exonerate any official in any bureaucracy or any scientist in any laboratory from his or her responsibilities as a thinking individual. Subordinates would no longer be able to hide behind the excuse of 'only obeying orders' and superordinates who sit behind desks planning atrocities would be as guilty as those who participated directly in their execution. Atrocities committed against one set of people (be it Jews or Poles or Roma) would henceforth be seen an affront not only to these people but to humanity as a whole.[1]

In *The Question of German Guilt* (Jaspers 1961, written 1945) Jaspers offered the quintessential cosmopolitan justification of the trials. He stressed the importance of prosecuting war criminals as an element in the more general re-evaluation of responsibility after Nazism. He argued that the trials provided a rational alternative to all collective forms of punishment, undercut a principle of national sovereignty which put a 'halo around heads of states' and made them inviolable to prosecution, extended the notion of guilt beyond that of mere war guilt, and made a necessary and valid distinction between those who were criminally guilty and the indefinite number of others capable of co-operating under orders. The treatment of mass murderers as mere *criminals* represented them, as he put it, in 'their total banality' and deprived them of that 'streak of satanic greatness' with which they might otherwise have been endowed. Jaspers resolutely rejected the various apologies and excuses invoked by the Nazi defendants as amounting only to an evasion of responsibility.

Jaspers addressed the question of German guilt as part of a larger investigation into a new organisation of human responsibilities: a political responsibility for how we are ruled, a moral responsibility for confronting the countless tiny acts of indifference' which make injustice possible, and a metaphysical responsibility for all 'the crimes that are committed in their presence and with their knowledge'. Jaspers's aim was not only to reorient the 'pariah nation' (Germany) back to the tradition of western humanism but to renew the tradition of western humanism itself. He acknowledged the legal defects of Nuremberg but what was more important was how it looked to the future. He described it as 'a feeble, ambiguous harbinger of a world order the need of which mankind is beginning to feel' and maintained that

> the trial as a new attempt on behalf of order in the world does not grow meaningless if it cannot yet be based on a legal world order but must still halt within a political framework . . . The world order is not at hand . . . but it has come to seem possible to thinking humanity; it has appeared on the horizon as a barely perceptible dawn.
>
> (Jaspers 1961: 60)[2]

At Nuremberg Jaspers saw the spirit of Kant and the eighteenth-century vision of cosmopolitan law coming to life. Kant had written that at the dawn of modernity 'each state saw its own majesty in not having to submit to any external legal constraint and the glory of its ruler consisted in his power to order the death of thousands of its people for causes which did not at all concern them' (Kant 1991: 103). Kant's hope and expectation, however, was that states would eventually abandon this 'lawless state of savagery' and introduce in its place a cosmopolitan system of justice based on the recognition that the peoples of the earth have 'entered in varying degrees into a universal community where a violation of rights in one part of the world is felt everywhere' (Kant 1991: 104–5). To Jaspers it seemed that the institution of crimes against humanity at Nuremberg transformed the idea of 'humanity' from a regulative idea into a substantial reality.

Arendt also welcomed the Nuremberg trials but both in her letters to Jaspers and in her own work she stressed the inadequacy of a merely legal response to the phenomenon in question. She emphasised the difference between mere criminality and mass extermination – between 'a man who sets out to murder his old aunt' and 'people who without considering the economic usefulness of their actions at all . . . built factories to produce corpses' (A&J 69). There was something about the latter which seemed to 'explode the limits of the law and shatter all legal systems' (A&J 54). She pointed to the disproportion between the few Nazis who were prosecuted and punished at Nuremberg and the vast number of perpetrators who committed the deeds in question. When the machinery of mass murder forces practically everyone in a society to participate in one way or another, 'the human need for justice can find no satisfactory reply to the total mobilisation of a people to that purpose. Where all are guilty, nobody in the last analysis can be judged' (EU 126). The effacement of visible signs of distinction between the guilty and the innocent – through a policy of making each individual dependent upon committing crimes or being complicit in them or at least appearing to be complicit – seemed to mark the limit of legal responsibility. And what role could the law have when perpetrators present themselves as if they were cogs in the mass murder machine and claim they do the job of killing 'only in a professional capacity, without passion or ill will'. For this 'modern type of man', conventional notions of legal responsibility seemed to have little purchase. In *Origins* she summed up her doubts thus: 'We attempt to classify as criminal a thing which, as we all feel, no such category was ever intended to cover. What meaning has the concept of murder when we are confronted with the mass production of corpses'? (*OT* 441).

Schmitt and Heidegger

The specific nature of Arendt's doubts may be illuminated by contrasting them with the objections to the trials raised by the Nazi defendants and their representatives at Nuremberg in their effort to challenge the proceedings. This attitude was thematised by the political theorist (and one-time Nuremberg detainee), Carl Schmitt, when he wrote of the trials:

> Genocide, the murder of peoples – a touching concept; I have experienced an example of it myself: the extermination of the German–Prussian civil service in 1945 . . . There are crimes against humanity and crimes for humanity. Crimes against humanity are committed by the Germans. Crimes for humanity are perpetrated on the Germans.
>
> (quoted in Habermas 1998)[3]

Schmitt employed the contemptuous formula 'Humanity, Bestiality' to designate what he saw as the sheer hypocrisy of cosmopolitan law. He argued either that 'humanity as such cannot wage war' because 'the concept of humanity excludes the concept of the enemy' (Schmitt 1996: 74), or if it does wage war, then 'humanity' turns the enemy into 'an inhuman monster that must not only be repulsed but must be totally annihilated' (Schmitt 1996: 36; cited in Habermas 1998: 198). The voice of Schmitt was later echoed in a comment made by Adolf Eichmann's lawyer concerning 'acts for which you are decorated if you win and go to the gallows if you lose'.

The trials themselves were faulted. The court was not international but rather enacted by the four victorious military powers. Its laws were applied only to the vanquished and all crimes committed by the victors were in principle excluded. The concept of 'crimes against humanity' may have violated the legal principle of specificity by containing vague phrases like 'other inhumane acts'. The principle of generality was arguably violated by the fact that they excluded crimes committed by the allies, and the principle of *nullum crimen sine lege* (no crime without law) was arguably violated by applying the retrospective application of the new offence to crimes committed before the law was passed. The actions designated as crimes against humanity were represented by defendants as normal routines of international politics as evidenced in the behaviour of the imperial powers to subject peoples in the colonies.[4] Arendt recognised that these arguments were self-serving and were certainly 'evasions of responsibility', as Jaspers put it, but they also revealed a measure of truth about the limits of this legal process.

A similar attitude to that taken by Schmitt was evident in the responses of the one-time Nazi philosopher, Martin Heidegger. Called upon by Herbert Marcuse to disavow the Nazi regime, Heidegger resorted to a version of the 'normalisation' defence, i.e. what the Nazis did to the Jews was no worse than what the Russians did to the Germans.[5] In a lecture entitled 'Con-figuration' he stretched the normalisation argument further when he stated that the 'manufacture of corpses in gas chambers and extermination camps' deserves no more attention than other practices of modern technology, like 'a motorised food-industry', and are 'in essence – the same'.[6] In a lecture entitled 'The Danger' he compared 'those who were liquidated inconspicuously in extermination camps' with 'the millions of impoverished people right now . . . perishing from hunger in China' and distinguished only between those who are 'capable of enduring death in its essence' and those who merely 'succumb' and are 'done in'.

Such responses were doubtless deliberately provocative, but Heidegger's Letter on Humanism, written in the fall of 1946, took the critique of humanism beyond these rather narrow limits. Heidegger's basic argument was that the consciousness that establishes 'humanity' as a standard against which to measure the violence of the age, conceals the fact that the principle of humanity allows us in the first place to elevate the human as the master of all things and cast the Other as inhuman, subhuman or a threat to humanity. According to Heidegger, Nazism proved to be a catastrophe only because it lost sight of its original opposition to western humanism – that it does not set 'the humanitas of man high enough' – and turned it instead into a 'defence of the inhuman'. He argued that the regression of Nazism made it all the more urgent 'to think the humanity of homo humanus . . . without humanism' (Heidegger 1976: 254; cited in Leaman 1997: 57–69). He said that he was not against laws that 'secure the existing bonds even if they hold human beings together ever so tenuously', and that he did not deny the need for 'rules . . . fabricated by human reason'; but his emphasis was on something more essential than any positive laws (Heidegger 1976: 255, 262; cited in Leaman 1997: 57–69). The 'higher call' was to overcome the will to power that marks the humanist tradition and assume in its place an attitude of 'guardianship and care in the clearing of Being'. We must learn to 'let beings be' and to 'will not to will' (Heidegger 1976: 250; cited in Leaman 1997: 57–69).[7]

Arendt saw in Schmitt and Heidegger's anti-humanism an echo of the 'spiritless radicalism' which had fed into totalitarian movements in the first place. Both arguments were in that same sense 'justified' and both illuminate the ground on which the attack on the idea of humanity was based. For Arendt, however, they were evidence that the legal category of 'crimes against humanity' was well chosen inasmuch as it caught the nature of the totalitarian project once the latter was stripped of its 'pretexts'.

The Eichmann trial

Arendt re-engaged with these issues in her account of the trial of Adolf Eichmann, *Eichmann in Jerusalem* (1960). By this time the cosmopolitan precedent set by Nuremberg had largely evaporated, international consensus had collapsed, cold war prevailed and the promise of a new cosmopolitan order was deeply distorted by nationalistic and other power-political ends. It is not true, as some critics have claimed, that Arendt was opposed to the trial. On the contrary, she upheld both its legitimacy and necessity in some hard-headed responses to the reservations now put forward by Karl Jaspers. She argued that the fact that Eichmann had been illegally kidnapped from Argentina was justifiable given that he had been indicted at Nuremberg, charged with crimes against humanity and was hiding in a country with such a bad record of extradition as Argentina. She argued that the use of an Israeli national court was justified in the absence of an international criminal court or a successor court to Nuremberg and in light of the fact that Eichmann's job was to organise the transportation of Jews. She argued that the contention that there were more important issues at stake than the trial of a single individual – the political character of modern anti-Semitism, the origins of totalitarianism, the nature of evil, etc. – was no reason not to seek justice in this particular case (A&J 419). She showed no compunction about the imposition of the death penalty: 'no member of the human race can be expected to want to share the earth', she wrote, with a man who 'supported and carried out a policy of not wanting to share the earth with the Jewish people and the people of a number of other nations'.[8] She also acknowledged the positive political effects generated by the trial: not least, after years of relative silence in the West, it publicised the facts of the Final Solution and opened it up as a field of moral, political and historical discussion. Indeed, most of Arendt's own text was devoted to a detailed account of what actually happened in the course of the 'Final Solution'.

The trial was for Arendt living proof that the idea of 'humanity' could once again be made *concrete*. However, she attacked what she saw as deformations of its cosmopolitan promise. She criticised the prosecution for its deference to Israeli nationalist aims, giving support to the contention that a Jew could be safe only in Israel, attempting to camouflage the existence of ethnic distinctions in Israeli society, attempting to conceal or downplay the co-operation of some Jewish leaders in the execution of the Final Solution, and most of all for its failure to understand that 'the supreme crime it was confronted with, the physical extermination of the Jewish people, was a crime against humanity perpetrated on the body of the Jewish people, and that only the choice of victims, not the nature of the crime, could be derived from the long history of Jew-hatred and antisemitism'. Arendt expressed a growing sense of lost opportunity: that the precedent set by Nuremberg was being ignored in the era of the cold war, that the universalistic import of crimes against humanity was being corralled back into a nationalist frame of reference, and that the ethical significance of totalitarian terror was being sacrificed to a moral division of the world between them and us, the evil and the good, which would serve only as an index of a world purged of all political profundity. Writing about the later trial of the 'butcher of Lyons', Klaus Barbie, Alain Finkielkraut captures the spirit of Arendt's criticisms when he speaks of the tendency to reduce the Holocaust to 'an exultant face to face confrontation between Innocence and the Unspeakable Beast' and to rewrite it as a 'meaningless idiot's tale' which signifies nothing and leaves only a 'gaping black hole' (Finkielkraut 1992: 60–1).[9]

It is well known that Arendt's criticisms provoked furious counter-criticism. Some of it was directed against her judgement that the actions of the Jewish leadership in the occupied countries represented 'the darkest chapter of the whole dark story' and was evidence of 'the totality of the moral collapse the Nazis caused in respectable European society' (*EJ* 117 and 125). Gershom Scholem denied the right to make such judgements on the ground that those who collaborated were 'compelled to make terrible decisions in circumstances that we cannot even begin to reproduce or reconstruct. I do not know whether they were right or wrong. Nor do I presume to judge. I was not there' (quoted in Beiner 1989: 99). To this criticism Arendt replied: '*we shall only come to terms with this past if we begin to judge* and to be frank about it' (quoted in Beiner 1989: 100). Elsewhere she writes: 'The argument that we cannot judge if were not present and involved ourselves seems to convince everyone . . . although if it were true, neither the administration of justice nor the writing of history would ever be possible' (*EJ* 295). The key point concerns less Arendt's particular judgement on Jewish leaders in the ghettos – they responded perhaps in ways that are not dissimilar to the responses of any other conservative leadership confronted by overwhelming force – but in the requirement that a cosmopolitan politics face up to the actions and responsibilities of the victims as well as the victimisers.[10]

The area that provoked the most criticism concerned Arendt's reflections on the question of evil. Arendt was accused of trivialising the Holocaust through the use of the term 'banality of evil' to characterise Eichmann's offence. Letters sent by Gershom Scholem offer a mild example of the diatribes levelled against her. He writes:

> your thesis concerning the 'banality of evil' . . . underlies your entire argument. This new thesis strikes me as a catchword; it does not impress me, certainly, as the product of profound analysis – an analysis such as you give us so convincingly . . . in your book on totalitarianism. At that time you had not yet made your discovery . . . that evil is banal. Of that 'radical evil' to which your then analysis bore such eloquent and erudite witness, nothing remains but this slogan . . .
>
> (Arendt 1978a: 245)

Arendt replied to Scholem thus:

> You are quite right: I changed my mind and do no longer speak of 'radical evil' . . . It is indeed my opinion now that evil is never 'radical', that it

is only extreme, and that it possesses neither depth nor any demonic dimension. It can overgrow and lay waste the whole world precisely because it spreads like a fungus on the surface. It is 'thought-defying' . . . because thought tries to reach some depth, to go to the roots, and the moment it concerns itself with evil, it is frustrated because there is nothing. That is its 'banality'. Only the good has depth and can be radical.

(Arendt 1978a: 250–1; cited in Bernstein 1996: 138)

The charge laid against Arendt, that her use of the term 'banality of evil' trivialised the Final Solution, was not true. Nothing could be plainer than that Arendt, no less than her critics, treated the Final Solution not just as 'another event' but as *the pivotal event* that separated the nineteenth century from the twentieth (*BPF* ch. 1 *passim*). It was for her the sign that something new had arisen in the world and that new concepts and categories were required to grasp it.

Radical and banal evil

I can see three reasons for the appropriateness of her use of the term 'banality of evil' in this context. First, at an empirical level she saw it as an accurate representation of Eichmann's own 'thoughtlessness' as a representative figure. His case seemed to reveal that the perpetrators of totalitarian terror can be pedestrian individuals, incapable of critical reflection or serious moral judgement, stuck in everyday concerns. She saw no evidence that Eichmann was even a convinced antisemite or that he had any motives beyond looking out for the advancement of his own career. One lesson Arendt took from Jerusalem was that such 'remoteness from reality' as Eichmann displayed can 'wreak more havoc than all the evil instincts taken together' (*EJ* 288). Although his deeds were 'monstrous', the doer was 'ordinary, commonplace, and neither demonic nor monstrous' (*EJ* 3–4). Arendt's judgement was based mainly on Eichmann's words and actions in the courtroom and on the evidence provided in the court. Of course, it is subject to modification in the light of further evidence concerning his conduct at the time he had power.

Second, Arendt used the term 'banality of evil' to highlight the fact that leading perpetrators of terror could be 'men like ourselves' who demonstrate only what *ordinary* human beings are capable of under extreme circumstances. It was a rejoinder to the image of a Nazi monster that has nothing to do with people like ourselves and to ways of thinking which paint the world in terms of a dichotomy between our own absolute innocence on the one hand and the unspeakable Nazi beast on the other. It expresses a refusal in other words to dehumanise the perpetrators as a response to their dehumanisation of their victims.[11]

Third, and in my view most importantly, Arendt had written in *Origins of Totalitarianism* of the '*appearance* of radical evil' (my emphasis) because the wrong committed against Jews and other victims of the Holocaust seemed lacking in any recognisable human motive. She sought to express the fact that 'evil has proved to be more radical than expected' and that our ways of thinking are inadequate in relation to the phenomenon itself. She wrote that

> it is inherent in our entire philosophical tradition that we cannot conceive of a 'radical evil' and that even Kant, the philosopher who coined the term 'radical evil', rationalised it as a form of 'perverted ill will' and explained it in terms of thoroughly comprehensible motives.
>
> (OT 459)[12]

In *The Human Condition* she defined 'radical evil' as evil which can 'no longer be understood and explained by the evil motives of self-interest, greed, covetousness, resentment, lust for power, and cowardice' or with any 'such humanly understandable sinful motives' (*HC* 241). It was to this end that she contrasted the evil committed by the SA 'brown-shirts', behind whose 'blind bestiality . . . there often lay a deep hatred and resentment of all those who were socially, intellectually and physically better off than themselves', with the lack of any humanly recognisable motives manifested by 'desk murderers' like Eichmann. Radical evil, in her view, is a form of evil in which conventional motives are lacking and the deeds are done without personal rancour. Arendt wanted to stress the *political* character of radical evil: that the perpetrators committed atrocities as elements of a *system* in which all human beings appear equally superfluous, including in the end the perpetrators themselves. In such a system conventional motives for murdering and tormenting other human beings may exist but are superfluous to requirements.

The *substance* of Arendt's analysis barely changed from her early use of the term 'radical evil' to her later use of the term 'banality of evil', which she unconsciously drew from her earlier correspondence with Jaspers (cf. Bernstein 1996: ch. 7). Her shift of terminology emphasised that it was necessary to demythologise the perpetrators of the Holocaust and not to endow them with any 'streak of Satanic greatness'. Her use of the concept 'banality of evil' also expressed the fact that the task of destruction requires 'no depth'. Killing people is relatively easy. It needs no elaborate organisation or technology. It leaves few traces. It offers a substitute for grand dreams of a thousand-year Reich – a *simulacrum of power* which manifests itself only in unlimited violence against defenceless victims. This is what I take Arendt to mean when she says that evil can never be radical and that only the good has depth.

However, to understand the significance both of Arendt's shift of terminology and of the criticism it engendered, we have to look further at the context in which it occurred. The Eichmann trial was an event that succeeded in 'breaking the silence' which had often submerged the memory of the Final Solution in the 1950s: a silence that had made it so difficult for survivors of the camps like Primo Levi to have their memoirs published, a silence that was experienced by survivors as a refusal to listen to or believe their stories. Arendt herself had played a major part in resisting this silence and her account not only of the trial but also of the history behind the trial continued to push the facts of the catastrophe to the fore. She insisted on the need to face up to the burden of this event and to construct new categories and standards to comprehend it. The term 'totalitarian terror' was the generalising concept she used to get to grips with an apparently senseless phenomenon, the 'manufacture of corpses' without utility, which had taken place on a huge scale in both Stalinist Russia and Nazi Germany.

In the wake of the Eichmann trial, however, there was emerging a new discourse: one which drew the concepts of the Holocaust and Shoah from Jewish theology; which represented the Holocaust as an 'event' beyond all human understanding – as something unique, singular, ineffable, unrepresentable and incomparable. Elie Wiesel put the perspective most clearly and succinctly when he urged his readers not to treat the Holocaust as if it were 'just another event' that we can 'understand':

> Whether culmination or aberration of history, the Holocaust transcends history . . . The dead are in possession of a secret that we, the living, are neither worthy of nor capable of recovering . . . The Holocaust? The ultimate event, the ultimate mystery, never to be comprehended or transmitted.
>
> (Roth and Berenbaum 1989: 2)

In a thought-experiment conducted some thirty years after Arendt wrote *Origins of Totalitarianism*, Jean-François Lyotard drew an analogy between the Holocaust and an earthquake so catastrophic as to 'destroy not only lives, buildings, and objects but also the instruments used to measure earthquakes directly and indirectly' (Lyotard 1988: 56). Lyotard imagined a situation in which not only vast numbers of Jews, Gypsies and other innocent victims are exterminated but the means to prove that this happened are also exterminated. If there are no indicators of the existence of the Holocaust that survive, if all documents have been destroyed, if there is nothing to preserve memory from oblivion, if surviving victims are themselves condemned to silence, if the authority of the tribunal supposed to establish the crime is discredited on the ground that the judge is 'merely a criminal more fortunate than the defendant in war' – if all this were true, then he concluded, Auschwitz would not be an historical event in the normal sense of the term nor would it be subject to the normal procedures of historical investigation: 'the name of "Auschwitz" marks the confines wherein historical knowledge sees its competence impugned'. For Lyotard, this was not of course to deny the reality of 'Auschwitz'; on the contrary, it was to affirm it as 'the most real of all realities'. As he put it, 'the impossibility of quantitatively measuring it does not prohibit but rather inspires in the minds of the survivors the idea of a very great seismic force'. But it signified that we have or should have a relation to 'Auschwitz' different from one of historical understanding, a relation that exceeds understanding, that puts out of play not only the claims of the 'Hegelian' or 'Marxist' dialectic but the validity claims of all theoretical discourse, a relation that is essentially ethical rather than social, a relation he calls the *differend*.

The ground for Lyotard's claim about 'Auschwitz' is not, as one might anticipate, its extreme horror but the destruction of what would render an account of what happened there *determinate*: namely, the voices of the victims and the signs of their extermination. The ultimate victims, the 'drowned', cannot testify to their murder and make their genocide determinate. No *historical* account of their slaughter can adequately account for what happened to them. The status of 'Auschwitz' is rather as the omnitemporal archetype of evil. What, after all, could be more evil than *this*?[13] Arendt too speculated on the possibility of a catastrophe so consuming as to destroy all our categories of thought, all our standards of judgement, and therefore our capacity for understanding itself: 'how can we measure length if we do not have a yardstick, how could we count things without the notion of numbers?' The Holocaust might have been like this if the voice of resistance had been silenced, if the endeavour to exterminate Jews had been carried to a successful conclusion, if the yardsticks which make possible human understanding, including the idea of humanity itself, had been destroyed. But for Arendt this thought-experiment was counterfactual: it highlighted not so much the limitations of human understanding as 'the necessary limitations to an experiment which requires global control in order to show conclusive results' (*OT* 459). We can certainly envisage the spectre of a catastrophe so terrible as to exterminate the possibility of 'knowing' the catastrophe itself – a nuclear holocaust, perhaps, which leaves behind no survivors, no witnesses, no traces, nothing human. However, after Auschwitz there was no shortage of signs, traces, documents or testimonies.

It was Arendt's refusal to 'singularise' the Final Solution, to isolate it from the wider phenomena of totalitarian terror, and her seeming reluctance to use the term 'Holocaust', that was her special offence from the standpoint of what Gillian Rose has called 'Holocaust piety'.[14] It was because she retained a secular, historical and political approach to the question of evil that she was so vehemently attacked. The terms 'radical evil' and 'banality of evil' became charged because they were emblems of this conflict. In a context in which human rights could no longer be entrusted to nation-states, nor to international bodies which operated in terms of reciprocal agreements between nation-states, least of all to supra-national movements which transcended the parochialism of the nation-state in pursuit of a global ambition, Arendt reaffirmed the *need* for 'new guarantees' of human rights whose '*validity* . . . must comprehend the whole of humanity and whose *power* must remain strictly limited, rooted and controlled by newly defined territorial entities'. This required a 'new political principle' and 'new law on earth' which were only just coming into evidence (*OT* ix). This essentially cosmopolitan perspective could not be contained in any idea of the uniqueness or sacredness of the Holocaust.

In thinking about the limits of totalitarianism, we may want to believe that there is something about the human condition – some capacity for 'beginning', some individual particularity, some voice of conscience, some sense of judgement – that cannot be reworked or destroyed according to plan. The text of *Origins* is punctuated by Arendt's attempts to find this 'something' that resists all transformation. In a world where lives were 'superfluous' and the notion 'I want you not to be' prevailed, she looked primarily among the victims, pariah peoples, stateless refugees to find those who would affirm 'the grace of love, which says with Augustine . . . "I want you to be" without being able to give any particular reason for such supreme and unsurpassable affirmation' (*OT* 301). In a world which suppressed uniqueness and portrayed difference as alien, she looked to those who would recognise 'the fact of difference as such and the disturbing miracle contained in the fact that each of us is made as he is – single, unique, unchangeable' (*OT* 300). In a world where spontaneity was denied, she looked to the capacity of human beings for creative action: '"that a beginning be made man was created", said Augustine' (*OT* 478–9). In a world in which friendship was subordinated to the duty to denounce disloyalty and inform on traitors, she looked to a conception of friendship (*philia*) which makes both personal and political demands (*MDT* 25). In a world where politics was equated with total domination and a single world view, she looked to a conception of politics whose *raison d'être* is freedom and whose premise is the plurality and exchange of opinions. Arendt did not idealise the modern pariah as the cradle of such values . When civilisation forces millions of people into conditions of savages, she recognised that it may equally well produce new barbarians (*OT* 302). People who have lost the rights and protection that nationality once gave them, often resort all the more desperately to some form of nationalism. Communal relationships, built in the hope of preserving some 'minimum of humanity in a world grown inhuman', often generate a 'worldlessness' that is vulnerable to its own forms of barbarism (*MDT* 13–17). The text of *Origins* is as punctuated by instances of those to whom evil is done doing evil in return – of resistance aping or mirroring the power against which it is set – as it is of unexpected acts of moral courage. In the end she concludes that what makes this planet 'a place fit for human habitation' is simply that there are always *some* people who will not comply with power even under conditions of terror (*EJ* 233).

Arendt had no fixed conception of human nature and preferred the term 'human condition'. In the book of that name, she writes:

> The human condition is not the same as human nature and the sum total of human activities and capabilities which correspond to the human condition does not constitute anything like human nature . . . The problem of human nature . . . seems unanswerable . . . It is highly unlikely that we who can know, determine and define the natural essences of all things surrounding us . . . should ever be able to do the same for ourselves – this would be like jumping over our own shadows. . . . Nothing entitles us to assume that man has a nature or essence in the same sense as other things.
>
> (*HC* 9–10)

There is nothing deep down in human beings that guarantees resistance to totalitarianism. It is possible that the organised attempts to 'eradicate the concept of the human being' might have succeeded in the past and might still succeed in the future; that the props of the 'human condition' can be cut away and that there is no 'human nature' that will necessarily protect us from their destruction. For Arendt, this was not a message of despair but of freedom. Everything depends on us – on what we do, how we act, whether we can find an adequate political response. None of this can be predetermined.

The call of modern philosophy is to understand a world which now knows Auschwitz and the Gulag and which is daily confronted by echoes of their hatred to humanity. It is at least one way in which, as Hegel wrote, we reaffirm our subjective freedom in the realm of the substantial. Worldliness. The word haunts Arendt's writings in its multiple meanings. Worldliness as a declaration of human right beyond parochial allegiance. Worldliness as a recognition that both reason and horror lie objectively in the world, not just in how we see the world. Worldliness as the practical wisdom of those who by hook and crook know how to construct a touch of humanity in the most forbidding of circumstances. Worldliness as the satisfaction of comprehending the present and the actual, not setting up some world beyond which exists God knows where. Worldliness as facing up to the burden of events, not to indulge the cold draft of despair, not to confess that things are bad but nothing better can be expected here, not to accept what is not justified in thought.

The research programme which this word expresses picks up a political and intellectual agenda that Hegel first set in his critique of Kant's critical philosophy and Marx followed in his comment that the task of philosophy is the critique of all existing conditions, including critique itself. It is an agenda which confronts the central perplexity of modern political life: that the critique of representation cannot rest content until it links hands with the critique of the critique of representation. It is not afraid of perplexity, it does not run away from it, it does not seek to resolve it with premature judgements and conclusions, nor does it use it as an excuse for inaction in the face of injustice. Rather than attempt to master perplexity and subsume it to the will of the subject, it is prepared to give it rope, to see where it takes us. It does not deny normative judgement but it dethrones it and puts it back from where it came: in the world where no sphere of innocence survives and the most dangerous man is he who nonetheless proclaims his innocence.

Notes

1 The Nuremberg Charter defined 'crimes against humanity' in terms of certain specific acts, namely murder, extermination, enslavement and deportation, other non-specific 'inhumane acts', and 'persecutions on political, racial or religious grounds'. The limiting factors were that these acts had to be committed against civilian populations, they had to have some connection with war (i.e. the concept did not apply in purely domestic situations), and they had to be carried out as part of a systematic

governmental policy and not merely as the result of individual initiative. The Charter upheld a strong notion of personal responsibility. Individuals were held responsible whether or not the crime is in violation of the domestic law of the country where it is perpetrated. According to Article Six, 'Leaders, organisers, instigators and accomplices participating in the formulation or execution of a common plan or conspiracy to commit any of the foregoing crimes are responsible for all acts performed by any persons in execution of such plan.' Article 7 added: 'The official position of defendants, whether as Heads of State or responsible officials in Government Departments, shall not be considered as freeing them from responsibility or mitigating punishment.' Article 8: 'The fact that the Defendant acted pursuant to order of his Government or of a superior shall not free him from responsibility, but may be considered in mitigation of punishment if the Tribunal determines that justice so requires.' Articles 9, 10 and 11 authorised the Tribunal to declare that a particular organisation, like the Nazi party, is criminal and that individuals who join such an organisation are personally responsible for both their membership and their participation in its criminal activities.

2 For further discussion, see esp. Rabinbach 1997: ch. 4 'The German as Pariah: Karl Jaspers' *The Question of German Guilt'*.

3 The quotation is from Carl Schmitt, *Glossarium 1947–1951* (Berlin, 1991).

4 This argument was echoed in the trial of Klaus Barbie in 1987 when Barbie's lawyers argued that their client's actions as police chief of Lyons during the occupation could not be called 'crimes against humanity' since this was merely a case of 'whites' doing to other 'whites' what all white Europeans have routinely done to non-Europeans (Finkielkraut 1992). By putting Barbie on trial, they claimed that the French camouflaged their own colonial history and scapegoated the Nazis for behaviour for which all Europeans had been responsible. Barbie's lawyers were the Congolese M'Bemba, the Algerian Bouaïta, and the French–Vietnamese Vergès.

5 'I can only add that instead of the word "Jews" there should be the word "East Germans" and then exactly the same holds true of one of the allies, with the difference that everything that has happened since 1945 is public knowledge world-wide, whereas the bloody terror of the Nazis was in fact kept a secret from the German people' (Heidegger, *Letter to Marcuse*, 20 Jan. 1948).

6 Heidegger, *Das Ge-Stell*, 1 December 1949 (cited in Lang 1997: 8–12).

7 Arendt read Heidegger's philosophy as an attempt to overcome the philosophy of the subject initiated by Kant and to reverse his destruction of the classical concept of Being by re-establishing the ontology of Being. However, by declaring that Being is Nothingness (*What is Metaphysics*), Arendt argued that Heidegger justified the arrogant idea that humanity stands in the same relationship to Being as the Creator stood before the world he created *ex nihilo*. According to Arendt, Heidegger's designation of Being as nothingness brought with it the attempt to put behind us the definition of Being as 'what is given' and to regard human actions as god-like, divine. Since nothingness appears as the truly free domain of humanity, *Dasein* is defined through the identity of its existence and essence (i.e. we can only ask of human beings Who but never What). Like the metaphysical view of God, *Dasein* becomes the 'master of Being' except that this mastery cannot be realised in world-creating but only in world-destroying. *Dasein* is brought back to the singular and unique self who, without any detour via the idea of humanity, hears the 'call of conscience from the ground of its being' and replaces being *human* with being a *self* in seemingly absolute isolation, and it was only after the fact, as it were, that Heidegger drew on mythologising and superstitious concepts like '*volk*' and 'earth' to supply his isolated selves with a common ground to stand on. Arendt presented Heidegger's existentialism as a kind of *Weltanschauung* which protects us from the real questions of our existence and gives

us a false sense of final results. She maintained that human existence is by its very nature social, not isolated, and only comes into being in communication with and awareness of the existence of others. We have to recognise that the reality of the world, the unpredictability of our fellow human beings, and the fact that I have not created myself provide the inescapable backdrop against which human freedom declares itself distinct. Human freedom has nothing to do with the god-like mastery of Being; on the contrary, it is a task of philosophy to free us from this illusion and to recognise that reality cannot be resolved into what can be thought, that the reality of the thinker precedes her thinking, and that the concept of human existence can only develop in conjunction with others (*EU* 176–87).

8 Arendt's views have often been confused in the secondary literature. It is not true that she objected to the use of an Israeli court, or that she insisted that there had to be an international court or nothing, or that she believed that the crimes Eichmann committed were too immense to be the subject of mere legal judgement, or that she held that Eichmann should have been executed without trial! These propositions have been advanced by Parvikko 1998: 49.

9 Arendt's sense of lost opportunity was echoed by Alain Finkielkraut. He analysed contemporary trends towards the 'banalisation' of crimes against humanity, as it became part of a 'competition of memories' between different national movements and was extended to include all those forms of man's inhumanity to man of which we might disapprove. Thus in the Barbie case Finkielkraut criticised the decision of the French court to muddy the distinction between the killing of Jews for what they *were*, and the killing of resistance fighters for what they *did*, and its decision to stretch the concept of crimes against humanity to include both. He also criticised the attempt on the part of Barbie's defence team to diminish the distinction between the extermination of the Jews and the violence of European colonialism. A certain 'emotional confusion' arises, he argued, when on the one hand the definition of crimes against humanity expands to include inhuman actions of every sort and on the other hand contracts to exclude those crimes that cannot be ascribed to Western imperialism.

10 The issue of judgement is not easily resolved. Primo Levi addressed its nuances when he wrote of the 'grey zone' of inmates in the camps forced into the role of functionaries and insisted that even in the case of the worst misdeeds 'the greatest responsibility lies with the system, the very structure of the totalitarian state' (Levi 1986b: 28). He pointed out that the creation of a grey zone in which all moral certainties are confused was the conscious aim of the Nazis and their 'most demonic crime' (Levi 1986b: 37). Levi suspends judgement on the *Sonderkommando*, the 'crematorium ravens', saying that 'no one is authorised to judge them, not those who lived through the experience of the Lager and even less those who did not' (Levi 1986b: 42) and comments that the question of the moral responsibility of more exalted functionaries who committed acts of brutality is 'more delicate' and that these 'ambiguous persons' may be 'rightful owners of a quota of guilt' (Levi 1986b: 33). He extends this argument to the collaborationist actions of Jewish leaders in the ghettos and in his account of Chaim Rumkowski, the President of the Lodz ghetto, though admitting the 'extenuating circumstances' of totalitarian rule, he eventually assigns him to the same 'band of half-consciences' who brutally served the regime of the camp (Levi 1986b: 49–50).

11 This is also a theme taken up by Primo Levi. He describes the SS as 'ordinary men' (Levi 1997b: 396) or as 'average human beings . . . save for exceptions, they were not monsters, they had our faces, but they had been reared badly . . . subjected to a terrifying miseducation' (Levi 1986b: 169).

12 Kant discusses what he calls the 'radical evil in human nature' in his *Religion within the Bounds of Mere Reason* (1998), where he associates radical evil with 'perverted maxims'. He writes: 'The depravity of human nature is . . . not to be named *malice*,

if we take this word in the strict sense, namely as a disposition (a subjective *principle* of maxims) to incorporate evil *qua* evil for incentive into one's maxim (since this is diabolical) but should rather be named *perversity* of the heart, and this heart is then called *evil* because of what results. An evil heart can coexist with a will which in the abstract is good. Its origin is the frailty of human nature, in not being strong enough to comply with its adopted principles' (60). The term 'radical evil' for Kant refers only to the 'natural propensity' to evil which resides in human nature by virtue of our 'free power of choice'. Kant illustrates what he considers to be the surrender to evil in the modern world in a comment made by an English Member of Parliament to the effect that 'every man has his price, for which he sells himself'. Arendt is right in saying that Kant's idea of 'radical evil' came far short of imagining the evil that was to come.

13 I am drawing here from Jay Bernstein's critique of Lyotard 'After Auschwitz: Grammar, Ethics, Trauma' in Fine and Turner (2000).

14 In her essay on 'Fascism and representation', the then Jewish philosopher, Gillian Rose, used the label 'Holocaust piety' to characterise this way of thinking. She writes: 'It is this reference to the "ineffable" that I would dub "Holocaust piety". How is it to be construed and what is its economics? "The ineffable" is invoked by a now widespread tradition of reflection on the Holocaust: by Adorno, by Holocaust theology, Christian and Jewish, more recently by Lyotard, and now by Habermas. According to this view, "Auschwitz" or "the Holocaust" are emblems for the breakdown in divine and/or human history. The uniqueness of this break delegitimises names and narratives as such, and hence all aesthetic or apprehensive representation . . . the search for a decent response to those brutally destroyed is conflated with the quite different response called for in the face of the inhuman capacity for such destruction. To argue for silence, prayer, the banishment equally of poetry and knowledge, in short, the witness of "ineffability", that is, non-representability, is to *mystify what we dare not understand*, because we fear that it may be all too understandable, all too continuous with what we are – human, all too human' (Rose 1996: 41–3). The questions Gillian Rose raises, echo those raised by Arendt: 'what is it that we do not *want* to understand? what is it that Holocaust piety . . . once again protects us from understanding?' (Rose 1996: 43).

BIBLIOGRAPHY

Adorno, Theodor W. (1990) *Negative Dialectics*, London: Routledge.
—— (1993) *Studies in Hegel*, Cambridge, Mass., and London: Massachusetts Institute of Technology Press Press.
—— (1996) *Minima Moralia: Reflections from a Damaged Life*, London: Verso.
Améry, Jean (1989) 'At the mind's limits: Contemplations by a survivor on Auschwitz and its realities' (originally published in 1966), in John Roth and Michael Berenbaum (eds), *Holocaust: Religious and Philosophical Implications*, New York: Paragon House.
Apel, Karl-Otto (1997) 'Toward perpetual peace as historical prognosis from the point of view of moral duty', in Bohman and Lutz-Bachman 1997: 79–110.
Arato, Andrew (1991) 'A reconstruction of Hegel's theory of civil society', in Cornell *et al.* 1991: 301–20.
Archibugi, Daniele *et al.* (eds) (1998) *Cosmopolitan Democracy: An Agenda for a New World Order*, Cambridge: Polity.
Arendt, Hannah (1958) *The Human Condition*, Chicago: University of Chicago Press (abbrev. *HC*).
—— (1968) 'Introduction', Walter Benjamin, *Illuminations*, New York: Schocken.
—— (1970) *On Violence*, London: Allen Lane.
—— (1976) *The Origins of Totalitarianism*, New York: Harvest (abbrev. *OT*).
—— (1977) *Between Past and Future*, New York: Penguin (abbrev. *BPF*).
—— (1978a) *Jew as Pariah*, ed. Ron Feldman, New York: Grove Press.
—— (1978b) *Life of the Mind*, New York: Harcourt Brace Jovanovich (abbrev. *LM*).
—— (1983) *Men in Dark Times*, New York: Harcourt Brace Jovanovich (abbrev. *MDT*).
—— (1990) *On Revolution*, Harmondsworth: Penguin (abbrev. *OR*).
—— (1994a) *Eichmann in Jerusalem: A Report on the Banality of Evil*, New York: Penguin: (abbrev. *EJ*).
—— (1994b) *Essays in Understanding 1930–1954*, New York: Harcourt Brace (abbrev. *EU*).
—— and Jaspers, Karl (1992) *Correspondence 1926–1969*, New York: Harcourt Brace (abbrev. *A&J*).
Arthur, Chris (1986) *Dialectics of Labour*, Oxford: Blackwell.
Avineri, Shlomo (1972) *Hegel's Theory of the Modern State*, Cambridge: Cambridge University Press.
Bauman, Zygmunt (1990) *Modernity and the Holocaust*, Cambridge: Polity.
Beardsworth, Richard (1996) *Derrida and the Political*, London: Routledge.
Beiner, Ronald (1989) 'Introduction' to Hannah Arendt, *Lectures on Kant's Political Philosophy*, ed. R. Beiner, Chicago: University of Chicago Press.

Bellamy, Richard (1988) *Modern Italian Social Theory*, Cambridge: Polity.

Benjamin, Walter (1968) 'Theses on the philosophy of history', in *Illuminations*, ed. Hannah Arendt, New York: Schocken.

Bernstein, Richard (1996) *Hannah Arendt and the Jewish Question*, Cambridge: Polity.

Bohman, James and Lutz-Bachmann, Matthias (eds), (1997) *Perpetual Peace: Essays on Kant's Cosmopolitan Ideal*, Cambridge, Mass.: Massachusetts Institute of Technology Press.

Bosanquet B. (1958) *The Philosophical Theory of the State*, London: Macmillan.

Browning, Christopher (1993) *Ordinary Men: Reserve Battalion 101 and the Final Solution in Poland*, New York: HarperPerennial.

Bullock, Alan (1983) *Hitler: A Study in Tyranny*, London: Odhams.

Calvino, Italo (1999) *Why Read the Classics?*, trans. Martin McLaughlin, London: Jonathan Cape.

Cassirer, E. (1946) *The Myth of the State*, New Haven, Conn.: Yale University Press.

Colletti, Lucio (1972) *From Rousseau to Lenin*, London: New Left Books.

—— (1973) *Hegel and Marxism*, London: New Left Books.

—— (1992) 'Introduction', *Marx's Early Writings*, Harmondsworth: Penguin.

Cornell, Drucilla *et al.* (eds), (1991) *Hegel and Legal Theory*, London: Routledge.

D'Hondt, Jacques (1988) *Hegel in his Time*, Peterborough, Ont.: Broadview Press.

Debord, Guy (1994) *Society of the Spectacle*, trans. Donald Nicholson-Smith, New York: Zone Books (first published in French 1967).

Derrida, Jacques (1992) 'Force of law: the mystical foundations of authority', in D. Cornell *et al.* (eds), *Deconstruction and the Possibility of Justice*, London: Routledge.

—— (1994) *Specters of Marx: The State of the Debt, the Work of Mourning, and the New International*, New York and London: Routledge.

Dickey, Laurence (1989) *Hegel: Religion, Economics, and the Politics of Spirit 1770–1807*, Cambridge: Cambridge University Press.

Fackenheim, Emil Ludwig (1996) *The God Within: Kant, Schelling, and Historicity*, ed. John Burbidge, Toronto and London: University of Toronto Press.

Fine, Robert (1985) *Democracy and the Rule of Law*, London: Pluto.

—— (1994a) 'Hegel's *Philosophy of Right* and Marx's Critique: A re-assessment', in Werner Bonefeld *et al.* (eds), *Open Marxism*, vol. 3, London: Pluto.

—— (1994b) 'The new nationalism and democracy: A critique of *Pro Patria*', *Democratization*, 1(3): 423–43.

—— (1994c) 'The rule of law and Muggletonian Marxism: The perplexities of Edward Thompson', *Journal of Law and Society*, 21(2): 193–213.

—— (1997) 'Civil society theory, enlightenment and critique', in R. Fine and S. Rai (eds), *Civil Society: Democratic Perspectives*, London: Frank Cass, 7–28.

—— (1998) 'The fetishism of the subject? Alain Touraine's Critique of Modernity', *European Journal of Social Theory*, 1(2): 179–84.

—— (2000a) 'Crimes against humanity: Hannah Arendt and the Nuremberg debates', *European Journal of Social Theory*, 3(3): 293–311.

—— (2000b) 'Hannah Arendt: Politics and understanding after the Holocaust', in Fine and Turner 2000: 19–45.

—— and Turner, Charles (eds) (2000) *Social Theory after the Holocaust*, Liverpool: Liverpool University Press.

Finkielkraut, Alain (1992) *Remembering in Vain*, New York: Columbia University Press.

Fraser, Ian (1997) 'Two of a kind: Hegel, Marx, dialectic and form', *Capital and Class*, 61: 81–106.

—— (1998) *Hegel and Marx: The Concept of Need*, Edinburgh: Edinburgh University Press.

Gentile, Giovanni (1961) *Opere complete di Giovanni Gentile*, vol. 4: *I fondamenti della filosofia del diritto*, Florence: Sansoni.

Gurden, Helen (2000) 'Primo Levi: Testimony, judgement and understanding', unpublished paper, Warwick University.

Habermas, Jürgen (1974) 'Natural Law and revolution', in *Theory and Practice*, London: Heinemann.

—— (1990) *The Philosophical Discourse of Modernity: Twelve Lectures*, Cambridge, Mass.: Massachusetts Institute of Technology Press.

—— (1991) *The New Conservatism: Cultural Criticism and the Historians' Debate*, ed. Shierry Weber Nicholsen, Cambridge: Polity.

—— (1997) *Between Facts and Norms*, Cambridge: Polity.

—— (1998) 'Kant's idea of perpetual peace', in *The Inclusion of the Other*, Cambridge, Mass.: Massachusetts Institute of Technology Press, and in Bohman and Lutz-Bachman 1997: 113–53.

Hardimon, Michael (1994) *Hegel's Social Philosophy: The Project of Reconciliation*, Cambridge: Cambridge University Press.

Hegel, Georg Wilhelm Friedrich (1956) *Philosophy of History*, London and Toronto: Dover (abbrev. *PH*).

—— (1975) *Early Theological Writings*, trans. T. M. Knox and R. Krane, Philadelphia: University of Pennsylvania Press (abbrev. *ETW*).

—— (1975a) *Natural Law*, trans. T. M. Knox, Philadelphia: University of Pennsylvania Press.

—— (1975b) *Lectures in the Philosophy of World History: Introduction*, trans. H. B. Nisbet, Cambridge: Cambridge University Press (abbrev. *LPWH*).

—— (1977) *Phenomenology of Spirit* , trans. A. V. Miller, Oxford: Oxford University Press (abbrev. *PS*).

—— (1984) *Hegel: The Letters*: Bloomington: University of Indiana Press.

—— (1991a) *Elements of the Philosophy of Right*, ed. Allen Wood, Cambridge: Cambridge University Press (abbrev. *PR*).

—— (1991b) *Encyclopaedia Logic*: Part I of *Encyclopaedia of the Philosophical Sciences*, trans. T. F. Geraetz, W. A. Suchting and H. S. Harris, Indianapolis: Hackett Publishing Co.

—— (1993) *Hegel's Science of Logic*, trans. A.V. Miller, Atlantic Highlands, NJ: Humanities Press.

—— (1995) *Lectures on Natural Right and Political Science: The First Philosophy of Right*, trans. J. Michael Stewart and Peter Wannenmann, introduction by Otto Pöggeler, Berkeley, Calif., and London: University of California Press.

Held, David (1995) *Democracy and the Global Order*, Cambridge: Polity.

—— (1997) 'Cosmopolitan democracy and the global order: a new agenda', in Bohman and Lutz-Bachman 1997: 235–51.

Hobbes, Thomas (1973) *Leviathan*, London, New York : Dent.

Hobhouse, L. (1951) *The Metaphysical Theory of the State*, London: George Allen and Unwin.

Honig, Bonnie (1993) *Political Theory and the Displacement of Politics*, Ithaca, NY: Cornell University Press.

Honneth, Axel (1997) 'Is universalism a moral trap? The presuppositions and limits of a politics of human rights', in Bohman and Lutz-Bachman 1997: 155–78.

Hyland, Richard (1989) 'Hegel: A user's manual', *Cardozo Law Review*, 10: 1735–1831.

Ilting, K.-H. (1984) 'Hegel's concept of the state and Marx's early critique', in Pelczynski 1984: 93–113.

Isaac, Jeffrey (1992) *Arendt, Camus and Modern Rebellion*, New Haven, Conn., and London: Yale University Press.

Jarvis, Simon (1998) *Adorno: A Critical Introduction*, Cambridge: Polity.

Jaspers, Karl (1961) *The Question of German Guilt*, New York: Capricorn Books.

Kant, Immanuel (1965) *The Metaphysical Elements of Justice*: part 1 of *The Metaphysics of Morals*, Indianopolis: Bobbs-Merrill (abbrev. *MJ*).

—— (1991) *Kant's Political Writings*, ed. Hans Reiss, Cambridge: Cambridge University Press (abbrev. *KPW*).

—— (1998) *Religion within the Bounds of Mere Reason*, trans. and ed. Allen Wood and George di Giovanni, Cambridge: Cambridge University Press.

Kedourie, Elie (1993) *Nationalism*, Oxford: Blackwell.

Kirchheimer, O. (1961) *Political Justice*, Princeton, NJ: Princeton University Press.

Knox, T. M. (1996) 'Hegel and Prussianism', in Stewart 1996: 70–81.

Kristeva, Julia (1991) *Strangers to Ourselves*, New York: Columbia University Press.

—— (1993) *Nations without Nationalism*, New York: Columbia University Press.

Lang, Berel (1997) 'Heidegger's silence and the Jewish Question', in Alan Milchman and Alan Rosenberg (eds), *Martin Heidegger and the Holocaust*, Atlantic Highlands, NJ: Humanities Press, 1–18.

Leaman, George (1997) 'Strategies of deception: the composition of Heidegger's silence', in Alan Milchman and Alan Rosenberg (eds), *Martin Heidegger and the Holocaust*, Atlantic Highlands, NJ: Humanities Press, 57–69.

Lefort, Claude (1986) *The Political Forms of Modern Society: Bureaucracy, Democracy, Totalitarianism*, Cambridge: Polity.

—— (1988) *Democracy and Political Theory*, Minneapolis: University of Minnesota Press.

—— (1998) 'The concept of totalitarianism', in *Papers in Social Theory*, Coventry: Warwick Social Theory Centre and Sussex Centre for Critical Social Theory, no. 2.

Levi, Primo (1986a) *The Periodic Table*, London: Abacus

—— (1986b) *The Drowned and the Saved*, London: Abacus.

—— (1997a) *If This is a Man*, London: Abacus.

—— (1997b) *The Truce*, London: Abacus.

Löwith, Karl (1967) *From Hegel to Nietzsche*, New York: Anchor.

Lukacs, Georg (1971) *History and Class Consciousness: Studies in Marxist Dialectics*, London: Merlin.

—— (1975) *The Young Hegel: Studies in the Relation Between Dialectics and Economics*, London: Merlin.

Lyotard, Jean François (1988) *The Differend: Phrases in Dispute*, Manchester: Manchester University Press.

MacGregor, David (1984) *The Communist Ideal in Hegel and Marx*, London: George Allen and Unwin.

—— (1998) *Hegel and Marx: After the Fall of Communism*, Cardiff: University of Wales Press.

Marcuse, Herbert (1979) *Reason and Revolution: Hegel and the Rise of Social Theory*, Boston: Beacon Press.

Marx, Karl (1968) 'Critique of the Gotha Programme', in *Selected Works of Marx and Engels*, London: Lawrence and Wishart.

—— (1972) *The Holy Family*, ed. Z. Jordan, London: Nelson.

—— (1973) *Grundrisse: Introduction to the Critique of Political Economy*, foreword by Martin Nicolaus, Harmondsworth: Penguin.

—— (1975) *Texts of Methods*, ed. T. Carver, Oxford: Blackwell.

—— (1990) *Capital*, vol.1, Harmondsworth: Penguin (abbrev. *Capital*).

—— (1992) *Karl Marx: Early Writings*, ed. L. Colletti, London: Penguin and New Left Books (abbrev. *MEW*).

—— and Engels, Frederick (1983) *Letters on 'Capital'*, trans. Edward Drummond, London: New Park.

—— (1998) 'The Communist Manifesto', in Leo Pantich and Colin Leys (eds), *The Communist Manifesto Now*, Socialist Register, Suffolk: Merlin Press.

McLellan, David (1980) 'Introduction' to *Marx's Grundrisse*, London: Macmillan.

Nancy, Jean-Luc (1997) *Hegel, l'inquiétude du négatif*, Paris: Hachette.

Neumann, Franz (1942) *Behemoth: The Structure and Practice of National Socialism*, London: Gollancz.

—— (1986) *The Rule of Law*, Oxford: Berg.

Nietzsche, F. (1969) *The Will to Power*, New York: Vintage Press.

—— (1983) *Untimely Meditations*, trans. R. J. Hollingdale, Cambridge: Cambridge University Press.

Nussbaum, Martha (1997) 'Kant and cosmopolitanism', in Bohman and Lutz-Bachman 1997: 25–57.

Parvikko, Tuija (1998) 'Hannah Arendt as judge: a conscious pariah in Jerusalem', in *The Finnish Yearbook of Political Thought* (University of Jyvaskyla: SoPhi), 2: 37–57.

Pelczynski, Z. A. (1984) *The State and Civil Society: Studies in Hegel's Political Philosophy*, Cambridge: Cambridge University Press.

Popper, K. (1996) *The Open Society and Its Enemies*, 5th rev. edn, London: Routledge.

Postone, Moishe (1986) 'Anti-Semitism and National Socialism', in A. Rabinbach and J. Zipes (eds), *Germans and Jews since the Holocaust*, New York: Telos Press.

—— (1996) *Time, Labour and Social Domination*, Cambridge: Cambridge University Press.

Rabinbach, Anson (1997) *In the Shadow of Catastrophe: German Intellectuals between Apocalypse and Enlightenment*, Berkeley: University of California Press.

Riedel, Manfred (1984) *Between Tradition and Revolution: The Hegelian Transformation of Political Philosophy*, trans. Walter Wright, Cambridge: Cambridge University Press.

Ritter, Karl (1982) *Hegel and the French Revolution: Essays on the Philosophy of Right*, Cambridge, Mass., and London: Massachusetts Institute of Technology Press.

Rosdolsky, Roman (1980) *The Making of Marx's Capital*, London: Pluto.

Rose, Gillian (1981) *Hegel Contra Sociology*, London: Athlone.

—— (1995) *Love's Work*, London: Chatto and Windus.

—— (1996) *Mourning Becomes the Law: Philosophy and Representation*, Cambridge: Cambridge University Press.

Roth, J. and Berenbaum, M. (1989) *Holocaust: Religious and Philosophical Implications*, New York: Paragon House.

Rousseau, Jean-Jacques (1973) *The Social Contract and Other Discourses*, London: Dent and Sons.

Rubin, Isaak (1972) *Essays on Marx's Theory of Value*, Detroit: Black and Red.

—— (1978) 'Abstract labour and value in Marx's system', *Capital and Class*, 5: 107–39.

Russell, Bertrand (1984) *A History of Western Philosophy*, London: Unwin.

Schmitt, Carl (1996) *The Concept of the Political*, Chicago: University of Chicago Press.

Smith, Steven (1991) *Hegel's Critique of Liberalism: Rights in Context*, Chicago: University of Chicago Press.

Stewart, Jon (1996) *The Hegel Myths and Legends*, Evanston, Ill.: Northwestern University Press.

Stirling, James (1971) *The Secret of Hegel* (1st edn 1865).

Taylor, Charles (1993) *Hegel*, Cambridge: Cambridge University Press.

Thompson, Edward (1978) *The Poverty of Theory and Other Essays*, London: Merlin.

Todorov, T. (1999) *Facing the Extreme: Moral Life in the Concentration Camps*, London: Phoenix.

Uchida, Hiroshi (1988) *Marx's Grundrisse and Hegel's Logic*, ed. Terrell Carver, London: Routledge.

Vatter, Miguel (1998) 'Arendt's theory of revolution', in *Papers in Social Theory*, Coventry: Warwick Social Theory Centre and Sussex Centre for Critical Social Theory, no. 3: 64–83.

Villa, Dana (1996) *Arendt and Heidegger: The Fate of the Political*, Princeton, NJ: Princeton University Press.

—— (1999) *Politics, Philosophy, Terror: Essays on the thought of Hannah Arendt*, Princeton, NJ: Princeton University Press.

Waldron, Jeremy (1988) *The Right to Private Property*, Oxford: Clarendon.

Walsh, W. H. (1998) *Hegelian Ethics*, Bristol: Thoemmes.

Warminski, Andrzej (1998) 'Hegel / Marx: Consciousness and Life', in Stuart Barnett (ed.), *Hegel after Derrida*, London: Routledge.

Weber, Max (1991) *From Max Weber*, ed. H. H. Gerth and C. Wright Mills, London: Routledge.

Weil, Eric (1998) *Hegel and the State*, trans. M.A. Cohen, Baltimore, MD: Johns Hopkins University Press.

Wolin, Sheldon (1994) 'Hannah Arendt: Democracy and the Political', in Lewis P. Hinchman and Sandra K. Hinchman (eds), *Hannah Arendt: Critical Essays*, Albany, NY: State University of New York Press, 289–306.

—— (1996) 'Fugitive Democracy' in S. Benhabib (ed.), *Democracy and Difference*, Princeton, NJ: Princeton University Press, 31–45.

Wood, Allen (1991) 'Introduction' to *Elements of the Philosophy of Right*, Cambridge: Cambridge University Press.

—— (1993) 'Hegel and Marxism', in Frederick Beiser (ed.), *The Cambridge Companion to Hegel*, Cambridge: Cambridge University Press.

Zolo, Danilo (1997) *Cosmopolis: Prospects for World Government*, Cambridge: Polity.

INDEX